The Battle of Magersfontein

Victory and defeat on the South African veld 10–12 December 1899

Gareth Benneyworth

Helion & Company

Helion & Company Limited
Unit 8 Amherst Business Centre
Budbrooke Road
Warwick
CV34 5WE
England
Tel. 01926 499 619
Email: info@helion.co.uk
Website: www.helion.co.uk
Twitter: @helionbooks
Visit our blog at blog.helion.co.uk

Published by Helion & Company 2023
Designed and typeset by Mach 3 Solutions (www.mach3solutions.co.uk)
Cover designed by Paul Hewitt, Battlefield Design (www.battlefield-design.co.uk)

Cover: 'Black Watch' infantryman, by Giorgio Albertini © Helion & Company 2023

ISBN 978-1-915113-79-5

British Library Cataloguing-in-Publication Data.
A catalogue record for this book is available from the British Library.

For details of other military history titles published by Helion & Company Limited contact the above address or visit our website: http://www.helion.co.uk.

We always welcome receiving book proposals from prospective authors.

Contents

Acknowledgments v
Foreword vii

1 The outbreak of war 9
2 Formation of the 1st Infantry Division 29
3 Advance on Kimberley 37
4 Battle of Belmont, 23 November 1899 47
5 Battle of Graspan, 25 November 1899 85
6 Battle of Modder River, 28 November 1899 93
7 The Boers prepare and entrench at Magersfontein 126
8 The Battle of Magersfontein, 10 December 1899 to 12 December 1899 148
9 Magersfontein. Burying the dead 205
10 Monuments, Memorials, and Graves 219
11 Conclusion: the aftermath 223

Bibliography 235
Index 242

Dedicated to my parents, Jill and Dennis Benneyworth.

Acknowledgments

This book unfolded over decades, 1977 being the first time that my parents took me to visit Magersfontein. The terrain was igniting, captivating, and drew me back throughout my life, leading to a lifelong fascination with the South African War and battlefields. All of it self-funded study thereon. A personal quest through libraries, archives and the terrains of war and conflict, yet all founded in that first visit, aged 11 years old.

Over decades, and particularly when appointed in 1999 to redevelop the Magersfontein Battlefield Museum exhibit, my reading of the then current works on the battle and its broader context, did not stand up to the personal account of combatants, and especially the archaeology of the battlefield. There was place for new work, yet that had to wait, while other journeys unfolded.

Finally, in 2020, the time was right. Drawing on over 30 years of research, my writing commenced. To address a historical hole in the body of literature, never published primary sources, letters, diaries, photographs, maps, battle orders, official histories and reports, personal reflections, regimental histories, and survivor interviews, collected over decades were consulted and incorporated. The archive of physical landscapes also weaves through the written archive and, after having walked the killing grounds for over three decades, my insights into the battlefield archaeology and its tangible and intangible record speaks.

My thanks to the publishers Helion & Company, and Dr Christopher Brice for enabling this work. Many people and institutions assisted this quest, particularly the South African War Museum (War Museum of the Boer Republics), Bloemfontein and its personnel and Director Mr. Tokkie Pretorius and the CEO of the McGregor Museum, Kimberley, Ms Sunet Swanepoel. The National Archives of South Africa and United Kingdom and other repositories referenced in this work, proved invaluable for accessing primary source material.

To my colleagues at Sol Plaatje University and the University of Johannesburg, thank you for your support. Amanda-Jane, my partner who stood by me during the write up, encouraging my work to its conclusion. Kedar Heritage Lodge and Conference Centre near Rustenburg, a majestic place where I retreated to write in peace and tranquillity-a special thanks to the Forsyth family, particularly Robert, Adele and Sarah. Another place being Matjiesfontein Village, itself a site that played a part in the war and, where I worked during my teenage years, to surround myself with history of that time. Last yet not least Magersfontein cottage atop the main hill, where in the stillness of nature, the intensity of combat could be thought through clearly, then committed to paper.

A special thanks to my family Dennis, Jill, Dirk, and Lance, and my many valued friends-you know who you are.

This work is the result of you all.

Dr Garth Benneyworth
24 May 2023.

Foreword

This presentation of events on the western front between November and December 1899, culminating in the Battle of Magersfontein, is a magnificent contribution to our knowledge of the South African War. This is the text that historians have been waiting for to do justice to a worthy topic.

Dr Benneyworth has made good use of primary sources, particularly in the McGregor Museum in Kimberley. His personal field work on the terrain over many years has also given him a very clear understanding of the issues at stake.

South African historians are usually in a good position to do research on the South African War, because they can tap both British (English) and South African (Dutch and Afrikaans) sources. In this work we therefore find that the most important primary and secondary sources in English, Dutch and Afrikaans have been consulted.

His intimate knowledge of the terrain on the western front has enabled Dr Benneyworth to come up with some fresh perspectives. For example: One of the captions for a photograph reads: "The 75th Battery Royal Field Artillery firing positions on Horse Artillery Hill, marked with a commemorative gun, erected in 1999 for the centenary of the battle. The author identified the exact site where to place this marker, based on T Friction firing tubes, used to fire the guns, found by the author on the ground." Another is his argument for the Boers making use of a pre-existing gulley (which they called a "sloot") for the Magersfontein positions. It is a very interesting point. This kind of input makes the author's contribution on Magersfontein invaluable and exceptional.

A wonderful read.

Fransjohan Pretorius
Professor emeritus
Department of Historical and Heritage Studies
University of Pretoria

1

The outbreak of war

Seeds of conflict

The South African War (1899–1902) has its roots decades before the birth of the 20th century.[1] After an initial British Occupation of the Cape of Good Hope in 1797, official British involvement in the African subcontinent commenced in 1806, with the annexation of the Cape from the Dutch. The next one hundred years saw this imperial power consolidate its hold over the Southern African subcontinent, achieved through the policy instrument of military conquest. Numerous campaigns were fought against the indigenous populations, particularly a hundred years' conflict with the amaXhosa in the Eastern Cape of South Africa. British conflicts in this region eventually induced some 17,000 Boer frontier farmers to evacuate this area between 1835–1837. They trekked into the interior, to escape British rule and establish independent republics for themselves. These Voortrekkers in turn subjugated indigenous populations with whom they came into contact. This fighting served to cement the commando system as the Boer military structure. Although Britain eventually recognised the independence of the South African Republic (also known as the Transvaal) in 1852 and the Orange Free State Republic in 1854, the Transvaal never shook off the long arm of British rule, being proclaimed a British Crown Colony in 1877. This served as a driving force for cyclical conflict, which first erupted in 1880, and again in 1899.

Until the discovery of diamonds during the late 1860s and 1870s, the South African interior was a backwater in the British empire. An uneasy peace ensued between the Cape and Natal Colonies under British rule, and the two Boer Republics enjoying their semi autonomy. Minerals would change this equilibrium forever.

The discovery of diamonds in the late 1860s and early 1870s, heralded the mineral revolution, with its concomitant political and economic wrangling. Britain ensured that this vast treasure chest on the featureless veld in an area

1 Also known as the Anglo-Boer War (1899–1902).

Kimberley Mine, 1874. The discovery of diamonds in what became Kimberley ignited the mineral revolution in Southern Africa, changing the course of history and laying the seeds of conflict. (Afrikana Library, with permission)

known as Griqualand West, would not slip under Orange Free State control. On 27 October 1871, Britain annexed the diamond fields.

Diamond mining was initially characterised by a diggers rush, as foreigners and the regional indigenous populations, in search of fortunes, trekked across the Southern Africa interior to the shanty town that sprung up around the workings. Their claims and small-scale mining operations resembled a massive spider web of pulleys and carts spun into the largest mine excavated by hand in human history, and sucked into this morass of activity, as cheap and expendable labour, were the indigenous populations.

An enduring result of this diamond rush was the formation of capital-wielding blocs under the guise of Cecil John Rhodes and his firm, De Beers Consolidated Mines. Rhodes created an immense business interest and built himself political influence both within the Cape Colony and the British Government. In a robber baron era, Rhodes, like his American counterparts, became synonymous with capital and the power it wielded. An ardent imperialist, he represented an agent of the British government, or it could be argued the British government represented De Beers, this niggling reality becoming prevalent in 1899.[2]

For the Boer Republics, near this centre of this economic critical mass, the impacts of this mineral revolution were soon felt, yet foremost on the minds of the Transvaal burghers was resolving the thorny issue of British

2 General Sir Redvers Buller. As quoted in: Maurice, *History of the War in South Africa*, vol. I, p.65.

An amaZulu Army outmanoeuvred and annihilated a British force at Isandlwana, inflicting one of the most humiliating defeats on a colonial army during the Victorian era. From *The Graphic*. (Public domain)

rule. Dissatisfaction with the British administration simmered throughout this period but increased British troop levels in Natal Colony during 1878 and 1879, dissuaded the Transvaal Boers from outright rebellion. In 1878, the British Government found itself being manoeuvred by its Colonial Secretary Sir Henry Bartle Frere, into conflict with King Cetewayo kaMpande's Zulu Kingdom. King Cetewayo kaMpande did not project any obvious signs of aggressive intent against the Natal or Transvaal territories yet, faced with an ultimatum that threatened the heart of Zulu society and his power base, refused to comply. Nor was this the last occasion that a Colonial Secretary manipulated local politics in pursuit of grandiose schemes, as events in 1899 demonstrate.

Consequently, during January 1879, the British army invaded Zululand and within days experienced a crushing defeat at Isandlwana. By late afternoon on 22 January 1879, the empire's soldiery lay disembowelled on the field of battle.[3] British reinforcements arrived in Natal and imperial firepower prevailed, resulting in the Zulu defeat at Ulundi later that year.

Following the 1879 Anglo Zulu War, discontent in the Transvaal against British rule erupted. Essentially, the 1880 uprising took the form of a tax revolt that led to full scale warfare, known as the 1880–1881 Transvaal War of Independence.[4] The military thinking and tactical application by the Transvaal forces during this conflict reveal a striking similarity to the tactics

3 John Laband, *Rope of Sand: The Rise and Fall of the Zulu Kingdom in the Nineteenth Century* (Johannesburg: Jonathan Ball Publishers Pty Ltd, 1995), p.227.

4 Also known as the First Boer War or Transvaal War of Independence. No official forces of the Orange Free State Republic participated in this conflict.

used by the senior Boer generals who rode off to war nineteen years later, during the spring of 1899. Notable were P.J. Joubert, later the Commandant General of the South African Republic in 1899 and General P.A. Cronjé, who played a prominent part in the hierarchy of the Boer leadership on the Western Front during 1899–1900. Their choice of tactics during 1880–1881 was a two-pronged approach to strategic and operational application, with the utilisation of topography to their decisive advantage. However, their replication of these tactics eighteen years later proved ineffective.

The first prong in 1880–1881 involved a lock up or siege strategy of the Transvaal British garrisons to force their capitulation. The second involved the commandos positioning themselves across the path of the anticipated British relief columns sent to break the strategic deadlock. The overall strategy behind these two tactical methodologies was to inflict defeat on the British forces, compelling the British Government to seek terms and thereby fulfilling the political strategy, namely recognition of the independence of the Transvaal.

It worked. A relief column under General Sir G. Colley attempted to enter the Transvaal from Natal. General Joubert's forces soundly thrashed the British forces in three engagements, their final victory at Majuba Mountain.[5] This defeat saw British troops fleeing before a non-permanent army. Peace negotiations followed. Britain conceded limited independence for the Transvaal, then renamed the South African Republic. This success by the Transvaal forces created a siege and settlement strategy, later replicated during the opening months of the South African War.

Peace did not prevail. Britain unknowingly handed over limited independence to a territory that would soon reveal the richest gold deposits found in the world to that date. In 1886, gold was identified on the Witwatersrand. Rapidly, the city of Johannesburg sprang up. Deep level gold extraction required both capital and mining technologies and this need saw the extension of capital wielding blocs under Rhodes, Werner Beit, and others. Capital wealth accumulated on the Kimberley diamond mines and, in the conquest of territory later named Rhodesia, consolidated itself on the Witwatersrand gold mines.

The consequent rush of 'uitlanders'[6] from all corners of the globe seeking their fortune on the goldfields resulted in their demands for an extension of the franchise by the Republic. This vast influx of foreigners created a quandary for the South African Republic, led by President S.J.P. Kruger. An extension of franchise would be an act of political suicide, as the uitlander population would soon outnumber that of the Transvaal's citizenry (burghers). The franchise was withheld, while fortunes were raked in by Kruger's state through taxation of various sorts, especially on the gold extracted from the mines. This led to the franchise cause and its extension being championed by an alliance that developed between the capitalist interests on the one hand and the political forces of the British Foreign Office on the other; both keen

5 Geo R. Duxbury, *David and Goliath: The First War of Independence, 1880–1881* (Johannesburg: SA National Museum of Military History, 1981), p.41.

6 Foreign nationals.

Cecil John Rhodes (1853–1902) came to South Africa in 1870, and in 1888 launched De Beers Consolidated Mines. He was a financier, statesman, and empire builder of British South Africa, and Prime Minister of the Cape Colony (1890–1896). He continually interfered and attempted to manipulate military matters during the Kimberley Siege. By his estate he established the Rhodes scholarships at Oxford University (1902) yet leaves today a contested legacy in South Africa and in the United Kingdom. (From M. Menpes, *War Impressions Being A Record In Colour* (London: Adam & Charles Black, 1901))

to extend their power over this mineral bearing wealth.

A badly planned raid on the South African Republic, known as the Jameson Raid of 1895–1896, had as its objective the toppling of the Kruger government through an armed invasion linked to an uprising in Johannesburg (which would, according to the plotters, bring about British military intervention). Rhodes, then Prime Minister of the Cape Colony, fully supported this endeavour to topple the South African Republic, also tacitly supported by Britain's Foreign Secretary Joseph Chamberlain. Yet it ended in an ignominious defeat at the battle of Doornkop, just outside of Johannesburg.

The Jameson Raid disgraced Rhodes, who resigned as Prime Minister of the Cape Colony in the wake of damaging disclosures, after a Premiership of six years (1890–1896). It soured the relationship between the British and the Kruger Governments and that of President M.T. Steyn of the Orange Free State Republic. These two Republics formed a military pact during 1897 and prepared to defend their independence, which based on their experience with the Jameson Raid, was clearly threatened. The Republics imported firearms, ammunition, and field guns from abroad. Kruger and Joubert re-equipped the Transvaal forces with modern German Mauser rifles, and the most up to date 75 mm Creusot and 75 mm Krupp guns, imported from France and Germany.[7] The Orange Free State did likewise, its artillery commanded by Major F.W.R. Albrecht, who later featured during the Western Campaign. The Boer Republics were militarily and politically united against a common foe, for the first and last time in their history.

7 The 75 mm Krupp was superior to the South African Republic's field artillery where they had different pattern guns, making ammunition supply more difficult. There were two types of Creusot guns. The 75 mm Schneider-Canet that was manufactured at Creusot in France, which were never used in the Kimberley area of operations and the 155 mm Long Tom gun made by Schneider et Cie; one of them being used at the Siege of Kimberley.

President Stephanus Johannes Paulus Kruger (1825–1904) was a dominant political and military figure in 19th century Southern Africa and President of the South African Republic (or Transvaal) from 1883 to 1900. He fled into exile after the fall of Pretoria. (War Museum of the Boer Republics, with permission)

President Marthinus Theunis Steyn (1857–1916) was a South African lawyer, politician, and statesman. He was the sixth and last president of the independent republic of the Orange Free State from 1896 to 1902. After the fall of Bloemfontein in 1900, he remained on commando until the end of the war. (War Museum of the Boer Republics, with permission)

The Bloemfontein Conference in May 1899 to June 1899 sought to address the question of the franchise for Transvaal uitlanders. However, it was an attempt by Britain's High Commissioner Sir Alfred Milner to manoeuvre the Kruger government into a corner and force a war. On 9 October 1899, an Ultimatum from the South African Republic was handed to the British Agent in Pretoria. The Ultimatum stated that because of the unlawful intervention of Britain in the internal affairs of the Transvaal, an intolerable state of affairs existed and requested:

- that all points of mutual difference be regulated by friendly arbitration or in some amicable manner agreed upon by both the Transvaal and British governments;
- that the British troops on the borders of the Transvaal be withdrawn immediately;
- that all reinforcements of British troops that had arrived in the Cape or Natal since 1 June 1899 be removed from these territories within a reasonable time (with a reciprocal guarantee that the Transvaal would not attack any British territory), and that the Transvaal would ultimately withdraw its own burghers from the borders, and;

- that all British troops on the high seas should not land in the Cape or Natal.

If no satisfactory answer were received by 5:00 p.m. on 11 October 1899, the action, or inaction, of the British government would be looked upon as a declaration of war. The Boer Republics did not expect the British government to comply, and it was a challenge that the British authorities welcomed. Between 32,000 and 35,000 burghers from both the South African and the Orange Free State Republics were mobilised for commando service. The Ultimatum expired and the Boer forces invaded the Natal and Cape Colony early the following day.

The overall Boer plan of action was for a campaign fought on four fronts, in itself an extremely risky undertaking. The Natal front, which would form the bulk of their offensive, aimed to smash the British garrison at Dundee before isolating Ladysmith. The Western Front comprised of two sub fronts, namely the Transvaal forces isolating British forces at Mafeking and elsewhere in British Bechuanaland, while the Orange Free State forces isolated Kimberley and Griequaland West. Additional Transvaal forces would secure the Northern Front border between the Transvaal and Southern Rhodesia; and the Central Front comprising the areas around Colesberg and De Aar areas in the central Cape Colony being secured by the Orange Free State forces. From these positions they could prevent a British advance into the Republics, by creating depth of defence, and as in 1881, terms could then be sought from a favourable military position.[8]

Prior to the outbreak of hostilities in South Africa, the British War Office, headed by the Commander in Chief, Field Marshal Lord G.J. Wolseley, devised a strategy whereby the British Army could swiftly defeat the Boer commandos and subjugate the Republics. Known as the War Office Plan, this strategy entailed a two-phase knockout blow, with the Orange Free State Republic forming the initial objective, prior to an invasion of the South African Republic. This plan assumed that upon the outbreak of war, the British military would hold the strategic advantage in terms of offensive operations and that prior to the outbreak of hostilities, an Army Corps was positioned in the North and central regions of the Cape Colony. This Army Corps would then cross two strategic bridges spanning the Orange River at Norvalspont and at Bethulie and, once across the only natural obstacle in its path, sweep across the open plains of the southern Orange Free State Republic to seize Bloemfontein, its capital city.

The Corps would then advance North across the Vaal River, invade the South African Republic and in capturing Pretoria, conclude the war. During this phase, the central railway infrastructure would provide the logistic routes to the Cape ports and rear supply dumps. Consequently, pre-war strategic and tactical thinking hinged around the western and central railway systems, both as the main points of entry into the Boer Republics and the conduits with which to sustain the critical mass required for successful conquest by

---

8 J.H. Breytenbach, *Die Geskiedenis van die Tweede Vryheidsoorlog, Vol. I* (Pretoria: Die Staatsdrukker, 1978), pp.153-158.

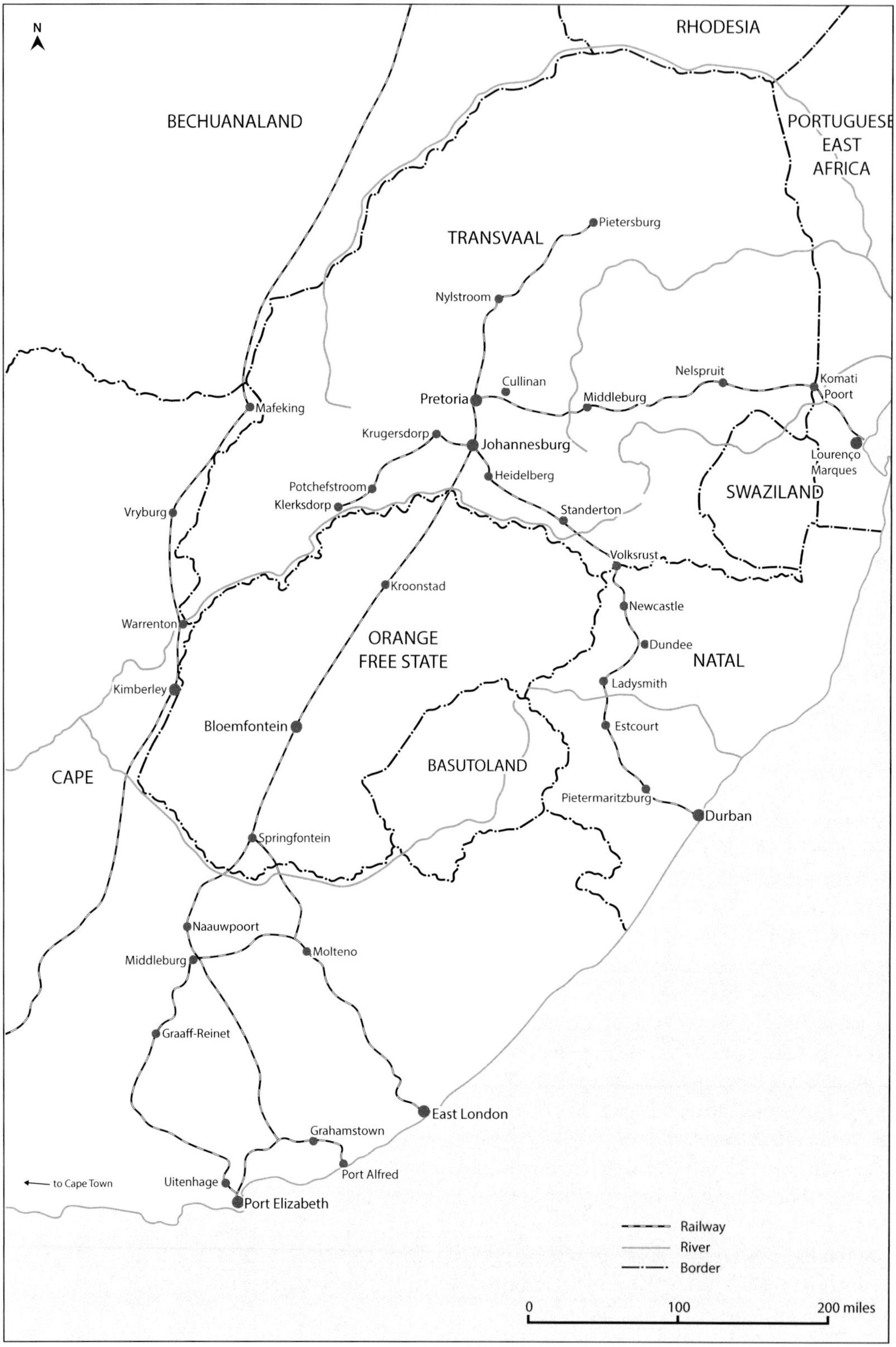

The entire war was going to be anchored to the railway network for supplies, reinforcements and moving troops, civilians and animals across a vast landscape during operations.

an army in the field. Lord H.H. Kitchener's feat of supplying his army by rail and river up to the critical point of the final battle at Omdurman underwrote War Office thinking.

While the plan assumed a degree of mopping up operations to finalise any spluttering resistance once the capital cities were occupied, it did not anticipate a protracted guerrilla war, which in fact occurred. Most importantly, it failed to take into account that the Boer forces might seize the initiative by striking first into the Natal and Cape Colonies, thus tilting the strategic advantage in their favour and jeopardising the basis of this strategy. Consequently, although this strategy was a central component of the War Office strategic framework, the Office did little by way of preparing itself for an actual conflict in South Africa.

Much has been written about its failure to do so with various writings apportioning blame to increasing meddling by the British Government's Secretary for War, Lord Lansdowne, in the Office and its affairs.[9] In 1895 the British government embarked upon a 'reform policy' of the Office, which saw increasing government control over this institution and a curtailing of Wolseley's authority within it. This raised the level of tension between Wolseley and the civilians whom he detested. However, it is worth noting that the War Office head, both literally and figuratively, was not functioning effectively.

In 1897, Wolseley succumbed to a bout of influenza and upon his return to duty, seemed incapable of making decisions and was prone to suffering from memory loss. His condition, being some form of dementia, isolated him further from both his subordinates and the civilian controlling body, both crucial instruments for instituting effective military policy to deal with a potential South African conflict.[10]

Added to this was an element of financial complacency and parsimony by the British Treasury who, used to easy and cheap military victories, saw no reason to allocate additional monies to the War Office. Lord Lansdowne believed that a political solution might be yet found and that increased troop levels in South Africa could undermine this process. This therefore negated the need for what was perceived by the British Government as unnecessary expenditure and, coupled with a non-interventionist policy, the Government instead followed a wait and see approach with regards to Republican intentions.

Consequently, troop numbers in the Natal and Cape Colonies remained low throughout 1899 and in June 1899 stood at some 10,000 strong (or weak). At the outbreak of war field commanders had no maps, or outdated maps so inaccurate that they proved of little value. For example, at the Battle of Modder River, Lord Methuen had a map reflecting only one river across his path, when in fact there were two. Events on the South African landscape inexorably rolled towards an outbreak of hostilities. On 6 June 1899, General Sir R. Buller was appointed as the Commander of the Army First Corps

9 Thomas Pakenham, *The Boer War* (Johannesburg: Jonathan Ball Publishers, 1979); and Rayne Kruger, *Goodbye Dolly Grey The Story of the Boer War*, 5th Edition (London: Pan Books, 1964).

10 J.L. Meriwether, 'The uncertain path: War Office administration and the journey into war, South Africa, 1896–1899', *Military History Journal*, 11:3/4, (1999), p.76.

which, in the event of conflict, would be dispatched to South Africa to implement the War Office plan.

Before the outbreak of war, the Boer strategy hinged on surrounding three key towns, each for differing reasons. Ladysmith – given the high numbers of British troops concentrated in the area, Mafeking – given the railway route into Bechuanaland and Southern Rhodesia – and Kimberley, for the economic role its diamond mines played in the economy of the Cape Colony. The immediate objective of this strategy was to lock up these garrisons, force their surrender and defeat these forces, while denting imperial prestige.

With the flames of rebellion fanning through British territory and behind the logistic lines of the British forces, the Republican forces could then inflict sufficient defeats on the British relief columns and force the British government to the negotiating table. This siege and settlement strategy should fulfil the political strategy, much as it had done eighteen years before during the Transvaal War of Independence (1880–1881), which culminated in the Majuba battle. Such was the power of Majuba to influence Boer thinking, despite the advances in weapons technology and tactical thinking by the British army during the preceding two decades.[11]

The Republics allocated the bulk of their military resources and striking power to the Natal front, as this colony contained the strongest British garrisons in Southern Africa. With the expiry of the ultimatum on 11 October, Joubert's commandos entered Natal the following day, outmanoeuvred General W. Penn Symons at Dundee and, swooping down on Ladysmith, locked up Sir G. White's army in Ladysmith. Additional forces invested Kimberley and Mafeking, while two smaller detachments entered the central and eastern districts of the Cape Colony over the Norvalspont and Bethulie bridges. The first, under General H.J. Schoeman, was tasked with seizing the British supply dump and central and western railway junctions at De Aar,

The Ficksburg Commando mobilising for war in the Ficksburg town showgrounds. These burghers played a key role in the Boer victory and British defeat on the South African veld at Magersfontein. (With permission, War Museum of the Boer Republics)

11 G. Benneyworth, MA Research Report, *Reinterpreting Military Landscape* (Johannesburg: University of Witwatersrand, 2002), pp.43–48.

The Winburg Commando mobilising in Winburg town square. (With permission, War Museum of the Boer Republics)

Centre burgher standing was Kommandant A.J. Naudé of the Winburg Commando at mobilisation. Amongst other actions, he fought at Belmont, Graspan, Modder River and Magersfontein, later being killed in action at Driefontein, 10 March 1900. (With permission, War Museum of the Boer Republics)

while the second, under General J.H. Olivier, had to shield Schoeman's left flank. Once they had seized their military targets, their primary objective would be raising the rebellion.

Schoeman had, in his sights, the most strategic target of the entire Western Campaign, namely De Aar. Had he seized this junction, he would have cut off the logistic route for the British column at Orange River Station, further isolated the invested Kimberley garrison and made the task of any counter invasion of the Orange Free State by a British force infinitely more difficult to achieve. Unfortunately for the Boer cause, Schoeman was incompetent, showing no sign of aggressive action and never fulfilled his objectives. Instead, allowing himself to be manoeuvred into Colesberg by Major General J.D.P. French's hastily formed cavalry division. While Schoeman threw away his strategic opportunity, Buller arrived in Cape Town and immediately set about formulating a crisis management plan.

Kimberley played a key role from the outbreak of war, when on 14 October 1899, the Republican forces besieged the city, heralding a 124-day siege. A scheme for Kimberley's defence was drawn up in 1896 and again in 1898 and 1899, which proposed defending Kimberley and Wesselton Mine, yet excluded Beaconsfield from the defence perimeter.[12]

With the arrival of Lieutenant Colonel R.G. Kekewich shortly before the outbreak of war, he revised this plan. Kekewich chose to include both Beaconsfield and the outlying Kimberley suburb of Kenilworth within a defended perimeter some 22 kilometres in length and containing approximately 50,000 residents. Wesselton Mine he would hold as an isolated strongpoint as it would provide the only adequate source of drinking water once the Boers cut the normal supply from the Vaal River, 35 kilometres away.[13] Despite there being two towns, namely Kimberley and Beaconsfield, each with their respective municipalities, the investment became known as the Siege of Kimberley.

The surrounding countryside for a radius of 100 kilometres was barren of trees, hacked down for firewood to supply the mines. Kimberley and Beaconsfield were set on a relatively flat landscape with no prominent topographic features within the urban limits. The only hills were the debris dumps generated from the diamond mines. It was the mining infrastructure and the dumps around which all the defences were anchored. The defence line that was constructed consisted of redoubts, trenches, minefields, and barbed wire entanglements all built by African compound workers supplied by De Beers Consolidated Mines to the military, headed by Rhodes who was trapped in the town.[14]

---

12 Maurice, *History of the War in South Africa*, vol. II.

13 D.E. Peddle, 'LONG CECIL The Gun made in Kimberley during the Siege', *Military History Journal*, 4:1 (June 1977), p.2.

14 J. Weale, *Paper III Siege of Kimberley Report of the Royal Engineers* (London: Royal Engineers, 1903), pp.70–77.

The brunt of the casualties during the Siege fell on the mine workers locked inside the compounds and not the civilian population. Many of them starved to death. (McGregor Museum, with permission)

The Siege of Kimberley, 14 October 1899–15 February 1900

The Boer force surrounding Kimberley dominated the battlefield with longer range artillery. This fire dominance enabled them to shell Kimberley without fear of effective counter-shelling. Nor were they selective about their targets. During the siege, the Boers fired approximately 8,500 shells, the overwhelming majority aimed at residences and the business areas of the two towns.[15] This situation changed slightly when, on 19 January 1900, a field gun with equal range, manufactured in the De Beers workshops, returned fire. To counter this, the Boers brought down from Pretoria a heavier artillery piece, the 155 mm Creusot Long Tom, which opened fire on the two towns on 7 February 1900, causing widespread civilian panic.

On 11 February 1900, 3,000 white women and children were sent down the mines for safety where they remained throughout this last week of the siege.[16] No such safety existed for the African mineworkers locked up inside their closed mining compounds. By return, the garrison fired 2,281 shells, most of which were manufactured in the De Beers Consolidated Mines workshops; the base of the shells stamped either with a diamond and De Beers or Compts CJR, which stood for Compliments of Cecil John Rhodes.[17]

15 Peddle, 'LONG CECIL', p.6.
16 Peddle, 'LONG CECIL', p.16.
17 Siege of Kimberley Display, McGregor Museum.

'Long Cecil', a 4.1 inch rifled breech loading gun designed by an American mining engineer, George Labram (pictured leaning the gun wheel), and manufactured in the De Beers Consolidated Mines workshops. Rhodes ordered its construction on Christmas day 1899, and it opened fire on 23 January 1900. On 9 February 1900, return Boer artillery fire killed Labram, who was buried with full military honours, his funeral procession being shelled by the Boers. Long Cecil fired 255 shells at the Boers over the last 21 days of the Siege. (McGregor Museum, with permission)

Earlier in the siege, on 31 October 1899, the De Beers Consolidated Mines Directors in Kimberley smuggled a telegram through the Boer lines to Britain's High Commissioner to South Africa Sir Alfred Milner in Cape Town, which hinted at all sorts of catastrophes for the British war effort, should military resources not be directed to their aid. This is important to note as this was not the last time that the company Directors attempted to manipulate the military to their advantage through using their political connections.

The Directors conveyed the possibility of an uprising among their African workers should the diamond workings remain closed due to a protracted siege and reported that food reserves were low. They suggested that food shortages would prove disastrous for the white civilians trapped inside the siege lines. The Directors mentioned that the Boer forces positioned between Kimberley and Orange River Station numbered no more than three thousand men, which was more than just a hint that the military authorities should take them seriously in their request for action. Were they not to respond then the Directors implied that they would surrender the town.

> We hope with the arrival of General Buller measures will be taken for the immediate relief of this place. Our information, which is reliable, gives not more than 2,000 to 3,000 Boers between this place and Orange River, and in our opinion we could already have been relieved without risk by the present force in Cape Colony. We have a very limited supply of coal, and when it is done we must close down the works, which will cause serious trouble amongst our 10,000 savages in our compounds, who are now kept quiet by being kept at work. If we discharge them, and send them home, they are sure to be driven back to the town by the Boers, which must lead to heavy loss of life. As to the question of food supply, though well provided with some things, we have only nine days tinned meat in

> case cattle are taken by the Boers, which of course, is probable. We do not know the reasons which have delayed our relief, but we think Your Excellency ought to weigh the risks caused by delay to this place with its 30,000 inhabitants, 10,000 of whom are raw savages. Now that the General has arrived we respectfully request to be informed as to the policy to be adopted regarding our relief, so as to enable us to take our own steps in case relief is refused. We are sending this by special messenger to Orange River, and will await your reply.[18]

General Sir Redvers Buller, VC, (1839 to 1908) a recipient of the Victoria Cross, saw extensive service in Canada, China, Ashantiland, Egypt, Sudan, and South Africa. The South African Field Force, initially, and then the Natal Field Force being his last command. (From L. Creswicke, *South Africa and the Transvaal War*, Volume 2 (Edinburgh: TC & EC Jack, 1900))

When Milner received the telegram he showed it to Buller, yet he appears to have sided with the Directors. Milner advised Buller to bear in mind that the African population attached immense importance to Kimberley. Should the city capitulate, this would damage British prestige and impact negatively on Anglo-African relations in South Africa. This appears to be an attempt to dictate policy to the military, in favour of De Beers Consolidated Mines.

Buller immediately requested Kekewich in Kimberley to clarify the matter. 'Civilians in Kimberley representing situation there as serious. Have heard nothing about this from you. Send appreciation of the situation immediately'.[19] When Kekewich received this signal, smuggled through by a runner, on 9 November 1899, he realised that Rhodes and his cohorts had transmitted conflicting and alarmist information behind his back. He immediately responded, informing Buller that while the situation was not critical and that the city could withstand a siege, the scenario could worsen should the Boers bring up heavy artillery, which they eventually did.[20]

Buller's first instinct was to trust an army officer, for he mistrusted these capitalists, yet he could not ignore the power that they wielded. If he did not come to their aid, then he feared the risk that they would undermine the defence of British interests and induce the surrender of the town. They had no power to surrender Kimberley given that martial law prevailed, yet they could withhold key resources, making it difficult to defend the town. On the matter he later stated that,

> I should have preferred to have diverted every possible man of my forces to Natal, for in Natal lay my true objective – the principle force of the enemy. But at the same time I felt it impossible to ignore Kimberley. That town represented to the native

18 Maurice, *History of the War*, p.65.

19 O'Meara, (1926), *Lt-Colonel Kekewich in Kimberley*, as quoted in T. Pakenham, *The Boer War* (Johannesburg: Jonathan Ball Publishers 1978), p.185.

20 T Pakenham, *The Boer War*, p.185.

Colonel Robert Kekewich (1854–1914) of the 1st Battalion The Loyal North Lancashire Regiment commanded the Kimberley garrison during the siege. For his services in the war he was made a Companion of the Order of the Bath. In August 1902, he was promoted to Major General, for distinguished service in the field. (McGregor Museum, with permission)

> the symbol of British power and property in South Africa, and I feared the effect of its fall upon the native mind in general and upon the Basuto's (sic) in particular. Moreover, though I felt the fullest confidence in the military commandant, Colonel Kekewich, I did not trust the other powers within the city. Very reluctantly, therefore, I decided to divide my forces.[21]

To deal with the Kimberley scenario, Buller ordered the 1st Infantry Division under Lord Methuen to assemble at Orange River Station, located 120 kilometres south of Kimberley, and to then lift the siege. However, he seriously underestimated the task, as events later proved.

At the start of the siege there were 11,106 African workers locked up inside the mining compounds.[22] Rhodes instructed his compound manager, W.D. Fynn, to remove as many workers as possible from Kimberley to reduce downtime labour costs resulting from the siege. Fynn was to lead the workers through the gauntlet beyond the Boer siege lines and leave them there to find their own way back to their homes. This would result in less mouths to feed enabling the mining company to slash its business overheads.[23] Yet by ejecting these workers, the Company knew exactly what risks they would face, given that they had highlighted this risk to Milner in their message, only seven days before.

On 7 November 1899, the Company tried to force 3,700 Basotho workers to vacate the compounds and return to Basutoland (Lesotho). On Rhodes's instructions, 1,700 workers from the De Beers mine compound and 2,000 from the Wesselton mine compound were to go.[24] The Boers were not about to allow this, as the more mouths to feed inside the town, the faster the food stockpiles would be eaten. The workers were turned back. In the weak light of dawn, the garrison artillery opened fire on the workers. When Kekewich realised the error, he permitted them back through the siege lines and into the compounds.[25]

21 Redvers Buller, *Evidence of General The Right Hon. Sir Redvers Buller Taken Before The Royal Commission on the War in South Africa* (London: Longmans Green and Co., 1904), p.10.
22 MMK: 2589: Mr W.D. Fynn's Reminiscences, Unpublished Manuscript, 16 April 1951, p.8.
23 MMK: 2589: Mr W.D. Fynn's Reminiscences, Unpublished Manuscript, 16 April 1951, p.8.
24 MMK: 2589: Mr W.D. Fynn's Reminiscences, Unpublished Manuscript, 16 April 1951, p.9.
25 MMK: 2589: Mr W.D. Fynn's Reminiscences, Unpublished Manuscript, 16 April 1951, p.10.

Waiting for rations. Nutrition and malnutrition varied, depending on race. (McGregor Museum, with permission)

Undeterred by this, additional attempts were made, and over time the workforce was whittled down to about 4,500 men.[26] By 4 December 1899, all mining operations ceased. Conditions in the compounds were dire. Due to starvation, 1,700 workers still inside the De Beers mine compound tried to break out and had to be subdued at bayonet point by soldiers.[27] W.D. Fynn later recorded that 1,600 Africans inside the compounds died from scurvy during the siege. He attributed this to Mr F. Gardner Williams, the General Manager, neglecting to provision the compounds adequately to withstand a siege, despite being instructed by Rhodes to do so.[28]

On 20 December 1899, rationing was only seriously enforced when the military commandeered all foodstuffs in Kimberley. Again racial policy prevailed as to who received the best and the worst nutrition. People designated as 'white' or 'coloured' individually received daily 14 ounces of bread or 10 ounces of Boer meel and flour, two ounces of mielies or corn, two ounces of rice, two ounces of sugar, ¼ of tea and ½ an ounce of coffee. Meat was half a pound per day. Those determined to be Indians received two ounces of mielie meal, four ounces of corn, eight ounces of rice and the same tea coffee and sugar allowance as whites. Those who were regarded as natives received six ounces of mielie meal, four ounces of corn, two ounces of samp, and tea, coffee, and sugar as per the others. It was the whites who had the only access to meat. All mine workers were to continue being fed by the mining companies, which was one tablespoonful of mielie meal per day.[29]

The Boer artillery pounded away and, although they killed and wounded a minimal number of civilians and troops and damaged property, they failed to induce surrender. Boer fire killed 51 and wounded 107.[30] Total deaths recorded during the siege were 1,679.[31] Of this 1,648 were those classified as natives, the chief cause of death being scurvy, followed by infantile diarrhoea,

26 MMK: 2589: Mr W.D. Fynn's Reminiscences, Unpublished Manuscript, 16 April 1951, p.9.
27 MMK: 2589: Mr W.D. Fynn's Reminiscences, Unpublished Manuscript, 16 April 1951, p.11.
28 MMK: 2589: Mr W.D. Fynn's Reminiscences, Unpublished Manuscript, 16 April 1951, p.12.
29 A.J. Beet and C.B. Harris, Kimberley under Siege, *Kimberley, Diamond Fields Advertiser*, 1950, p.43.
30 Siege of Kimberley Display, McGregor Museum.
31 Africana Library (Africana), Kimberley Corporation Mayors Minute, Municipal Year ending 31 December 1899, pp.110–121; Africana: Kimberley Corporation Mayors Minute, Municipal Year ending 31 December 1900, pp.72–85.

A Boer 75 mm Krupp field gun shelling residential and business areas during the Siege. (McGregor Museum, with permission)

and pneumonia.[32] The death rate for African babies was 935 out of every 1,000,[33] and 50 percent for white babies.[34] W.D. Fynn recorded 1,600 deaths in the compounds alone.[35] Boer shellfire claimed the lives of nine civilians.[36] The brunt fell on the mineworkers in the compounds who starved to death. Fifty buildings were damaged and six destroyed.[37]

One final point on the Siege of Kimberley. In all the histories and sources consulted on the siege and the war, the point never presented is that the Boer shelling of civilians would later result in a retaliatory response – particularly in the case of Kimberley where civilians were directly targeted by artillery fire. Most of the garrison's key defence works were built on top of mine dumps, the only high points in the area. These forts made excellent artillery targets, yet they were never shelled into destruction. The author's view is that because of the Boers indiscriminate targeting of civilians, in Kimberley, Beaconsfield, Ladysmith and Mafeking, views hardened in the British high command and in the minds of soldiers who later encountered Boer civilians. Added to this hardening response, yet to follow, was the looting and ransacking of Boer occupied Natal by the commandos.[38]

Kekewich had little option other than to sit tight and await the arrival of the relief column. He attempted to co-operate with the 1st Division's advance by retaining Boer troops around the city and thus preventing them from moving south to block Lord Methuen's advance. Garrison troops attacked the Boer redoubts and gun positions at Carter's Ridge on 25 November 1899, and again two days later. The first assault inflicted some casualties amongst the burghers but the second proved disastrous, resulting in unnecessarily

32 Africana: Kimberley Corporation Mayors Minute, Municipal Year ending 31 December 1899, p.83.
33 J. Beet and C.B. Harris, *Kimberley under Siege*, p.61.
34 Siege of Kimberley Display, McGregor Museum.
35 MMK: 2589: Mr W.D. Fynn's Reminiscences, Unpublished Manuscript, 16 April 1951. p.12.
36 Information supplied by the McGregor Museum, Kimberley to the author in 1998.
37 Siege of Kimberley Display, McGregor Museum.
38 See: H Rethman, *The Natal Campaign: A Sacrifice Betrayed* (Gloucestershire: Amberley Publishing, 2017).

Civilians in Kimberley and Beaconsfield sought shelter not only in bomb shelters, they also tunnelled into the mine debris dumps for safety from shellfire. (McGregor Museum, with permission)

high loss of life amongst the garrison troops. Aside from the Boer shelling, Kekewich's single greatest 'sniper' was Rhodes, who continually harassed, bullied, and pestered him. More so, when news leaked out of the plan to remove the civilian population.

Rhodes remonstrated and offered to raise 2,000 colonial volunteers at his own expense to reinforce the garrison once the relief column arrived. Were this not allowed, he threatened to shut the mines, dismiss all the white employees and hand over 13,000 African mine workers to the military for them to dispose of. Kekewich forwarded this information to Lord Methuen on 7 December 1899, who replied the following day. 'Please understand that I can give you one and a half battalions and a Naval brigade, and you must cut your coat according to your cloth. I am arranging military defence with you, and Rhodes must understand that he has no voice in the matter'.[39]

Rhodes expressed his loathing of the military for not pandering to his requirements saying to Kekewich: 'You damned soldiers are so loyal to one another that I verily believe if God Almighty even was in a fix you would refuse to get him out of it should it interfere with your damned military situation'.[40]

On 11 December 1899, while the Magersfontein battle was underway, Kekewich received a written despatch from Methuen that not a single civilian or African were to remain in Kimberley after the relief, unless required for essential services. Fifteen trains would be assigned to convey food supplies and thirty to remove the civilians, after the railway was opened on 15 December 1899, as hoped, and the evacuation finalised by 22 December 1899.[41]

39 *The War in South Africa*, p.62
40 Siege of Kimberley Display, McGregor Museum.
41 *The War in South Africa*, p.63.

The only memorial commemorating a black civilian who perished during the Siege. The plaque is inset in the pavement outside of the Kimberley Club. (Author's collection)

Kekewich had his orders; he ignored Rhodes, desisted from further offensive action, and awaited the British breakthrough. He later said that: 'Rhodes during the siege did excellent work for welfare, town and defenders: also when his views on military questions have coincided with mine; but he desires to control the military situation. I have put up with his insults so as not to risk safety of defence'.[42]

Criticism is easy in hindsight, yet the fact remains that the Boer siege lines around Kimberley absorbed some 7,000 burghers with nine field guns, and this constituted a major strategic misappropriation of the Republican fighting power. Unlike at Ladysmith and Mafeking, they made no attempt to capture Kimberley and Beaconsfield. Had the Republican Generals not become distracted by the relatively weak Kimberley garrison, which lacked sufficient striking power in any event to threaten the Republics, and had their commandos captured De Aar and penetrated deep into the Cape Colony, the outcome of the war might have been completely different.

42 Siege of Kimberley Display, McGregor Museum.

2

Formation of the 1st Infantry Division

Although the War Office Plan called for a concentration of forces in the central Cape Colony, this had to be tempered against the emergency unfolding in Natal. The Boers had locked up Ladysmith and little lay between them and Durban. Already their commandos were within striking distance of Pietermaritzburg. Buller later claimed to have received intelligence information that should they seize Durban then an undisclosed foreign power would enter the war in support of the Boer cause. Intelligence reports indicated that the bulk of the Boer strength was allocated to the Natal front and that Durban might indeed form their primary military objective. He believed that should he implement the War Office plan, this would not apply sufficient pressure against the Republics to affect a Boer withdrawal from Natal.[1]

Buller's main priority therefore was defending Natal and rescuing Ladysmith, but also balancing other regional issues against his need to achieve this. As an immediate stop gap he arranged with the Admiral of the Cape Station to land some naval guns at Durban to secure the port. The bulk of the Army Corps reinforcements would have to be split up with the majority of arriving troops being sent to Natal, while the remainder would shore up the central and western fronts of the Cape Colony. Once the situation in Natal had been stabilised and the Boers ejected from the colony, then the troops would be re-routed back to the Cape Colony to implement the War Office Plan. Buller decided that he would base himself in Natal as this seemed to be the centre of the crisis. Apart from this, he knew the territory, having won his Victoria Cross during extensive service in the 1879 Anglo-Zulu War.

Nevertheless, events in the central and eastern Cape could also not be ignored. Major General J.D.P. French was on route to Noupoort to undertake a holding action in order to shore up the central front and so secure De Aar and the line back to Cape Town. Buller ordered General W.F. Gatacre at Queenstown to remain on the defensive and frustrate any further Boer

1 Evidence of Buller *Royal Commission*, p.10.

Lord Methuen, despite his defeats and being captured by General J.H. De la Rey in 1902, remained popular with the British hierarchy, later rising to the rank of Field Marshal. After the war he became General Officer Commanding-in-Chief in South Africa in 1908, Governor and Commander-in-Chief of Natal in 1910 and then Governor and Commander-in-Chief of Malta in 1915. (McGregor Museum, with permission)

invasion into the Eastern Cape districts and to supplement his numerically weak force with locally raised volunteers.

To deal with the Kimberley scenario, Buller decided to send an infantry division under Methuen to lift the siege. Once the division reached Kimberley it was to extract the civilian population and rail them down to the Cape, while throwing in reinforcements so that the garrison could hold its own. The division would then fall back on Orange River Station, before cutting across country to Colesberg where it would link up with French and the reinforcements constituting the Army Corps. Then, hopefully, the plan could unfold and Buller, having managed a crisis that had initially caught everyone off guard, could get on with the job of seizing the Boer capitals and winning the war. However, he seriously underestimated the task allocated to Methuen, as events later proved.

First shots

On 19 October 1899, Kommandant P.T. van der Merwe's 300 strong Fauresmith Commando occupied Belmont station and laagered their wagons behind the hills in a hollow on Kaffir Kop farm, known as Frederick's Kop.[2] Their scouts reported that a numerically stronger British force was assembling at Orange River Station and, as General J. Prinsloo's commandos were shortly expected to reinforce his weak force, van der Merwe desisted from any offensive action further south. However, as a British advance would in all likelihood follow the railway line, he ordered his burghers to destroy the culverts and telegraph poles located within an area four miles North and three miles south of Belmont Station.[3] Having done so, he awaited reinforcements.

Isolated from the mainstream of the war, rumours ran rife amongst the Orange River Station garrison of an impending Boer attack. Mr E.F. Knight, a newspaper correspondent attached to the force, summed up the situation:

> The township which surrounds the railway station, is merely a congregation of a few houses belonging to people connected with the railway. It stands in the midst of a desert—a dusty treeless plain covered with low sparse sage bush and enclosed

2 The National Archives of the United Kingdom (TNA) WO 32/7884: Lieutenant Colonel G.H. Gough, Despatch of Reconnaissance to Belmont, 11 November 1899, p.2.

3 TNA: WO 32/7884: 'Despatch of Reconnaissance to Belmont', p.2.

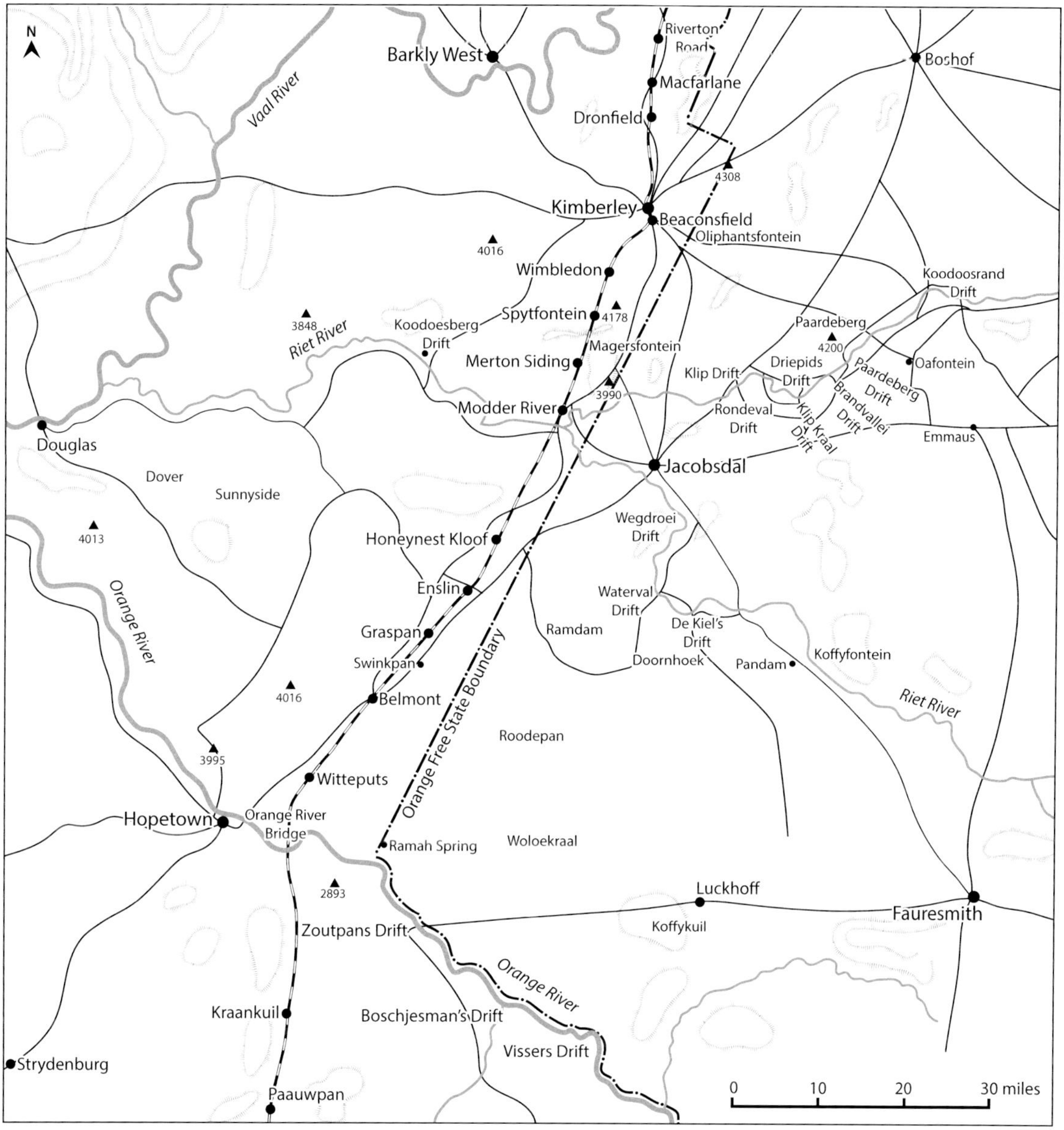

Area of operations. For the Boer forces they had depth of defence, offering battle at Belmont, Graspan, Modder River, Magersfontein and Spytfontein. The supplies were transported from Jacobsdal which in turn was victualled by Bloemfontein. The British forces faced a weakness of depth of offence by moving further North from Orange River Station. They risked being outflanked and running out of water between that place and the Modder River.

> by rocky ridges. It is wonderful, indeed, that the Boers did not attempt to seize this valuable prize a week or so ago, when the camp was practically undefended, and when our officers, momentarily expecting attack, were sleeping in their boots. Our position is far from secure even now; our force here is insignificant, and it seems the Boers are getting closer. They have crossed the river at various points. It is rumoured today that they are close to, and that the attack on De Aar is but a question of hours. But still the heavily laden trains come in with their valuable freight and the military stores accumulate.[4]

Buller meanwhile telegraphed Major General E. Wood, the Officer Commanding Orange River Station, that he required a 'strong wish for news about Belmont.'[5] This request, coming from Natal, seemed easier said than done, for Wood had no knowledge of exactly where the Boer force was positioned or what its intentions and numbers were.

The countryside North of the station stretched away into a horizon studded with hills and broken ground, all of which could conceal large bodies of Boer forces that might swallow up a scouting patrol. The Boer forces to date remained completely out of sight, invisible on a landscape where the only movement noticeable to the sentries and through the officers' field glasses and telescopes from the surrounding heights were the swirling dust devils, shimmering heat haze and an occasional ostrich prancing across the great plains.[6]

The veld seemed to swallow all that entered it.

> The surface of the veldt looked level, yet it was far from that as to cause a body of our troops at one time, and at another time a railway train, to disappear suddenly, though the surface seemed flat all around them. They vanished at a few miles distance, and though we imagined ourselves to able to look down upon the whole plain, their further progress entirely was hidden from our view.[7]
>
> It looks level because it is a dead and dull monotony of baked earth, sage tufts, and stones, any single acre being precisely like the next hundred or ten thousand. Instead of being smooth, it rises and falls in earth billows, and often in the depression behind the ridge of such a billow an army can move…But there is far better cover for the Boers than these afford. There are the so-called nullahs and spruits, which seam the veld in millions of places. No one can see them until he is almost upon them, yet their troops can move unseen on horseback. In hundreds of them the whole Boer army could ride invisible for miles.[8]

Consequently, any reconnaissance entering this landscape and running into difficulty would require strength and firepower to extricate itself, should the main Boer force materialize in large numbers. Lieutenant Colonel B. Gough

4 E.F. Knight, Correspondent, *The Morning Post*, 1899.
5 TNA: WO 32/7884: 'Despatch of Reconnaissance to Belmont', p.1.
6 Julian Ralph, *Towards Pretoria: A Record of the War between Briton and Boer to the Hoisting of the British Flag at Bloemfontein* (London: C Arthur Pearson Ltd, 1900), pp.144, 145.
7 Ralph, *Towards Pretoria*, pp.146, 147.
8 Julian Ralph, *An American With Lord Roberts* (New York: Frederick A. Stokes Company, 1900), p.5.

9th Lancers scouting. (McGregor Museum, with permission)

then undertook, 'a reconnaissance and demonstration to the North with Cavalry and artillery, to shell Belmont, and to show enemy we are alive.'[9] Simply put, to show aggressive action. On 9 November 1899, Gough set off with the 9th Lancers, some Mounted Infantry and two field guns. On reaching Fincham's farm, a mile West of Witteputs railway siding, they pitched camp. Patrols were then dispatched towards Belmont and a two man probe to investigate the area as far North as Heuningneskloof Siding.[10] Although the Burghers near Belmont sniped at and chased some of these patrols back to Witteputs, no serious clash of note occurred.

Gough reported back to Wood and Lieutenant Colonel W. Verner, that he recruited the services of some local Afrikaans-speaking guides who knew the terrain and reported the Boer strength at some 700 strong with one field gun. Gough also indicated that he would return to Belmont the following day to pinpoint the laager. Some infantry were then railed up from Orange River Station to secure his camp at Fincham's Farm.

The following morning the mounted troops set off towards Belmont but were soon drawn into an engagement on ground of the Boers' choosing. Some forward British scouts whose horses were dropped by sniper fire had to be rescued by the main force, which then pressed forward towards Luiperds Kop.[11] The guides advised Gough that this feature screened the Boer laager and the Boer artillery opened fire, confirming that they were in fact defending a position. Gough's field guns returned fire and he ordered his troops to dismount and form a firing line but when pressing closer towards the hills,

9 TNA: WO 32/7884: 'Despatch of Reconnaissance to Belmont', p.1.
10 TNA: WO 32/7884: 'Despatch of Reconnaissance to Belmont', p.1.
11 TNA: WO 32/7884: 'Despatch of Reconnaissance to Belmont', pp.8–9.

Boers firing on the cavalry. The picture accurately depicts the terrain and that many of the older Orange Free State burghers were armed with the Martini Henry rifle. (From *Penny Illustrated*, Public Domain)

they came under rifle fire. Gough ordered a mounted detachment to turn the Boer left flank, but they rode into an ambush prepared by twelve Boer riflemen who promptly emptied seven British saddles. Gough immediately broke off the engagement and returned to Witteputs.

The explosions reverberated to Orange River Station. While the soldiers and correspondents scrambled up the hills hoping for a view of the distant action,[12] Verner railed up additional infantry to Witteputs. They arrived in time to load up the broken bodies of the dead, dying and wounded before returning to camp. British losses were two dead and five wounded and Boer casualties two wounded.[13]

The following day Methuen heard of this skirmish when about to dine at Government House in Cape Town. He later severely criticised Gough's management of this encounter and on 14 November 1899, two days after his arrival at Orange River Station, added an addendum to Gough's despatch of the operation:

> I consider this operation was unsatisfactorily conducted – this main …for distant reconnaissance can only be maintained by keeping mostly all their time along a new track – To fall back, sleep, and go in again was in my opinion an unnecessary

12 Ralph, *Towards Pretoria*, pp.142–143.

13 Maurice, *History of the War*, vol. 1, p.213.

> risk. Also I think that to allow a reconnaissance to develop into a half hearted fight was a mistake— … I do not think the operation was a good one.[14]

This clash saw a deteriorating relationship between these two officers, heralding the creation of a scapegoat for subsequent tactical failures, during the Belmont and Graspan actions. Buller's response to Gough's reconnaissance was: 'When will officers learn that fighting is fighting, reconnaissance is reconnaissance'.[15] Methuen was angry about the death of Keith Falconer: 'Poor Falconer, married only 6 months and this news broken to her whilst we were going into dinner at Government House. A real bungle losing 2 good officers, a milder man than Gough and Verner I never saw. I think Weitz or Seymor could lick the two.'[16]

Methuen later claimed that on or around 18 November 1899, Buller instructed him to remove Lieutenant Colonel G.H. Gough from his command and send him to Stellenbosch as Commandant of the remount depot. Being Stellenbosched was for officers in South Africa a disgrace, and sounded the death knell of their military careers. In Gough's case this would take a different turn. Methuen left him in his position and only relieved him of his command after the Graspan action, a week later. This 'Stellenbosching' of Gough occurred at convenient moment when Methuen was desperate for a scapegoat to which he could attach the blame for his hollow victories at Belmont and Graspan. The resultant disgrace of his dismissal drove Gough to suicide.

For Kommandant van der Merwe's burghers, their success at driving back a numerically superior British force boosted their morale, instilling a false sense of confidence that their Belmont position was impregnable to British attack.

> The troops made an advance on Belmont yesterday. When we advanced last night they retired to Witteputs. This morning they again moved forward to attack us. We took up position on a ridge. The fight lasted about four hours, after which three ambulance wagons arrived to load up the dead and wounded. The loss of the enemy, although unknown, appears to be considerable. Jacobus van Rooyen and Andries du Preez were slightly wounded on our side. Also three horses wounded. We had 350 men, the enemy about 700 men, 3 guns and 2 maxims. We captured two horses, with saddles, etc. Our artillerists worked their guns very smartly. The enemy retired in the direction of Orange River Bridge.[17]

What this action also resulted in was that the two Boer governments realised that they needed to reinforce van der Merwe's forces to thwart the imminent British advance on Kimberley. Kruger withdrew forces from the Northern and Western borders to be rapidly dispatched to this front. On 16 November

14 TNA: WO 32/7884: Despatch of Reconnaissance to Belmont, pp.17–18. The gaps in this transcript are due to illegible handwriting in sections of the original document.

15 MMK: P.S. Methuen, Diary of War, 1899, Unpublished Manuscript, p.7.

16 MMK: 7654/194 a: P.S. Methuen, 1899, Letter to Wife, Unpublished Manuscript, 18–24 November 1899, p.2.

17 South African Library (SAL) AZF. 1991–15: Copy of Kommandant P.T. van der Merwe War Telegram, 11 November 1899.

1899, Steyn advised Kruger that Belmont had been reinforced comprising 1,500 burghers who arrived from the siege lines around Kimberley on 16 November 1899, and another 100 from Wepener. By 23 November 1899, the day of the Belmont action, Prinsloo had a force 2,000 strong in position on the hills and another 950 men either on route or at various points along the railway line.

3

Advance on Kimberley

'Of course, it is so easy now to find fault with our not having had better sketches of the Transvaal and Free State. I happened to be Deputy Adjutant-General in the Cape for some time, and if we had sent anybody up to the Transvaal or Free State sketching promiscuously they would have got back pretty quickly'.[1]

A cornerstone for any successful military operation is the acquisition of accurate intelligence information about the topography of the designated operational area and the available natural resources, such as water and foodstuffs, required to sustain an army in the field. Intelligence preparations by the British army for the impending conflict against the Boer Republics proved ineffective. Yet although there may be some merit in the opening statement by Methuen that espionage activities could not effectively or safely be undertaken in the Republics, this can hardly be true regarding the complete lack of preparedness, which existed in terms of the Cape Colony.

The route to Kimberley from Orange River Station ran through British territory, yet the lack of topographical intelligence meant that it formed for Methuen, an unknown landscape. He had no accurate maps, indicating the topography to be encountered along the road to Modder River and Kimberley and no detailed sketches, other than a map indicating farm boundaries, which in any event was not to scale.[2] This was a serious issue, as mistaken topography became a characteristic of the Belmont action while complete ignorance of the topography a critical feature of the Modder River battle.

The post war histories mention this topographical information deficit. Yet it is worth noting that Methuen participated in the 1885–86 Warren Expedition, which had, as one of its objectives, surveying of the Transvaal/Orange Free State/Cape Colony border area of the Colony as far North as Mafeking. By his own admission Methuen was the Deputy Adjutant General in South Africa 1888-1890, yet silence pervades within the official histories

---

1 P.S. Methuen, *Minutes of Evidence, Royal Commission on the War in South Africa* (London: Wyman and Sons Ltd, 1903), Volume 2, pp.130, 132.

2 Methuen, *Minutes of Evidence*, pp.130, 132.

and the Methuen papers as to why the Colony had not been effectively charted by the military before the outbreak of the war.[3]

The only accurate information compiled to date was obtained by Lieutenant Colonel B. Gough during his recent reconnaissance. His report included descriptions of the various roads and tracks approaching Belmont, with an assessment of their suitability (or lack thereof) for wheeled transport. He assessed the damage wrought to the railway and communications infrastructure, while identifying the drinking wells located between Orange River and Belmont Stations. Gough included an estimate of their pumping capacities and gallon volumes and assessed the available cattle and sheep stock resources on the farms in the vicinity. His skirmish with van der Merwe's forces indicated to Methuen and his Staff that the Boer force at Belmont was intent on holding the position. Gough's intelligence from local informants enabled Methuen's Intelligence Officer, Major R.N.R. Reade an opportunity to assess the Boer strength.[4] On 18 November 1899, Reade estimated that at Belmont this stood at around some 700 to 1,200 burghers with four guns, and that a commando had successfully recruited new members from the ranks of the disloyal farmers in the Barkly West, Campbell, Douglas and Griquatown districts.[5]

Most importantly of all, Gough had sketched the southern end of the Boer position (later known as Sugar Loaf), albeit while under fire and included this map into his reconnaissance report.[6] Yet, the official histories[7] and Methuen are silent on the fact that this sketch map offered him a first glance into the topography of what subsequently became the Boers left and southern flank during the Belmont engagement. However, it was Verner who later received the credit for being the 'past master at the art of reconnaissance'.[8] This wartime and post war praise was seriously misplaced.

Before advancing into an unknown landscape, Methuen had to consider his logistics and communication lines with his rear supply dumps and the route of his advance, through Boer held territory. Both considerations were determined by only one factor, that of the route of the western railway line between Orange River Station and Kimberley. This was because:

> I had to keep to the railway, because I could only carry a certain amount, I forget how many days of supplies with the mule transport, for most of that was required for the blankets, and so on, that had to go with the regiments, and the remainder of my provisions were carried by the railway, which followed me day by day.[9]

Methuen would rely upon this line for the speedy re-supply of both troops and munitions when required and the rapid transmission, by train, of Kimberley's populace south once he had reached the beleaguered towns. The line connected his force with the supply dumps at De Aar and the Cape ports

3 This refers to all sources listed in this book.
4 TNA: WO 32/7884: 'Despatch of Reconnaissance to Belmont', pp.2–8.
5 Maurice, *History of the War*, pp.213–214.
6 TNA: WO 32/7884: 'Despatch of Reconnaissance to Belmont', p.9.
7 This refers to all sources listed in this Bibliography.
8 Methuen, *Minutes of Evidence*, vol. 2, p.125.
9 Methuen, *Minutes of Evidence*, p.120.

and French's forces at Noupoort junction, which effectively formed his right flank.

Methuen's route was a non-negotiable option; the railway line was crucial to the fulfilment of his orders and the broader military objectives. Yet by following it, the Boer forces were left with no doubt as to where to position their forces to block his advance on Kimberley, in accordance with their objectives. These odds weighed heavily against Methuen in this respect, yet his route, like the many war memorials that currently mark its path, was set in stone. However, it did not rule out the option for outflanking manoeuvres.

Buller's orders were, that upon reaching Kimberley, the non-essential white civilians and the entire black populace be evacuated, provisions offloaded and the garrison reinforced with infantry and four naval guns before the Division returned to Orange River Station.[10] This planned forced removal of the civilian population was kept secret, as many would resist this dislocation, yet ironically, the 1st Infantry Division became known as the Kimberley Relief Column.

Major General (later Field Marshal) John Denton Pinkstone French led a distinguished career as a cavalry officer, seeing active service in Egypt, the Sudan, India and South Africa where he made his name, serving right through the conflict. He later commanded the British Expeditionary Force for the first year and a half of the First World War. (From M. Menpes, *War Impressions Being A Record In Colour* (London: Adam & Charles Black, 1901))

Methuen's orders from Buller were:

> To clear out, I think, something like 11 000 useless mouths, who were black men, and so on. I was to send up the trains holding provisions sufficient for Kimberley to go on with for some time, and clear out all these black men and send them down country or where I could; at any rate get them out of Kimberley. I was to move Mr Rhodes too, and having done that to get back as quick as I could.[11]

Having done this, he was 'to return to Orange River, where I have got a million rations. You will probably be cut off from us all; you must fight the enemy where you meet him; and you must make your way across to Colesberg to join French'.[12]

Buller believed that the breakthrough to Kimberley would induce the besieging Boer forces to pull back on Bloemfontein to counter a potential invasion of the Orange Free State from the south, thus leaving the Kimberley garrison strong enough to safely stand-alone.[13] Once back at Orange River Station, Methuen was to cut across country to link up with General French's forces near Colesberg, who by this stage should have blocked the Boer invasion of the central Cape Colony and then seize the Bethulie and Norvals

10 12 pr 12 cwt Quick Firing 'Long 12' naval guns.
11 Methuen, *Minutes of Evidence*, pp.119–120.
12 Methuen, *Minutes of Evidence*, Telegram: Buller to Methuen, p.120.
13 Methuen, *Minutes of Evidence*, Telegram: Buller to Methuen, p.120.

Pont bridges. Once additional reinforcements had arrived Methuen's force would then invade the Orange Free State, in line with the War Office Plan.[14]

Yet were these two officers in agreement with this plan? The official histories make no mention of any disagreement between the Commander in Chief and his subordinate, but a confidential despatch written by Buller to the Under Secretary of War reveals a somewhat different picture of Buller's assessment of Methuen. It indicates that Methuen may not have been the type of General that the official histories have subsequently made him out to be while offering insight into why he might have made some serious misjudgements before and during the Belmont, Modder River and Magersfontein engagements.

> In a conversation with Lord Methuen before he started to Orange river, I told him that, after he got to Kimberley, helped them to get rid of the 9000 natives and 7000 women and children who now endanger their defence, reinforced the garrison, and left the heavy naval guns I am preparing to send them; I wished him to drop back to Orange River, by which time I hoped to be in a position to send some of his force through De Aar by rail to Noupoort and to march the rest on Colesberg. He said that going back was a great mistake and strongly advocated his advance for Pretoria direct on Bloemfontein. At the time he made this proposition he was fully aware of the facts of the situation, and knew that my available force was so small that I was intending to leave the communications with Kimberley unprotected. I consider it so reckless a proposition and one that shows so little real military knowledge, that it has certainly shaken my confidence in him. I feel it my duty to report this.[15]

In terms of potential Boer opposition Methuen later claimed that Buller had advised that he 'Had no reason for anticipating a determined resistance from the enemy in any very large numbers between Orange River and Kimberley, though they would elect to fight on the Modder.'[16]

Methuen's statement is of particular interest in that the post war written histories all state that Buller advised him to expect the Boer forces to offer resistance at Spytfontein, which is located North of Magersfontein and some distance from the Modder River.[17] This is offered by these histories as an explanation as to why Methuen expected no serious Boer resistance at Modder River and consequently was ambushed by Generals Cronjé and De la Rey's commandos when his army approached this crossing point on 28 November 1899.[18] However if, as Methuen states, he was forewarned to prepare for an action when approaching Modder River, then again some doubt is cast on his generalship, for he marched his force straight into a Boer ambush at that place.

---

14 Methuen, *Minutes of Evidence*, p.120, and Maurice, *History of the War*, pp.209–213.

15 National Archives of South Africa (NA): Notes from Micro Film No. A. 355 W.O. Box 32 / 851, File 196: Confidential – General Redvers Buller to Under Secretary of State for War, Cape Town, November 1899.

16 Methuen, *Minutes of Evidence*, p.119.

17 All sources consulted, as listed in the bibliography.

18 All sources consulted, as listed in the bibliography.

Methuen only received mule drawn transport with which to carry five days' provisions for his troops while on the march. This enabled a degree of flexibility from being bound to the railway line and once over the Modder River, to leave the line and split his force, so that he might outflank a potential Boer position at Spytfontein. Instead of the 367 mule wagons promised, he received 190, hardly enough to attempt a cross-country manoeuvre of any depth.[19] Furthermore, the carrying capacity of the mule drawn carts was less than that of ox wagons, so again any potential flexibility from the line in effect was neutralised from the outset. He later stated that this transport column proved insufficient for his needs.[20]

Regarding grazing for his cavalry and artillery horses, the summer grazing around and North of Orange River Station was speedily exhausted. This again reduced the mobility of his artillery and cavalry. Buller was grossly mistaken when he told Methuen: 'Mind, you will find there is grazing up there, and you will make them graze; don't listen to anyone if he says they want more for their horses.'[21] To worsen matters, the 9th Lancers horses had been badly knocked about during a storm on the voyage out from India. Their saddlery was worn out and unfit for service. The incidence of sore backs amongst the horses increased dramatically, debilitating Methuen's only regular cavalry unit from the outset of his campaign.[22]

His next consideration was that of adequate water. He was about to march his force into an area caught in the grip of a drought. Without adequate water his advance would grind to a rapid halt. However, Gough's report indicated sufficient water resources available on the various farms for the Division, at least up until Belmont.

His route to Belmont would replicate Gough's reconnaissance. The Division's first halt would be at Witteputs Siding and Fincham's Farm and its second at Belmont Farm (also known as Thomas's Farm) before any offensive action, should the Boers still be in possession of the Belmont heights. Although told to expect resistance closer to Kimberley, he was confident that he would see his first action at Belmont and was keen to start as soon as the last of his reinforcements arrived.

In a letter to his wife on 13 November 1899, Methuen wrote that, 'Buller thinks I leave here 24th. I shall go 20th if my soldiers come and I hope to have a good fight near Belmont about 23rd and to get to Kimberley 27th.'[23]

In the same letter, Methuen offered a prophetic view of what the military outcome may be, were he unsuccessful in crushing the Boer force and provides a glimpse of what lay ahead, until the conclusion of hostilities. 'Either the next fortnight will clear the air, or we have a desperate war to face, because our lines of communication are so great, and all around us are enemies.'[24]

19 Methuen, *Minutes of Evidence*, questions 14147–52, p.120.

20 Methuen, *Minutes of Evidence*, questions 14147–52, p.120.

21 Methuen, *Minutes of Evidence*, questions 14147–52, p.120.

22 The Marquess of Anglesey, *A History of the British Cavalry* (London: Secker & Warburg, 1986), vol. 4, p.80.

23 MMK: 7654/194 a: Methuen to Wife, 18–24 November 1899, p.1.

24 MMK: 7654/194 a: Methuen to Wife, 18–24 November 1899, p.10.

Julius Jeppe,[25] with the Boer forces at their Belmont laager, recorded his private thoughts on 13 November 1899.

> I am more impressed than ever by the wonderfully fair and manly spirit shown by the Free State Boer – the utter absence of brag and bounce – the quiet resigned way they speak of Britain's power and their own small chance of victory. It is the conviction of the justice of their cause and their strong belief in the help of the Almighty that makes them such dangerous foes; every Boer fights for what he considers rightly or wrongly, his liberty and country and if he perseveres he will be most difficult to beat. But it is yet to be proved if he possesses the required stamina for prolonged war.[26]

By 23 November 1899, the day of the Belmont action, Prinsloo had a force 2,000 strong in position on the hills and another 950 men either on route or at various points along the railway line.[27]

Nor were the Boers sitting idle at Belmont. They steadily reinforced themselves and, on 18 November 1899, Major Albrecht, State Secretary Blignaut and additional burghers arrived at the laagers, topping the strength up to 2,500 men. Albrecht, Officer Commanding Orange Free State Artillery Corps, brought with one 75 mm Krupp field gun and one 37 mm Pom-Pom machine gun firing high explosive shells, increasing the Boer artillery strength to two field guns.[28]

Prinsloo, like many of the older Boer generals at the outset of the war, proved most unfortunate for the Boer cause and, after his third defeat at Modder River, resigned his position, being replaced by General I. (Naas) Ferreira.[29]

The Boer officers believed that the Belmont hills comprised a natural fortress, impregnable to a British attack and fortified the position. Carl Von Heister later recalled that, 'We always had time to prepare a position and strengthen it with entrenchments and emplacements. Without these it is probable not a man of us would have been left'.[30] Their recent action with the British cavalry showed that the hilltop boulders were seemingly ideal positions to fire on approaching British troops, with apparent effect. The hilltops commanded the surrounding approaches for as far as the eye could see and the features all interconnected with ridges or valleys, enabling mounted parties the means to reinforce or pull back from a given position. Furthermore, the British reliance on railing infantry reinforcements to

---

25 For more about J. Jeppe see: https://www.sahistory.org.za/people/sir-julius-jeppe , accessed 29 April 2021.

26 TNA: WO 32/7884: 'Despatch of Reconnaissance to Belmont'; and TNA: WO/32/7891: J. Jeppe, 'Captured Diary', p.5.

27 J.H. Breytenbach, *Die Geskiedenis van die Tweede Vryheidsoorlog, Vol. II* (Pretoria: Die Staatsdrukker, 1978), pp.17-18.

28 TNA: WO 32/7884: 'Despatch of Reconnaissance to Belmont'; and TNA: WO/32/7891: J. Jeppe, 'Captured Diary', p.5.

29 WMBR: 03213/00001: Recollections by J.S. Kruger

30 Carl Von Heister (1901): 'The Orange Free State Artillery', *Royal United Services Institution Journal*, 45:276, pp.188–189.

Albrecht, who served in the Prussian Army during the 1870–1871 Franco Prussian War, was a veteran of conventional warfare but subordinated to Kommandant (Lappies*) Prinsloo who assumed the mantle of General. (McGregor Museum, with permission)

* Lappies was an unfortunate nickname, as translated into English, it means small rags. See War Museum of the Boer Republics, Bloemfontein (WMBR): Unique ID: 03213/00001: Recollections by J.S. Kruger.

General I.S. Ferreira before the war. He was later accidently shot dead during the night of 18 February 1900, near Paardeberg while trying to awake a sleeping Boer sentry. (McGregor Museum, with permission)

Gough suggested that any British advance would be reliant on the railway line and that, given the topography and heat, the infantry would not be able to stray too far from this line. This in turn reduced the risk of an outflanking attack by the British infantry of their position.[31]

Two parallel series of hills running North to South and East of the railway offered the Boer officers a double defensive position, which in turn screened their laager and campsites and the well at Kaffir Kop Farm.[32] The first series of hills (Table Mountain and the Gun Hill/Coldstream Hill complex) were located within effective rifle range from the railway line and Belmont Station. The second comprised a higher series of ridges terminating in a valley at its southern end, which then joined the highest hill of the entire position (Mount Blanc). This high hill was connected to its South by a smaller series of hillocks and ridges (Sugar Loaf), behind which was Kaffir Kop Farm.[33]

31 The author has walked over every part of the Belmont battlefield between 1989–2002 and formed these conclusions.

32 Historical name. No negative connotation implied.

33 The author has walked over every part of the Belmont battlefield between 1989–2002 and formed these conclusions.

Should the worst case scenario manifest in the form of a possible encirclement by the British force, or an attack by overwhelming numbers, the burghers could abandon their positions and retire to the next possible position, further North up the railway line. The defiles behind the reverse slopes of the hills enabled their African Auxiliaries (Agterryers) to conceal the burgher's horses within easy reach. The valleys between the various positions facilitated a rapid withdrawal over soil as opposed to rock, and the re-entrants behind the second tier of defence meant that the burghers could retire to and take up position along these heights. Due to their mounted mobility they could switch fronts within minutes if only a portion of their entire position was attacked or threatened.

Although the Boer officers believed that these were good defensive positions, the second tier of ridges and hills were undefendable, as the summits are slightly set back from the crests, thus rendering the base of the positions invisible to the riflemen on the top. Although all the post battle maps mimic those of the Official Histories of the war by reflecting that the Boer forces positioned an artillery piece on what is reflected as Mount Blanc and a Pom-Pom on what is shown as Razor Back Ridge, this could not have been so.

In the entirety of the areas where these guns are supposed to have been in position there is no surface or terrain evidence to indicate that they were. There are no prepared positions for these guns in the form of boulder emplacements, nor are there any cleared areas on the ground where these guns might have been positioned. There are no cleared paths along the summits or the reverse slopes of these hills to enable dragging these guns over the very rocky ground and into position. Finally, if they were positioned here, they would have had no clear field of fire from the set-backed summits, apart from some long distance shelling of the distant ground (3,000 metres), which is visible from the summits.[34]

The commando strengths, after cross referencing the sources listed and other non-listed material, concludes that the maximum number was 2,500 burghers at Belmont with only one field gun present during the opening shots, the day before the action, on 22 November 1899. Apart from the Orange Free State Artillery Corps, the other forces present were the Bloemfontein, Jacobsdal, Fauresmith, Winburg, Hoopstad, Kroonstad, and Boshof Commandos. The exact positions occupied by each commando is impossible to determine with any degree of accuracy.

Jeppe, an experienced land surveyor and map maker, said this about the Boer position. 'I cannot imagine the British troops coming in here; they would gain nothing by driving us back and would run a good chance of being defeated as our position is very strong and they can never corner us'.[35] A Boer prisoner later told a British officer after the action that, 'They had been told that half of Europe wouldn't turn them out.'[36]

34 The author has walked over every part of the Belmont battlefield between 1989–2002 and has formed these conclusions.

35 TNA: WO/32/7891: J. Jeppe, 'Captured Diary', p.7.

36 MMK: 7654/291: H.G. Chandos Pole Gell, 2nd Battalion Coldstream Guards, Unpublished Diary, p.8.

Orange Free State Artillerists with a 75 mm Krupp in Jacobsdal, while on their way to the front. (McGregor Museum, with permission)

During the night of 19 November 1899, and the following morning it rained heavily throughout the region. Jeppe recorded that: 'Many of them (the Boers) take this as a sign of the Almighty's favour of our cause–pasturage will be excellent in a few weeks and the empty dams replenished. On the other hand it will also enable the enemy to move a big body across the desert between this and Kimberley'.[37]

Methuen was aware that this downpour worked in both his and the Boers favour and that he could not continue waiting for the naval guns and Naval Battalion still on route. Recent intelligence reports confirmed that Transvaal reinforcements were moving South to join Prinsloo's commandos.[38] Therefore it was imperative that the 1st Division reach Belmont and possibly the Modder River, before they arrived. If he tackled the Orange Free State commandos on their own at Belmont then he stood a greater chance of defeating them and thus gaining ground before coming up against stiffer opposition, but if faced with both forces simultaneously while still some distance from Kimberley his task would be infinitely more difficult. Buller had expressly told him that, 'I have already told you that I am sending with you a Naval brigade with four 12-pr-cwt. Guns; these guns range 6,000 yards. You will not start without

37 TNA: WO/32/7891: J. Jeppe, 'Captured Diary', p.7.
38 Maurice, *History of the War*, p.208.

them, will leave them at Kimberley.' Although instructed to wait, the Navy would have to catch up, as he was ready to strike North.[39]

During a recent patrol, Methuen met with Mr Fincham who reiterated that between two to three thousand burghers were in laager to the East, behind the Belmont heights.[40] During this meeting Methuen obtained permission for his force to camp on Mr Fincham's property: "Now Mr Fincham may I come and breakfast with you and 2 or 3 officers on Tuesday at 9" – He said; "Quite delighted, to whom have I the pleasure of speaking?" "Lord Methuen" said I and at 7-am- he will see Lord Methuen, 8000 Infantry, 1500 cavalry, 390 sailors, 12 guns, 190 vehicles after 12 miles march.'[41]

On 20 November 1899, Methuen ordered the advance.[42] Since speed and mobility were crucial for a rapid strike North that would hopefully catch the Boer forces unprepared, the Division's baggage was slashed to a bare minimum. Tents would remain and additional supplies be railed up when required. Even the medical unit had to cut their equipment complement and would take only half their number of operating and ward tents. For the rest, they would have to utilise farmhouses, sheds and buildings en route. Officers were each permitted two blankets and one waterproof sheet but the troops had to share their sheet and blanket between two men.[43]

---

39 Maurice, *History of the War*, p.213.

40 MMK: 1st Division Diary: 13 November 1899; and MMK: 7654/194 a: Methuen to Wife, 18–24 November 1899, pp.5–7.

41 MMK: 1st Division Diary: 13 November 1899; and MMK: 7654/194 a: Methuen to Wife, 18–24 November 1899, pp.5–7.

42 MMK: 1st Division Diary: 13 November 1899; and MMK: 7654/194 a: Methuen to Wife, 18–24 November 1899, pp.24–45.

43 W. Wood, *The Northumberland Fusiliers* (London: Grant Richards, 1900), p.21.

4

Battle of Belmont, 23 November 1899

On 20 November 1899, just before sunset, the 1st Infantry Division crossed the Orange River bridge and bivouacked. Exposed to the elements, the troops spent a miserable night in the open. 'The previous night had been so cold I spent it walking all over several camps between the prostrate bodies of restless, shivering soldiers. Some made no pretence of sleeping, but divided their time between gathering sticks, and building little fires to huddle round while they lasted.'[1]

Before dawn the Division advanced, following the route that the steel tracks and wooden sleepers cut through the landscape. Apart from their rifles and ammunition, they carried additional kit rolled inside the greatcoats, strapped to their backs. A few personal items included cutlery and pocketknives, while non-fighting equipment was an army issue field cap, a spare shirt, shoes, socks, laces sewing kit, a cap to stave off cold nights and cooking mess tin.[2]

The burghers at Belmont and their forward scouts observed the increased activity between Witteputs and Orange River Station. They realised that the British forces were afoot. The following day, Johannesburg learnt of this advance from information supplied to the media by the Boer forces. 'General De La Rey's Laager, November 21st (Special) – The British troops are crossing the Orange River today and advancing towards Kimberley'.[3]

Many soldiers in the 1st Division were veterans of the Sudan campaign or army reservists with prior service.[4] Yet the march proved strenuous and numerous men collapsed on route.[5]

---

1 Ralph, *Towards Pretoria*, p.199.

2 Wood, *The Northumberland Fusiliers*, p.163.

3 *Standard and Diggers News*, Johannesburg, 22 November 1899, p.4.

4 For example, Corporal W. Wilson in the 1st Scots Guards who saw service in the 1882 Egyptian campaign and action at Tel-el-Kebir. Wilson was killed in action at Belmont.

5 The author walked this exact route at the exact time of the advance on the 100th anniversary of the event and in peak fitness at age 33, found the ground between Orange River Station and Witteputs rather strenuous to traverse.

> On and on we marched, in heavy sand, or over stones, or stumbling across furrowed ground–all gasping like fishes thrown on a beach. The hair shrivelled on our hands, and our feet grew dry as devilled bones. Here and there a man fell forward on his hands and knees, or stumbled out of the ranks, and lurched prone on the veld.[6]

By 8:00 a.m. they reached Witteputs. Those not detailed on outpost duty cooked breakfast and sought water from a nearby reservoir. First to drink were the mounted troops and horses. Once they cleared out and disappeared into the distance towards Belmont, the transport drivers and mule column followed. Then it was the turn of the infantry who 'Crowded like bees around a honey pot, filling their cloth-clad bottles out of a stone tank, while other Tommies walked round and round a sort of windlass that pumped new water into the tank. Every man filled his bottle, emptied it down his throat, and filled it again. A water mania, a thirst madness was upon the troops.'[7]

While the infantry rested, the mounted troops approached Belmont Station. They drew fire from the hills and pulled back to Thomas's Farm situated beyond Boer rifle range. This hamlet, surrounded as it is by some low hills and rocky ridges, formed an ideal vantage point from which to observe the Boer positions. The men left their horses with a watering party at the farm reservoir and, together with a signal section, scrambled up a nearby hill from where they opened heliograph communication with Headquarters back at Fincham's Farm. This hill offered a clear view of the railway line, the Belmont hills and the direct approach routes to the Boer position.

Verner, reputedly one of the British army's most skilled cartographers, climbed the hill and, from a point marked D in his subsequent sketch, drew a

Refilling water carts whilst on the march. Water resources dictated strategy and tactics throughout the war and, particularly in the dry, almost desert conditions where the forces found themselves. (McGregor Museum, with permission)

6 J. Ralph, *Towards Pretoria*, p.200.
7 J. Ralph, *Towards Pretoria*, p.202.

map of the immediate area.[8] Methuen and his Staff Officers later joined him. Verner's work would play a critical role in the battle plan so, responsibility for attention to detail was vital. The entire force would soon rely on this map to navigate themselves onto their objectives during the impending action. However, the map contained key errors, glossed over by British apologists who subsequently attributed his misrepresentation of the military landscape to factors such as a heat haze or mirage distorting his perspective of the terrain. Major General H.E. Colvile later referred to this as 'an impressionist map issued for their guidance'.[9]

Nevertheless, was this true? If one examines this map when standing on the actual spot where he did his reconnaissance and compares it against the landscape, it is apparent that Verner made some serious errors.[10] First and foremost, he sketched from one fixed vantage point when in fact he could have cross-referenced the terrain from various positions. Therefore, the broken ground between himself and the Ganger's Hut (captioned the Tin House on his map) obscured his view and determined his perspective of the distance to the Boer position. Had he, albeit at some personal risk should the Boers open fire on him with artillery, located himself on the edge of this broken ground, the true distance would have become apparent and enabled him to compile a map to which he could have attached some degree of scale.

Although Verner focused on the two prominent hills closest to him, namely Table Mountain and Gun Hill, he took no compass bearing to the Ganger's Hut, Gun Hill, or Mount Blanc (Razor Back Ridge).[11] This seems inexcusable, as the time required to do so, for someone of his experience would have taken seconds.[12] Why not, remains unknown, yet it was obvious that these hills formed part of the Boer position.

Although Verner sketched Thomas's Farm with accuracy, this did not form a part of the Boer defences and was currently occupied by British troops. Nor did he ask Thomas if he might examine his Title Deed map that would reflect the distances to the railway line.[13] Perhaps if interviewed, Thomas might have filled in some of the gaps. After all, he knew the area better than Verner and enjoyed neighbourly relations with Mr Van Eck of Kaffir Kop Farm, which, behind the Belmont hills, formed the site of the main Boer laager. Thomas could have provided distances from his homestead to Kaffir Kop farm and the

8 Methuen, *Royal Commission on the War*, p.125.

9 H.E. Colvile, *The Work of the Ninth Division* (London: Edward Arnold, 1901), p.2.

10 The author conducted an experiment on both the 99th and 100th anniversaries of Lieutenant Colonel W Verner being on this hill. This involved comparing a copy of his original map to the actual terrain. The result was that through an ordinary set of field glasses the author was able to easily distinguish all the prominent features of the Belmont heights and the landscape between them and Verner's Hill. On both occasions it was exceptionally hot but climatic conditions had no influence on visibility. The conclusion was that although it would have been possible to compile an accurate map, Lieutenant Colonel W. Verner's map was hastily drawn and not totally completed.

11 The author identified in a 2002 MA thesis that if one consults the primary sources then the names given to various hills in the official histories and subsequent writings are incorrect, as covered in this chapter. The incorrect yet mistakenly accepted names are in brackets and the correct names in the main body of the text.

12 It took the author fifteen seconds to do this during 1998.

13 Thomas was at home that day.

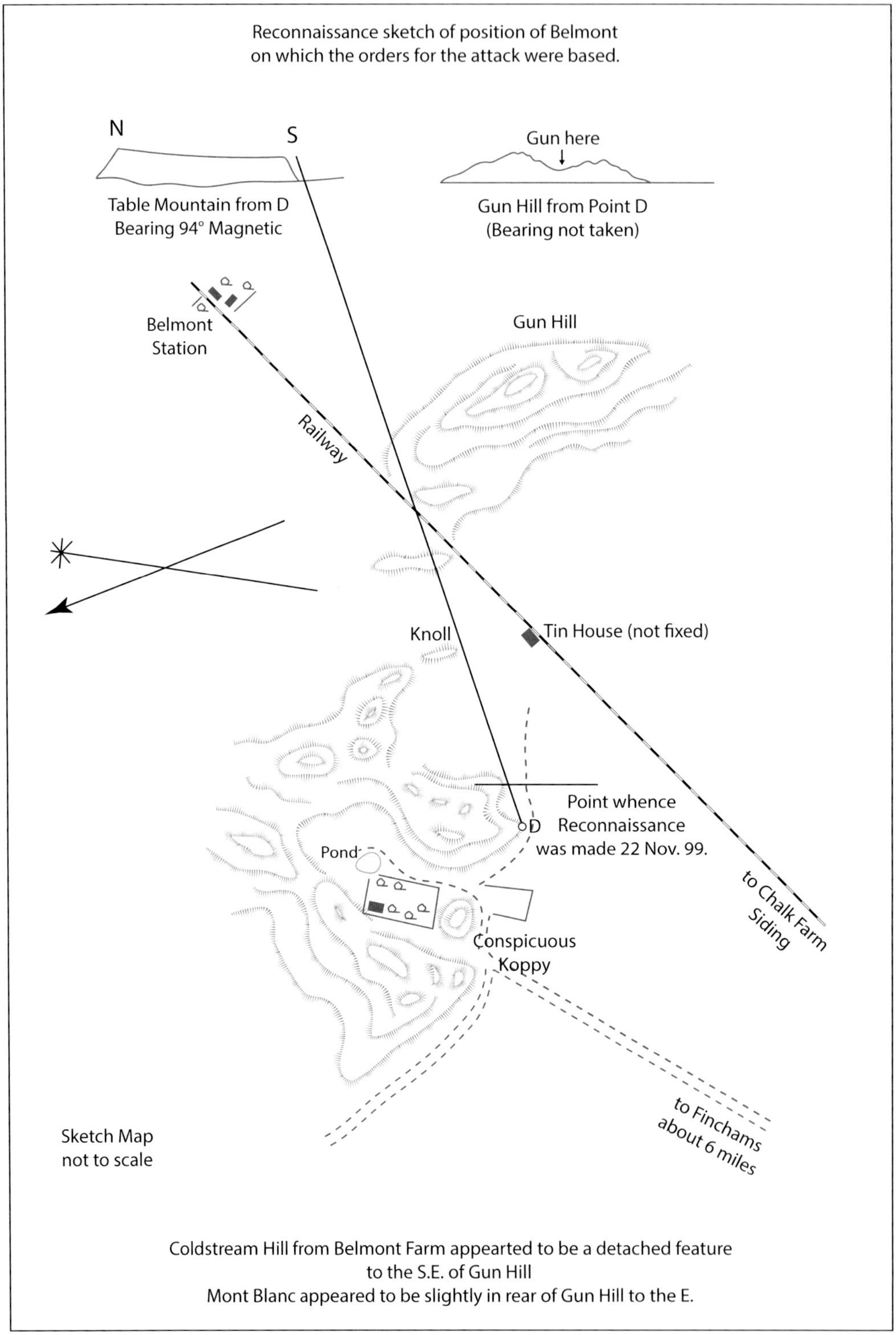

The information in this map is all that the battalion commanders had to rely on when trying to identify their objectives in the dark during the opening stages of the action. The sketch includes only the profiles of two hills when in fact at least six are visible from Point D on the map and of which two hills share a similar profile. (From South African Library, A 355 31 GRE: 1899, 'Staff Diary of the Guards Brigade,' with permission)

various hills occupied by the Boers, yet it is apparent that neither Verner, nor any of the other Staff Officers cared to ask him or utilise his local knowledge. Thus the map, without a scale of distances, was incomplete.

Major Reay, the Divisional Intelligence Officer, later visited Thomas on 6 December 1899 and recorded:

> With Mr. Thomas I chatted over the events of the campaign and the battle of Belmont. My host is one of the English farmers who decided to stand by their homesteads and see the trouble through. He has an extensive property and, is (sic) married to a lady of Dutch descent, from the Free State. Thomas who knows every inch of the surrounding country, told me that he strongly advised Lord Methuen to go on to Jacobsdal, and thus menace the Free State capital, as the best way of relieving Kimberley. "I don't know anything about soldiering," added Mr. Thomas, "but I know the country".[14]

Despite Verner's inadequate reconnaissance and his deficient cartography, he was never censured. Although Methuen expressed prior reservations about him after Gough's reconnaissance, for some inexplicable reason, later sang Verner's praises in 1903.

> From the time I left Orange River to the time I left Modder River to take up my command at Kimberley (1900), the reports and sketches were as clear and comprehensive as they could well be under the conditions of modern warfare – that is the difficulties entailed by smokeless powder and long range fire. *Later on in the war the short reports sent to me from the front were seldom misguiding…* [Emphasis is the author's] Of course before I went to Modder I had the advantage of Colonel Verner, who is a past-master at the art of reconnaissance. I was speaking to Dr. Warre, and he said, "You took picked men," and I said, "Naturally, because I wanted my work done as well I could"; but all I know is that better work could not have been done". I must honestly say that I have never had any complaint to make.[15]

In the History of the War in South Africa 1899–1902, it's recorded that, 'Lieut.-Colonel Willoughby Verner, DAAG; for topography to the army corps, sketched the Boer position from the low hill East of Thomas' farm. These sketches were subsequently reproduced and distributed among the officers of the column before the action.[16]

Verner was not the only officer confused by terrain that lay before him. Colvile also muddled himself around what was apparent to the naked eye, for he too later misjudged the distance to the Ganger's Hut.[17]

Rather than later blaming a poor map, Colvile pointed to other deficiencies prior to the outbreak of hostilities.

---

14 W.T. Reay, *Australians in War: With the Australian Regiment from Melbourne to Bloemfontein* (Melbourne: A.H. Massina & Co., 1900), p.51.

15 Methuen, *Minutes of Evidence*, p.125.

16 Maurice, *History of the War*, p.216.

17 Gangers were railway employees who maintained a section of track. Also known as platelayers.

Major-General Sir Henry Edward Colvile, (1852–1907) joined the Grenadier Guards in 1870, seeing service in the Sudan, Central Africa, Gibraltar, and finally South Africa, with a specialisation in Intelligence. He was fired from his command of the 9th Division by Field Marshal Lord Roberts in 1900, and retired from the army in 1901. (McGregor Museum, with permission)

It had not the drawback of being due to somebody's mistake, for I do not see that, as far as we were concerned, anything else could have been done which would have altered its course. The Staff Officer who made the sketch map on which we worked could only draw what he saw, and if anyone was to blame, it was 'the person or persons unknown' who might have mapped the ground on the other side of the double hill in the days before the Boers came on to it.[18]

Verner's omissions had severe consequences; resulting in a near debacle and certainly cost the lives of many men. Despite this, these statements later made by officers who were present when he compiled his map all form a rather tame historical narrative or an apology on behalf of the role of this so-called mapping expert.

British Battle Plans

Standing on Verner's Hill, Methuen could, for the first time since arriving in South Africa, appraise his opposition and their choice of topography from which they presented battle.[19] Although forewarned by Buller to expect Boer resistance at Modder River, it was obvious that Belmont was his first battleground, confirming what he anticipated.[20] Prinsloo's position, astride the railway, invited a British attack. However, Methuen's Staff Officers suggested that he bypass Belmont altogether. Instead of engaging the burghers on ground of their choice, they recommended a Western detour across the countryside to Modder River. After all, an outflanking manoeuvre can unlock the inherent potential of ejecting an opponent from their position, without firing a shot.

These officers were not the only ones in the vicinity to have seen the merit of a hook turn around a static defensive position. Thomas, the stock farmer, saw this, as did Jeppe, ensconced on the Belmont hills.

18 Colvile, *The Work of the Ninth Division*, p.4.

19 This hill is immediately East of Thomas's Farm and overlooks the farmhouse and was named such by the author during the lead up to the centenary commemorations.

20 Or at Spytfontein, depending on which source one accepts.

> I cannot imagine the British troops coming in here [The Belmont heights]; they would gain nothing by driving us back and would run a good chance of being defeated as our position is very strong and they can never corner us; it is, quite possible that the enemy is only making a big demonstration with a few thousand men for the purpose of keeping us here while they are rushing a column past us towards Kimberley; our intelligence Dept. is very poor and I should not be a bit surprised if we found tomorrow or day after that they had slipped past us.[21]

Although this seemed an obvious option, Methuen weighed the risks of a flanking manoeuvre. If ejected from their position by such a manoeuvre, the commandos might pose a greater risk, left free to roam a countryside that held no corners. Such a manoeuvre would necessitate breaking loose from the railway line, risking an undefeated force in a position within striking distance of the Orange River bridge and supply depot. Should the Boers take the initiative and seize these strategic positions, he would be cut off from his communication and logistic routes. Trapped in the wilderness in the dry environment, his Division would soon run out of water and provisions. Recent intelligence indicated that the Transvaal reinforcements were heading south, so in detouring West he might find them in front, with Prinsloo's commandos behind him, trapped between two forces. Such a prospect is anathema for any military commander. Therefore, he was justified in balancing his options against this scenario.

Furthermore, if he left the commandos intact near Belmont, they might strike deeper into the Cape Colony, seize the line between De Aar and Noupoort, presently weakly held by Major General A.G. Wauchope's Highland Brigade. This would cut French off from his logistic centres and collapse the British Central Cape front, unravelling Buller's entire holding strategy for the central Cape. The political consequences of a British defeat in the central Cape Colony would prove catastrophic and further fan the flames of a simmering Cape rebellion. The last thing that, for the sake of avoiding an engagement, leave the Cape ports vulnerable to a Boer attack. This point was impressed on Buller who in turn made it clear to Methuen that the only option was to press forward and engage the commandos where they presented themselves.

He summed it up in a comment to his censor officer, Colonel Streatfield. 'It is not possible with so mobile a foe to get round the flank. Therefore one has to accept the inevitable and attack the position in front, trusting to the courage and stubbornness of our troops to gain the day'.[22] He would attack the Boer position.

The Boer forces were stationary, thus inviting attack. Most importantly, having occupied the hills, it seemed that they had forfeited their mobility. This presented an opportunity to surprise and overwhelm them with superior infantry numbers and inflict a crushing defeat that in turn would undermine Boer morale, break the back of further resistance and open the road to Kimberley.

Methuen commanded some of the best infantry battalions in the British army to deliver the knockout blow. Some 9,000 troops versus at most 2,500

21 TNA: WO/32/7891: J. Jeppe, 'Captured Diary', p.8.

22 W.B. Pembarton, *Battles of the Boer War* (London: Leo Cooper, 1964), p.40.

Some of the Intelligence Staff with Rimington's Guides. Every member of the unit had to speak Dutch and at least one indigenous African language, with many speaking more. Also known as The Tigers because of their tiger skin hatbands, they were armed with carbines and revolvers, riding light, ahead of the main army. (War Museum of the Boer Republics, with permission)

Boers. He enjoyed superior artillery. Two batteries of 12 guns versus Albrecht's single gun which, following the infantry up onto the heights, could blast apart any fleeing stragglers. A dawn attack would facilitate the element of surprise while minimising the attacking force's losses when crossing the veld, which rolls up towards the heights. The crucial difference lay in his lack of horse artillery and sufficient mounted troops, only two batteries and some 900 horsemen. This lack of mounted striking power would be the undoing of any elaborate plan, for there would be no follow-up to ground gained and the destructive pursuit of a fleeing enemy. The impending action would not see a cavalry charge as its Grand Finale, as at the earlier battle at Elandslaagte in Natal the month before where the Dragoons and Lancers waded into a retreating Boer force, leaving heads rolling about the veld. Instead, it would be a grimly fought infantry battle.

Yet how to deliver the dawn attack?

Methuen returned to Witteputs to finalise this. He ordered his infantry, artillery and engineer Brigadiers to Verner's Hill the following day to show them the terrain, before finally deciding. He designated Thomas's Farm as the next Divisional Headquarters, ordering the mounted troops to occupy Verner's Hill during the dawn of 22 November 1899, secure this position, then probe the Boer laager at Kaffir Kop Farm. The Royal Engineers would follow, improve the water facilities and repair the damaged sections of railway track North of Witteputs. As the coming day promised its usual heat wave with the temperature cooling slightly during the afternoon, the infantry would leave Witteputs at 4:00 p.m. The 10 kilometre march should not prove too exhausting[23] and, to lighten their load, they would leave their greatcoats and surplus equipment behind.[24]

23 The author has walked the exact route followed by the infantry between Witteputs at the exact hour of their advance on both the 99th and 100th anniversaries of their advance. For the 99th anniversary the author wore replica British equipment and kit and although 'tired' when reaching Verner's Hill, he did not find the 'march' exhausting.

24 SAL: A 355 31GRE: Staff Diary of the Guards Brigade, 1st Division, South African Field Force, 1st Division Orders, 1899, p.25.

At dawn the mounted troops occupied Thomas's Farm yet drew fire when approaching the southern end of the hills. They fell back and occupied Verner's Hill. Here they found Methuen, his staff and the Brigadiers who had 'cantered over to Belmont (Farm) at 04:a.m.'[25] Methuen then issued verbal orders as to his plan of attack, later typed up at Witteputs.[26]

These were:

> At three A.M. Guards Brigade to advance from small white house near railway on Gun Kopje, supported by battery on right plus Naval Brigade; 9th Brigade on west side of Table Mountain; at same hour, bearing already taken, supported by battery on left, 9th Lancers, two squadrons, one company, Mounted Infantry, marching north of Belmont Station, keeping one to two miles on left flank and advanced; Rimington's Guides, one squadron Lancers, one company Mounted Infantry, to east of Sugar Loaf, one company Mounted Infantry on right of Naval Brigade, protecting right; the force having got over open ground should arrive at daybreak on enemy; 9th Brigade having secured Table Mountain to swing round left and keep on high ground, and then advance east to west on A (on plan; not printed); Guards Brigade confirm, being pivot; then Guards advance on East edge of Mount Blanc, guns clearing entire advance with shrapnel; cavalry to get round rear of enemy, securing horses and laager.[27]

* * *

> 1st Division Orders[28]
> (Dictated)
> *Witte-Putts Farm*
>
> 22/11/99
>
> ...2. At 3 a.m. on the 23rd 9th Brigade will move from its camp on a bearing previously taken on the southern face of Table Mountain. O.C. R.A. with one Battery will support the attack north of this bearing.
>
> Guards Brigade will move at 3 a.m. on Gun Kopje, supported by one Battery on its right.
>
> The 9th Lancers will move at 3 a.m. by west of Belmont Station to the front, about one to two miles to the left and front of IX Brigade.
>
> The IX Brigade having secured Table Mountain will swing its left round and take the ridge of heights beyond, running from north to south.
>
> The Guards Brigade will conform to the movement, and will take as its first objective the north shoulder of Mont Blanc. The Batteries R.A. will support the advance of the two Brigades by clearing the heights with shrapnel.

---

25 MMK: Military History Collection: Methuen, 'Diary of War', p.10.

26 MMK: Military History Collection: Methuen, 'Diary of War', p.10.

27 L. Creswicke, *South Africa and the Transvaal War* (Edinburgh: T.C & E.C. Jack, 1900), vol. 2, pp.86, 87.

28 SAL: A 355 31 GRE: 1899, 'Staff Diary of the Guards Brigade', pp.48, 49. Error in original document: should read 1st Battalion 1st Scots Guards.

It is probable that the 9th Brigade will have to ease off somewhat to the east to allow Guards Brigade to attack Mont Blanc from the north.

9th Lancers will accompany these movements, their object being to prevent the escape of the enemy towards the east.

Rimington with his Regiment will advance at 3 a.m. from Whiteman's Farm, taking a point S. of Sugar Loaf Hill, and aiding in preventing the escape towards the S.E.

The Infantry will continue the advance until the ridge is cleared, and when the Cavalry have done their work the two parties Mounted Troops will join and proceed to the laager at Kam's Kop, and bring the entire laager back to Belmont Farm.

* * *

The following orders were later added to the Divisional Orders:

1. The 3rd Battalion Grenadier Guards and 2nd Battalion Scots Guards will parade at 2 a.m. to-morrow morning in fighting order. They will be drawn up in line of quarter columns at twenty yards interval, will be led by the Brigade Major to the Tin House, on the railway. The battalions will deploy for attack after crossing the railway, and will be led to Big Gun Hill, which will be taken by assault.
2. The 1st and 2nd Battalions Coldstream Guards will rendezvous at 3 a.m. under the west brow of hill, east of camp, in line of quarter columns. They will act in reserve to the attack of the first position, and will then swing round the north of Big Gun Hill and attack Coldstream Hill. When this is taken then the whole Brigade will assault Mont Blanc.

Although not much different in terms of content from the Division orders, additional Brigade Orders were issued once the infantry had arrived at Belmont (Thomas's) Farm during the evening of the 22nd.[29]

* * *

BRIGADE ORDERS.

Belmont Farm,

22/11/99

1. PARADE

The 3rd Battalion Grenadier Guards and 1st Battalion Scots Guards will parade at 2 a.m. to-morrow morning in fighting order with extra ammunition. They will be drawn up in Line of Quarter Columns – 20 yards interval – and be led by the Brigade Major to Big Gun Hill, which will be taken by assault.

29 SAL: A 355 31 GRE: 1899, 'Staff Diary of the Guards Brigade', p.49.

2. The 1st and 2nd Battalion Coldstream Guards will rendezvous at 3 a.m. on the west brow of the hill, east of camp, in Line of Quarter Columns. They will act in reserve to the attack of the first position, and will then swing round "Big Gun Hill" and attack "Coldstream Hill." When this is taken then the whole Brigade will assault "Mont Blanc.

* * *

These orders reflect that the various hills and features, comprising the prominent parts of the Boer position, Methuen christened during his reconnaissance on 21 November 1899. This is borne out by the fact that, 'It was during this reconnaissance that Lord Methuen named the prominent features of the Belmont kopjes, Table Mountain, Mount Blanc, and Sugar Loaf'.[30]

This offers a clue to which hills were christened Table Mountain, Mount Blanc, Gun Hill, and Sugar Loaf, enabling an understanding of what transpired during the subsequent confusion of battle and the later recording of these events. Gun Hill received its name due to the Boer artillery position on 22 November 1899, and is marked as such on Verner's map. No dispute exists between this descriptor at the time and later representations of it, the same being true for Table Mountain.

Important to note is that Methuen was severely criticised for his so-called reliance on frontal attacks during the Belmont, Graspan, Modder River and Magersfontein actions. This became more vociferous after his defeat at Magersfontein.[31] In studying the written histories and maps of the Belmont action one is left with the impression that his entire plan hinged upon this choice of sledgehammer tactics. Yet the question to be raised is, did he intend to deliver a purely frontal attack against what visually appeared to be a strong position, or has this perception arisen after the action based on what transpired during the battle? Did Methuen, therefore, plan an unimaginative frontal attack from the outset? The answer rests in his orders, the topography and the troop numbers and relative strengths at his disposal.

First and foremost, when standing at Witteputs it is apparent that the Southern approach to Belmont is dominated by a single hill rising out of the plain to a height of 1,300 metres above sea level and shadows the surrounding hills. The official historical accounts and subsequent post war accounts refer to this hill as Razor Back Ridge. It is currently crowned with a trigonometry survey beacon, as it is the highest peak for many miles around. This height is most certainly not a 'ridge' as its descriptor implies.

30 MMK: 7654/134: Lieutenant Colonel C.H. Burtchaell, 1912, Journal of the Royal Army Medical Corps, United Services Medical Society, Volume XVIII, p.299.

31 During the build up to the Magersfontein action and, after Lord .Methuen's force had seized Modder River Station, Major General A. Wauchope tried to rally the support of Major General H.E. Colvile and Major General. R Pole-Carew, to remonstrate with Methuen against his use of frontal assaults. Major General A.J. Wauchope had expressed the opinion to one of subordinates, Brigade Major Lieutenant Colonel S. Ewart, that Lord Methuen's tactics bordered on madness. See: MMK: 7654/37A: General Sir J.S. Ewart, Unpublished Autobiography.

Immediately to its South are some lower hills, which appear as pendants on the landscape, referred to as the Sugar Loaf with varying heights above sea level of 1,281 metres and 1,286 metres. Behind the Razor Back Ridge and Sugar Loaf, the reverse slopes are filled with re-entrants within which is located Kaffir Kop Farm and the Boer laager. Like every camping ground, it was located near a well. This position was screened by a ridge running East of and at right angles to the Sugar Loaf and terminating in Luiperds Kop, where the mounted troops saw action on 10 November 1899. To its North, the Razor Back Ridge is separated from a series of ridges of almost equal height by a valley. This series of ridges is referred to as Mount Blanc in post battle representations and according to them, supposedly formed the main Boer position during the action.

To the West of these positions and located between them and the railway line another series of parallel ridges are visible, yet only distinguishable to the naked eye on a clear day, as being lower, they blend in against the hills behind them known as the Razor Back Ridge and Mount Blanc. The most northerly of the two is a flat topped hill called Table Mountain with varying heights above sea level of 1,269 metres and 1,265 metres, and which is connected to the northern slopes of the Gun Hill/Coldstream Hill complex to its south by broken rocky ground. Coldstream Hill forms a separate feature to Gun Hill and is separated from the Razor Back Ridge by a valley. To avoid later confusion, Coldstream Hill became known as Grenadier Hill, after the 3rd Grenadier Guards attacked this position, due to their Commanding Officer, Colonel E.M.S. Crabbe, confusing his objectives in the dark.

All the positions described are covered with large boulders and rocks and offer unparalleled views of the surrounding landscape. From Razor Back Ridge one can see with the naked eye Orange River Station to the South and over the tops of the ridge immediately North of Witteputs and Fincham's Farm. The terrain surrounding Belmont (Thomas's) Farm and Verner's Hill is clearly visible from all the hilltops that formed the Boer positions. The names used to describe these hills are drawn from the post battle maps.

However, when examining Methuen's orders and the pre battle descriptions of the Boer positions only the following hills are referred to:

A. Gun Hill, otherwise known as Gun Kopje (varying heights to a total of 1,250 metres above sea level)
B. Coldstream Hill[32]
C. Table Mountain (1,269 metres and 1,265 metres above sea level)
D. Sugar Loaf (1,281 metres and 1,286 metres above sea level).
E. Mount (Mont) Blanc (1,301.1 metres above sea level)
F. Ridge of heights (High Ridge) (at its highest point 1,296 metres above sea level)

It is therefore apparent and crucial to note that, at the time of the action, the Razor Back Ridge was a non-existent entity and this descriptor only came into use when Major General F. Maurice constructed the Official History

32 Height not reflected on the South African Cadastral mapping system, yet of a similar height to Gun Hill.

during 1906 and the Southampton Ordnance Survey Department produced its 1906 battle map. The various regimental histories written much later, along with numerous other 20th and 21st century accounts of the action mimic the terrain descriptors used in these works, as did the Boer Official History written during 1969–1977.

However, if these post battle descriptors for the Belmont military landscape are indeed correct then they overtly imply that Methuen set himself purely on a frontal attack and that, for some inexplicable reason, had no intention of attacking the Razor Back Ridge and Sugar Loaf Hill, since these were presumably unoccupied by the burghers. This was not the case, as shown by the casualties from the reconnaissance of 10 November 1899.

Belmont was his first combat command of a divisional strength formation and while it is true that he lacked accurate maps and could not push his reconnaissance too close to his opponent's position, to behave in such a matter would have constituted gross incompetence. Therefore, this begs the question: what were his intentions and what was the actual military landscape at Belmont at the time of the action?

First and foremost, Mount Blanc is the highest mountain in Europe, and it seems logical that this descriptor was attached to that peak which visually appeared the highest of all the hills from Methuen's vantage points at Witteputs and Belmont Farm. Remembering that he had no pre-war survey maps depicting the heights and contours of the Belmont position. The Mount Blanc of 21–23 November 1899, is therefore that high point which later became known as the Razor Back Ridge, as reflected on Map 1. This position is shown as having the highest altitude of all the hills that constituted the Boer position in the contemporary South African Cadastral maps.[33] Therefore, the actual Mount Blanc of the Belmont action and the military landscape of the time, is that feature, later known as the Razor Back Ridge.

The battle plan entailed a two-phased enveloping attack of the Boer positions thus surrounding the commandos and laager with the infantry, considering that infantry formed his dominant force. To minimise casualties and avoid exhaustion during the approach, phase one of the attack was timed for first light on 23 November 1899. The infantry brigades would leave their bivouacs at 2:00 a.m. rendezvousing one hour later at two different points alongside the railway. Colvile's 3rd Grenadier Guards and the 1st Scots Guards would rendezvous at the Ganger's Hut (Tin House) and Major General R.S.R. Fetherstonhaugh 9th Brigade at a point south of Belmont Station. In line with Buller's orders, on 9 November 1899, he delegated, 'the first chance of fighting to Fetherstonhaugh's Brigade,'[34] which would push home the enveloping attack against Mount Blanc (Razor Back). Their first objective was Table Mountain and after seizing this position the 9th Brigade

---

33 It seems incredible that the entire spectrum of post battle authors, have not noticed the discrepancy between the height of the hills and their linked descriptors, when using any of the maps, which reflect the height of the hills as a tool to interpret the action in their construction of the military histories. Incredible, yet that is the record as presented by the sources.

34 MMK: Sir R. Buller, Correspondence to Lord P.S. Methuen, 9 November 1899, and MMK: Methuen, 'Diary of War'.

Major Michael Frederic Rimington (1858-1928) joined the 6th (Inniskilling) Dragoons in 1881. Stationed to South Africa, he served in the 1884 Warren Expedition, with Lord Methuen and in the 1888 Zulu civil war. Sent to South Africa as a Special Service Officer in July 1899, he served right through the campaign, receiving 10 clasps to his Queens South Africa medal. In 1907 he went to India and in 1914, commanded of the 1st Indian Cavalry Division in France. In December 1914, he was promoted to command the Indian Cavalry Corps and during 1916 to 1918, commanded a reserve centre in the United Kingdom; and retired from the Army in 1919. (McGregor Museum, with permission)

would then swing North, deploying along a line running East to West and occupy the northern end of the ridges. The Brigade would then advance south along this high ground and block potential Boer escape routes off Mount Blanc (Razor Back).

While their initial attack went in against Table Mountain, the 3rd Grenadier Guards and 1st Scots Guards would attack and seize Gun Hill. The two Coldstream Guards Battalions would form the Guards Brigade reserve and once Gun Hill fell then seize Coldstream Hill. With this first tier of Boer positions in British hands and 9th Brigade deploying itself along the Ridge of Heights, the stage would then be set for the final assault on Mount Blanc. The Guards Brigade would launch this attack and strike at an oblique angle against the northern slopes of Mount Blanc (Razor Back Ridge) so as to reduce casualties, as not all the Boer riflemen along the summit would be able to bring their rifles to bear on the infantry advancing towards them in broad daylight, and to effect a junction with the 9th Brigade to their North. In brief, those burghers defending the ridges and Mount Blanc (Razor Back Ridge) would be trapped between the two infantry Brigades and overwhelmed, while those burghers defending Sugar Loaf would be cornered between the infantry and southern cavalry pincer.

During their attack, the infantry brigades would be supported by artillery fire from the 18th RFA and 75th RFA, and the naval guns, still on route from Orange River Station. The mounted troops, divided into two columns would operate both to the North and South of the Boer position. The left pincer was led by Gough, which seems unusual considering that he had not seen the country to the North before but was already familiar with the topography of the southern end of the Boer position. Nevertheless, Major Rimington with his Rimington's Guides and some cavalry and mounted infantry would command the southern pincer. Their combined job was to prevent the fleeing Boer forces from regrouping or retreating southwards, seize their laagers and frustrate their retreat.

In summary, the path to victory was, 'Securing the high ground and walking all along it'.[35]

35 MMK: 7654/194 b: 'Methuen', 26 November 1899, p.3.

However, once the infantry was at Thomas's Farm, the last thing that was needed was for a Boer force to then swoop past Methuen's right flank and raid Witteputs, so he instructed half a battalion of infantry to remain behind and secure the bivouac. [36] Apart from guarding the stores they were to build bonfires along the hilltops thus exaggerating the true number of troops holding the position.[37] As a final precaution, Rimington's pincer would bivouac halfway between Witteputs and Verner's Hill at White Chalk Farm (today Spes Bona Farm) and positioned there, screen both campsites, before forming the far right flank during the coming action.[38]

However, if the commandos abandoned their positions in time, there was little chance of annihilating them due to the weakened cavalry force. He was conforming his movements to the Boer choice of terrain and, compelled to take the offensive, would bear the brunt of casualties. Most critically, the entire operation hinged on a night advance reaching rendezvous points at designated times. Should these points not be timorously reached or the troops become lost, then the entire plan could go horribly awry.

Their order group finished, the Brigadiers took compass bearings to their designated objectives, and returned to Witteputs. The all-important map was copied and distributed to the unit commanders who had not yet seen the position. The mounted troops remained yet as the day wore on the temperature soared, reaching 93 degrees Fahrenheit by midday. This was the hottest recorded day of the western campaign.[39] For the men and horses of both sides, heat proved torturous. 'I spent my day hunting for a little shelter from the burning sun and scorching stones, looking in vain for an enemy on the broad expanse of plain.'[40]

The mounted troops emptied their water bottles and their horses, already in a pitiful state, rapidly dehydrated. By late afternoon most were close to collapse.[41] The Engineers duly arrived and unwittingly heralded in the opening shots of the Belmont action. They drilled for water beneath the trees adjacent to Thomas's reservoir and, as the water table is less than a metre below the surface, soon filled their newly erected canvas reservoirs.[42] The sight of water being pumped into the reservoirs proved too strong to resist and watering parties arrived, thronging about the yard, desperate for a drink for themselves and their horses.[43]

36 Loyal North Lancashire Regiment.

37 The author observed in 1997 that the site where these bonfires were built and lit was still marked by ash deposits in the topsoil and rusted British army ration tins.

38 SAL: A 355 31 GRE: Staff Diary of the Guards Brigade, Brigade Orders, Belmont Farm, 22 November 1899. Yet despite this primary, the official histories and their subsequent mimics all show Major M.F. Rimington's column leaving the vicinity of Verner's Hill before its advance around the southern end of the Boer position.

39 MMK: Kimberley Meteorological Report, November 1899.

40 TNA: WO/32/7891: J. Jeppe, 'Captured Diary', p.10.

41 For the condition of horses see: Methuen, *Minutes of Evidence*, p.120, and Maurice, *History of the War*, p.217.

42 Interview conducted by author with the then landowner Mr L Liebenberg in 1998.

43 SAL: Microfilm 75/12: B.J. Bridges, p.99.

9th Lancers watering their horses. (McGregor Museum, with permission)

These activities indicated that a British force would soon arrive.[44] If the Boer artillery could damage the reservoirs and pumping equipment they might delay the British advance by a day, enabling the Transvaal reinforcements, now in the Graspan vicinity, to reach them before the inevitable action. Besides which, the troops clustered around the watering points offered an ideal artillery target. At 3:00 p.m. Albrecht's gunners opened fire; the shells shrieked down on the unsuspecting horsemen and engineers, scattering them into cover among the rocky ridges around Verner's Hill.[45] Half a dozen shells detonated around Thomas's house, a fragment knocked a hole through the roof, while another exploded within a few feet of a back veranda where the Thomas family sat taking tea.[46]

Although the gunners fired with great accuracy, most of the air burst shrapnel shells contained faulty fuses and failed to explode. In all, only two men were slightly wounded.[47] For the New South Wales Lancers undergoing their baptism of fire, they didn't care. Most ran about picking up shell fragments for souvenirs.[48]

44 SAL: *Standard and Diggers News*, 25 November 1899, p.4.

45 J.H. Breytenbach has two Krupp field guns and the Pom-Pom firing on the British force. Yet there is no other archival evidence to support this, nor is there any evidence on the ground to suggest three prepared gun positions. Had three guns opened fire it is unlikely that only one hill would have been called and designated as Gun Hill by the British forces. See: Breytenbach, *Die Geskiedenis van die Tweede Vryheidsoorlog*, *Vol. II*, p.21.

46 Reay, *Australians in War*, pp.50–51.

47 TNA: WO.108/83: South African Field Force Casualty List, 1899–1902.

48 Also known as the Fighting 28, a nickname in use at the time for the twenty-eight Australian cavalrymen of the New South Wales Lancers attached to the 1st Division; See: R.L. Wallace,

Advance to contact

The explosions echoed back to Witteputs. Soon the 1st Scots Guards outposts saw, in the distance, the heliograph flickering on Verner's Hill:

> 'Enemy going in position 1500 yards east side of railway immediately opposite BELMONT FARM shells dropping in round pond aiming at watering party'.[49]

Methuen was not about to tolerate this threat to his bivouac. 'They had the cheek to send shells into my drinking water here, therefore I sent for my two batteries who arrived at 4.50 – two horses dropping down dead'.[50]

To hurry the guns up from Witteputs, Colonel F.H. Hall ordered them to trot the entire distance with dire consequences for the horses. Five dropped dead on route and the rest arrived exhausted, unable to raise so much as a trot during the forthcoming battle.[51] At 05:00 p.m. the gunners dragged their guns into position along a low ridge lying North of and immediately adjacent to the farm entrance, 2,743 metres from Gun Hill. [52] Opening fire, they plastered the Boer gun positions with shrapnel fire, keeping up this one-sided duel until sunset, killing and wounding at least six Boers.[53]

Outgunned, Albrecht pulled his artillery off the hills. This retreat, in the face of the enemy, seriously undermined Boer morale. For most of the burghers, this shellfire was their first taste of combat and the booming guns and shells exploding above their heads unnerved them.[54] Many must have doubted their ability to hold their positions, especially with what transpired next.[55]

Looking towards Witteputs, they saw the dust kicked up by the infantry advance and, for the first time, realised the full strength of the British force.[56] To date they had heard countless rumours regarding their opponent's strength

---

The Australians at the Boer War (Canberra: The Australian War Memorial and Australian Government Publishing Service, 1976), p.60.

49 Authors' collection, copy of Heliograph message, 22 November 1899.

50 MMK: 7654/194 b: Methuen, Letter to Wife, 26 November 1899, p.1.

51 Methuen, *Minutes of Evidence*, p.120.

52 The author found the T Friction Tubes on this position on 30 April 1999. These tubes were used to fire British artillery guns during the war and as the British artillery only fired from this area on the 22 November 1899, these tubes verify that this was the artillery position.

53 Lord P.S. Methuen, *Despatch of Belmont Action*, 26 November 1899, as reproduced in *The True History of the War Part II* (London: Harrison & Sons, 1902), p.6. Their aim was spot on target, as shrapnel and shell pieces observed on the ground by author in 1998 testify.

54 The author during 1989 and 2001 observed numerous shell fragments and shrapnel amongst the Boer positions, particularly on Gun Hill, which was not shelled on 23 November 1899. The conclusion is that these airburst shells detonated above many of the burgher's heads, as airburst shells were designed to explode between 0-50 metres above the target. The British shell fire was right on target.

55 Authors' interpretation of all sources consulted and from having walked over the topography of the battlefield since 1989 to present.

56 From the Boer positions the slightest movement by so much as an ostrich on the landscape between Verner's Hill and Witteputs is immediately visible though field glasses and on a clear day with the naked eye.

and most had never yet seen a British soldier.[57] In the waning light of day, out on the open plain before them, the panoramic stage of battle unfolded. In a long sinuous khaki column with hundreds of mules, carts and auxiliaries, some 7,000 infantrymen advanced towards Verner's Hill.

Yet the outnumbered burghers did not know that their artillery had struck a significant blow against this seemingly invincible force, yet not in men and material. Insidious in nature, it struck to the core of the 1st Division. By forcing the British artillery to retaliate, this debilitated the gun team horses, reducing the British batteries to the status of the mounted troops, an ineffective fighting force. Methuen sacrificed the full striking power of his second key tactical arm and could only rely upon his infantry to crush the Boers. The chance of this succeeding hung in the balance. Should his plan fail, then scapegoats would be required and scapegoats there were.

Down amongst the scrub and hot sand the infantry tramped toward the farm, its trees a blob on the horizon up ahead.[58] To their right, in the distance, Belmont lay beyond the railway line, with Mount Blanc (Razor Back Ridge) clearly visible above the plains. For Padre Eustace St Claire Hill, these were his first steps along the road to war, marching with the 1st Northumberland Fusiliers. Hill chatted with Captain E.B. Eager and Lieutenant R.W.M. Brine, both veterans of the recent Sudan Campaign. They discussed their children and other personal matters with the Padre. Perhaps, on the eve of battle, they welcomed the Padre's presence, yet unbeknown to them, Hill would soon officiate over their open graves. When nearing Belmont (Thomas's) Farm, Eager pointed out a puff of white smoke in the distance, remarking, 'That's the first shot in anger you have experienced.'[59] They watched the artillery action and Brine, 'a cheerful fellow seemed to regard the whole thing as sport'.[60]

The troops loaded their magazines and reached their bivouac between Verner's Hill and Belmont (Thomas's) Farm shortly after sunset. No sooner did the shellfire stop, then thousands of murmuring soldiers stood between the farmhouse and Verner's Hill, queuing for their turn at the reservoir. The track behind choked with transport carts. On cue, the mules refused to cooperate, tempers flared, and cracking their whips, the shrieking African drivers dragged their stubborn beasts into the farmyard. Thomas's lawns and gardens disappeared between the hooves and wheels. The family's howling dogs added to the cacophony, joined by the mournful braying of the mules. This animal chorus set the tone for Armageddon.[61]

The 9th Brigade and Divisional Field Hospital carts arrived at 9:00 p.m. The medical personnel prepared for the broken bodies, erecting surgical tents behind the homestead. They cleared the adjacent sheds and schoolhouse,

57 TNA: WO/32/7891: J. Jeppe, 'Captured Diary', p.5.

58 As already indicated this was the hottest recorded day of the Western Campaign. The author has also walked the exact route at the exact hour on 22 November 1998 and again the same date in 1999.

59 Author's collection: Padre Eustace St Claire Hill: Unpublished Diary, 1899, p.16.

60 Author's collection: Padre Eustace St Claire Hill: Unpublished Diary, 1899, p.16.

61 Authors' collection: Padre Eustace St Claire Hill: Unpublished Diary, 1899; and J. Ralph, *Towards Pretoria*, pp.203–204, and J. Hall, *The Coldstream Guards 1885–1914* (Oxford: The Clarendon Press, 1929), pp.29–30.

Captain E.B. Eager. (McGregor Museum, with permission)

Lieutenant R.W.M. Brine. (McGregor Museum, with permission)

Padre Hill first saw action at Belmont and served throughout the war. In 1915 he served in the German South West Africa campaign and the Senussi campaign in 1916, thereafter being transferred to the Western Front. In July 1916 he was intimately involved in the Somme battles of Longueval and Delville Wood. At Butte de Warlencourt, he lost his right arm, being awarded the Military Cross in late 1916. On 24 March 1918, at Marrières Wood he was captured and served the remainder of the war as a prisoner of war. He was released in November 1918. (McGregor Museum, with permission)

yet their lanterns failed to reveal a small farm cemetery, 200 metres beyond the buildings. For those queuing for their dinners and thronging about the reservoir, some would soon be buried there. The night shroud proved a blessing.[62]

The cooks stripped the surrounding trees, lit cooking fires behind Verner's Hill, and brewed the men's dinners. The 1st Coldstream Guards and two companies of the 1st Royal Munster Fusiliers still on the road from Witteputs jettisoned their baggage and ration carts to hasten their advance. Ahead, the kitchen fires formed a clear beacon and they tramped into the bivouac at 10:30 p.m. Dinner consisted of stew and potatoes and a rum ration. Once fed, the troops filled their water bottles with cold tea.[63] It was a bitterly cold night without greatcoats.[64]

The cacophony and pre-battle tension kept most awake. To the strains of harmonicas, the men sang choruses late into the night. Methuen recorded that he 'never got a wink of sleep'.[65] As for the Naval Battalion and the long awaited naval guns, they arrived at 3:00 a.m.[66]

The battalion commanders gathered for their first and only pre-battle order group. This briefing was crucial, as their clear comprehension of the overall battle plan would determine the outcome. Colvile called together his four commanding officers and imparted his orders to them through the Brigade Major H.G. Ruggles-Brise and provided compass bearings for their route to the Ganger's Hut and Gun Hill. Yet his competency left much to be desired both during this and other subsequent actions.[67] Colvile misjudged the distance to the Ganger's Hut and Gun Hill, did not explain the complexity of the overall battle plan,[68] nor provide duplicates of the Divisional orders. Instead, 'By the light of a lantern they were given a glimpse of Colonel Verner's sketch'.[69] This dubious map later proved sorely deficient and such unclear instructions to subordinates who would lead troops into action against a complexity of hills courted disaster.

Colvile's briefing alarmed both Crabbe and Ruggles-Brise who doubted its accuracy. When the order group broke up, they dragged Lieutenant A.V.F.V Russell, who had shown good navigation skills during a night march at Orange River Station, into the darkness with them.[70] At this late hour the

62 MMK: 7654/134: Lieutenant Colonel C.H. Burtchaell, 1912, 'Journal of the Royal Army Medical Corps', United Services Medical Society, Volume XVIII, pp.299–300.

63 SAL, A 355 31 GRE, (1899), 'Staff Diary of the Guards Brigade', pp.25, 48–49.

64 MMK, 7654/291, H.G. Chandos Pole Gell, Unpublished diary, p.8.

65 MMK: 7654/194 b: P.S. Methuen, Unpublished letter to Wife, 26 November 1899, p.1.

66 Captain R. Prothero, Despatch of Belmont and Graspan Actions, 4 December 1899 as reproduced in *The True History*, p.24.

67 Field Marshal Lord Roberts later dismissed Colvile for incompetence during 1900. During the 11 December 1899 Magersfontein action Colvile refused to attack a section of the Boer position although twice ordered to do so by Methuen. See MMK: 7654/205.

68 Major General Sir H.E. Colvile, Despatch of Belmont Action, 26 November 1899, as reproduced in *The True History*, p.7.

69 J. Hall, *The Coldstream Guards*, p.32.

70 SAL: A 355 31 GRE: (1899), 'Staff Diary of the Guards Brigade', pp.22, 23 and A.V.F.V. Russell, *Letters from South Africa During the Boer War of 1899–1902* (London: JJ Keliher & Co. Ltd, 1909), p.15.

hills were a discernible dark mass along the horizon.[71] As Gun Hill is lower than the surrounding peaks, Crabbe's objective was totally invisible. However, Mount Blanc (Razor Back Ridge) stood out amongst the dark morass and, sharing the same profile as that portrayed as Gun Hill by Verner, confused these officers, then and later. They rechecked their bearings and compared his map copy against the topography visible to them. Once familiar with their night advance route, they returned to their units. That they tried, at this late hour, to rectify Methuen, Colvile, and Verner's shoddy reconnaissance stands to their credit. However, unlike the unfortunate Guards Brigade, Fetherstonhaugh gave clear and concise orders to his 9th Brigade battalion commanders, for they experienced no difficulty reaching their rendezvous point at the designated time.[72]

Just before 2:00 a.m. the men arose, gulped down a mug of hot cocoa and paraded in quarter column beneath a bright starlit sky.[73] The two Brigades left camp for their respective objectives. Julian Ralph, an American war correspondent, marched with the 2nd King's Own Yorkshire Light Infantry and 1st Royal Munster Fusiliers who formed the 9th Brigade's reserve, 1,000 paces behind the spearhead of their formation:

> Like a colossal centipede with twenty thousand legs, the column moved along the shadow of the more friendly hills, crawling a few score yards, then halting, then crawling a little farther. At each halt the officers and men sank upon one knee. The orders to march, to halt, to kneel, and to rise were given by movements of the hands of the commanders, no word being spoken. Here and there a few men whispered now and then, but the light breeze which sifted through the wild sage of the veldt was louder than these hushed voices.[74]

The Bloemfontein Commando had put out sentry outposts, so they knew the attack was on its way. They would not have been the only commando to do so. 'We could hear the English cannon wheels on the stones'.[75] Ahead of the British force, dawn glimmered above the hills while the clouds turned an ominous red. At 3:07 a.m. the 9th Brigade rendezvoused correctly against the railway line and crossed it.[76] Groups of burghers were observed in the weak light moving around on Table Mountain. The 9th Brigade deployed into attack formation. The 1st Northumberland Fusiliers extended to their left while the 2nd Northamptonshire Regiment opened rightwards to link with the 1st Scots Guards, who should have been in position to their right.[77]

---

71 Author has tested this on numerous occasions at night on the site and again between at the exact time on 22 November 1999.

72 Major General R.S.R. Fetherstonhaugh was wounded during the action and later replaced by Major General R. Pole-Carew, just before the Modder River action.

73 Russell, *Letters from South Africa* p.15; Ralph, *Towards Pretoria:* p.202; Author's collection: Hill: Unpublished Diary.

74 Ralph, *Towards Pretoria:* pp.158–159.

75 WMBR: 02005/00001: War Memories by P.J. Horak, Bloemfontein, pp.12–15.

76 Major General R.S.R. Fetherstonhaugh, Despatch of Belmont Action, 26 November 1899 as reproduced in *The True History of the War*, p.8.

77 Fetherstonhaugh, *The True History of the War*, p.8.

However, they were not. Although their marching boots were clearly audible in the cool air, the Guards Brigade was not in position. This delay, at the crucial moment, threatened to jeopardise the entire attack.[78] Dawn with its accompanying blast of Boer rifle fire was moments away.

Action

The 1st Scots Guards and 3rd Grenadier Guards reached the Ganger's Hut at 3:30 a.m., 30 minutes late. Although Verner's map indicated Gun Hill some 730 metres away, the reality was that it was at least 1,640 metres away. The blame for losing their way in the dark was later attached to their compasses proving unreliable over the rocky ground causing the guides to find their way through the dark by sense of direction[79] as opposed to the commanders, where in fact the fault lay.[80] Consequently, the battle plan was about to unravel as the confusion of battle unfolded and, for the Guards Brigade, confused objectives were about to compound the problem.

Once across the railway line the 1st Scots Guards deployed and, when one 137 metres from Gun Hill, fixed bayonets.[81] Crabbe's 3rd Grenadiers lagged some 180 metres behind their right flank, losing direction in the weak light. Crabbe mistook Coldstream Hill as the southern knoll of Gun Hill and ordered his battalion to attack this position's steep western slopes. Veering right (East), the 3rd Grenadier Guards advanced on the wrong objective. Their failure to reach the dead ground before first light ruled out all chance of a surprise attack.

Two hundred and seventy metres up ahead, Coldstream Hill beckoned, a dark and an ominous mass. The burghers showed no activity. Some optimists thought, there might not be an action. Turning to Crabbe, Lieutenant Russell whispered, 'I am afraid they have bolted.'[82]

Suddenly, as if on cue, 'When from the whole hillside came a tremendous burst of fire, and the bullets fairly spattered round us, and they seemed to grow thicker and thicker, and there was a tremendous noise.'[83]

> Julian Ralph recalled that, 'At that moment too there ran along the crest of the great southern kopje quick, vivid jets of fire, like jewels flashing in a coronet on the hills brow. It was the flame of a volley from the Boers fired at the nearest British.'[84]

---

78 Maurice, *History of the War*, p.221.
79 SAL: A 355 31 GRE: (1899), 'Staff Diary of the Guards Brigade', p.26.
80 The author has tested numerous compasses, both contemporary and of the pattern used during 1899 and found them all to work most reliably on the terrain, which between Verner's Hill and the Ganger's Hut can hardly be described as excessively rocky.
81 SAL: A 355 31 GRE: (1899), 'Staff Diary of the Guards Brigade', p.222.
82 Russell, *Letters from South Africa*, p.15.
83 Russell, *Letters from South Africa*, p.15.
84 Ralph, *Towards Pretoria*, p.161.

A representation of the Belmont action depicting the Guards Brigade attack against what might be Gun Hill or Coldstream Hill (Grenadier Hill). The hill to the right could be Mount Blanc (Razor Back) with the High Ridges to its left. The casualties and the fixed bayonets convey something of the horror of the dawn attack. (From L. Creswicke, *South Africa and the Transvaal War*, Volume 2 (Edinburgh: TC & EC Jack, 1900)

Drawing their whistles, the officers blew the charge yet the men required no inducement. Leaping forwards, they raced towards the rows of rifles flashing ahead of them. Bounding up Gun Hill, the 1st Scots Guards quickly overran the south-western summit, then drew flanking fire from the Hoopstad Commando defending a ridge to their left (North). Lieutenant Colonel W. Pulteney promptly led one company in a bayonet charge against this position and the burghers fled, leaving some 30 ponies behind. He mounted some of his troops on these abandoned steeds and gave chase but as there were no British cavalry operating in this area, the 75th Battery Royal Field Artillery promptly opened fire on them. The men leapt off their horses and continued on foot, bayoneting several Boer stragglers en-route but rifle fire from Table Mountain eventually forced them into cover along a rocky spur south of the position.[85]

The burgher's marksmanship left a lot to be desired. Crabbe, on its receiving end later stated. 'I do not think that the shooting of the majority of the Boers was any better than ours. And in the battle of Belmont, in the early hours of the morning the Boer firing was very wild indeed'.[86]

However, the 3rd Grenadier Guards, caught in the open, suffered heavy casualties. Coldstream Hill's narrow frontage forced them to close ranks

85 F. Maurice, *The History Of The Scots Guards* (London: Chatto and Windus, 1934), vol. 2, pp.155–157.

86 F.M.S. Crabbe, *Minutes of Evidence, Royal Commission on the War in South Africa* (London: Wyman and Sons Ltd, 1903), vol. 2, p.421.

as they ran towards it. Bunched together, a deadly hail of bullets dropped men screaming to the dust, leaving the veld behind strewn with dead and wounded. On reaching the dead ground at the base of the hill they paused, caught their breath and fixing bayonets, scaled the slopes. The burghers leant over their breastworks to fire into the dead ground, pouring a lethal fire into the Guardsmen clambering toward them, sometimes at point blank range. The infantry returned fire, supported by the reserves behind them, aiming at the rifle flashes and the burgher's hats, silhouetted against the skyline. Amidst the din of well over a thousand rifles, the officer's commands were inaudible. Some exposed themselves, waving their troops forward. Rising up to do so, Lieutenant L.F. Fryer fell dead; shot through his mouth, his skull exploding on the bullet's impact.[87] Russell charged up armed only with a Drill Sergeant's swagger stick. Struck above the eye with fragments from a ricocheting bullet he muttered, 'Mere scratch' and, covered in blood, stumbled on, passing a wounded burgher who greeted him with a cheerful, 'Good Morning'.[88]

At 4:00 a.m. the battalion's reserves reinforced the firing line. Together at bayonet point, the troops seized the crest. Unable to flee, pockets of burghers fought on relentlessly from behind the boulders. Lieutenant W.A. Blundell turned to assist a wounded burgher and, approaching him with a water bottle, shouted that he 'remain here and you will be looked after.'[89] The burgher shot him at point blank range; mortally wounding him. Another wounded burgher shot Crabbe through his wrist and thigh. Both burghers were promptly bayoneted.[90] During the ferocity of close combat it became impossible 'for the officers to keep a hand over the men' and some enraged troops bayoneted some of the Boer wounded. [91]

Those burghers who escaped this bayonet assault, fled under covering fire towards the High Ridge (Mount Blanc) to regroup. The summit of Coldstream Hill was a ghastly sight. 'Here and there Boer wounded lying in pools of blood'; men staggered about or lay dying between the boulders.[92] Eventually all remaining Boer resistance was snuffed out and at 4:20 a.m. a resounding cheer announced control of Gun Hill. 'I gathered the Boers had been driven off it too as I saw a guardsman doing a gleeful war dance on the top and waving his helmet about on the tip of his fixed bayonet'.[93] Three cheers for Her Majesty the Queen followed from Coldstream Hill (Grenadier Hill). For the wounded strewn along its summit, the slopes and across the veld below, their ordeal was far from over. Only the doctors, arriving in the wake of their attack, could save them.

> Soon, however, I had news that there were a large number of wounded lying under Grenadier Hill. When I got there men seemed to be lying about in scores, and it looked as if there was work for half a dozen medical officers. However, I

87 Russell, *Letters from South Africa*, p.17.
88 Russell, *Letters from South Africa*, p.15, 17.
89 Russell, *Letters from South Africa*, p.17.
90 SAL: A 355 31 GRE: (1899), 'Staff Diary of the Guards Brigade', p.52.
91 Russell, *Letters from South Africa*, p.17.
92 Russell, *Letters from South Africa*, p.15.
93 Author's collection: Padre Eustace St Claire Hill: Unpublished Diary, 1899, p.18.

This stylised and dramatic sketch reflects the British infantry attack hitting home against a Boer position at Belmont. British war artistry usually depicted the British soldier in full warrior pose and was similar to art depicting hunting scenes, where the startled quarry lies awaiting death at the feet of the hunter. However, the reality was that had these soldiers silhouetted themselves in such an exposed manner, they would have been shot. (McGregor Museum, with permission)

> set to work and rendered what aid I could, applying tourniquets and using up all the dressings in the field companion, and as many first field dressings as could be found. The two essentials most vividly impressed on my mind were the relief of pain and thirst. Luckily we had plenty of water in the water bottles to give a sip to those who most needed it. A 2-oz. bottle of morphia solution and a good hypodermic syringe are invaluable.[94]

Meanwhile, the 9th Brigade faced stiff opposition. Boer fire from Table Mountain and its southern ridges and flanking fire from a rocky outcrop swept through the 1st Northumberland Fusiliers, pinning the battalion down in the open. To their right, the 2nd Northamptonshire Regiment fixed bayonets. Charging towards this outcrop, they drew flanking fire from Gun Hill's northern slopes. Forced to their stomachs, they wriggled across the last hundred metres towards the outcrop, gained the dead ground and cleared the burghers from their position. This released the 1st Northumberland Fusiliers to recommence their attack. Linking up, the two battalions swept across the open veld towards Table Mountain.[95]

94 Captain Profeit, as quoted in MMK: 7654/134: Lieutenant Colonel C.H. Burtchaell, 1912, 'Journal of the Royal Army Medical Corps', United Services Medical Society, Volume XVIII, p.301.

95 R. Gurney, *History Of The Northamptonshire Regiment 1742–1934* (Aldershot: Gale & Ploden Ltd, 1935), pp.288–289; and M. Barthorp, *The Northamptonshire Regiment* (London: Leo

This sketch, drawn by an officer who witnessed the attack, depicts the 3rd Grenadier Guards clambering up Coldstream Hill, while under fire from concealed burghers. The infantry attempted to screen themselves behind boulders and, while some put down covering fire, others moved forward. The high ground to the left bears an uncanny resemblance to how the profile of Gun Hill appears from this sector of the battlefield. (McGregor Museum, with permission)

Taken during the action, the 1st Scots Guards are seen descending Gun Hill after capturing the position. Although the imprint of these soldiers onto the actual landscape has passed with the passage of time, the military landscape is little different from when the action was fought there. (War Museum of the Boer Republics, with permission)

The Face of Battle. The 1st Scots Guards regroup after seizing Gun Hill. Combat induces increased adrenaline production and insatiable thirst, hence the water bottle slung around the soldier's neck for easy access. This is the only known photograph taken of discernible individual combatant at Belmont during the action. (War Museum of the Boer Republics, with permission)

Some soldiers sprinted towards a spur where, in the dim light, they thought they saw burghers hiding in the shadows of the dead ground at its base. Opening fire, they exchanged shots with Pulteney's Guardsmen. The 1st Scots Guards pipers, lying on their backs, quickly played a rather flat version of Cock of the North, stopping this second friendly fire incident before damage was done.[96]

For the infantrymen scaling Table Mountain their experience was similar to that of the 3rd Grenadier Guards. The Boers leant over their breastworks, firing into their faces and at those troops crossing the veld below.[97] Padre Hill, at this stage of the action was in the area of the railway embankment and, in the wake of the 9th Brigade's attack, and came under fire. He witnessed an act of bravery by Private J. Kidd, which earned the only Distinguished Conduct Medal awarded for the action.

> The bullets seemed hitting around us and I told the 2 tommies next to me if they know how to pray they better offer a prayer up. However my interest was soon diverted by seeing Percival with the 5th Fusiliers maxim pulled by 2 mules coming toward the line, as he was crossing it one of the mules was hit and fell fouling the trace. P. seemed in his element with the sort of look on his face you like to seen worn at a footer match. He had a mule carcass cut free and I saw a Tommy moving up to take its place, his face was pale but the grey light made his expression very clear cut. His lips were tightly shut and a look not of enjoyment

Cooper Ltd, 1974), p.55; and W. Wood, *The Northumberland Fusiliers*, p.165.

96 Barthorp, *The Northamptonshire Regiment*, p.55.

97 Wood, *The Northumberland Fusiliers*, p.165.

Hill ministered to the wounded and dying, later being reprimanded by Methuen for being too far forward, which is where the Padre believed he was most needed. From H.W, Wilson, *With the Flag to Pretoria: A History of the Boer War of 1899–1900* (London: The Amalgamated Press Ltd, 1902)

> but of determination to do his duty was there all right and the maxim moved onto the koppies. [98]

A bullet struck the Padre's boot heel. Undaunted, he proceeded towards Table Mountain and, finding some wounded, waved his bamboo cane about to attract the stretcher bearers. Having organised their evacuation, he reached the base of Table Mountain to make an interesting discovery. 'At the foot of the kopje I found a cart and several rugs around it and better still bottles of all kinds of spirits–evidently the owners had come for a picnic and had made a hurried bolt for safety or else they would have never have left their liquor'.[99]

Hill clambered up the slopes and took cover with some officers behind a boulder and surveyed the scene. Boer riflemen held sections of the hill, sweeping the summit with a murderous close range fire. Eager lay dead, shot while trying to retrieve his wounded servant who fell ahead of him. He 'was hit as he stooped over him. He stood up crying, "Oh my God" when a second hit him in the heart.'[100] Brine, peered over a rock and fell dead with a bullet through his neck.[101] Pockets of burghers refused to give way, holding up the 9th Brigade from seizing their objective. The action in this area deteriorated into a series of isolated firefights, often at point blank range.

The two battalions of Coldstream Guards advanced immediately after the first blast of rifle fire but had not proceeded far before Codrington felt that they were moving too far to their right (East). He ran across to Stopford and suggested they follow a more northerly course but Stopford, who directed the advance, disagreed.[102] For the second time that morning, the hill profiles in the weak light deceived yet another experienced officer. On reaching the railway embankment, Codrington reported his concern to Colvile who instead agreed with Stopford and instructed him to stay on course.[103] Colvile remained with the 2nd Coldstream Guards until Gun Hill fell, then ordered them to reinforce the assault and support the 9th Brigade. However, as the sun rose above Mount Blanc (Razor Back) it blinded the troops and Stopford mistook this position as Coldstream Hill. He advanced both Coldstream

98 Author's collection: Padre Eustace St Claire Hill: Unpublished Diary, 1899, p.16.

99 Author's collection: Padre Eustace St Claire Hill: Unpublished Diary, 1899, p.16.

100 Author's collection: Padre Eustace St Claire Hill: Unpublished Diary, 1899, p.18.

101 Author's collection: Padre Eustace St Claire Hill: Unpublished Diary, 1899, p.19.

102 MMK: 7654/264: Lieutenant Colonel A. Codrington, Unpublished Diary, 1905, p.4; and Hall, *The Coldstream Guards* p.33.

103 Hall, *The Coldstream Guards*, p.3.

Lieutenant Colonel Alfred Edward Codrington (1854–1945) entered the Coldstream Guards in 1873. He saw active service during the 1882 Anglo-Egyptian War of 1882, was wounded twice during the South African War, the first incident at Magersfontein and later retired as Major General in 1916. (Public domain)

battalions towards the position and at 5:45 a.m. when eight hundred yards from Mount Blanc (Razor Back Ridge) and the Sugar Loaf Hills to its south, the 1st Battalion Coldstream Guards drew fire from their right flank. To meet this, the company commanders swung right to attack the positions yet in doing so committed both of the battalions to a frontal attack.[104]

By this stage, Colvile had climbed Gun Hill. He saw that the 9th Brigade's attack on Table Mountain was grinding to a halt. Seeing the Coldstream Guards' turning movement he dispatched Ruggles-Brise to stop them. Ruggles-Brise secured four 2nd Battalion Coldstream Guards companies and led them back to Gun Hill where a detachment re-established contact with the 9th Brigade and supported Pulteney's attack against Table Mountain.

Although Colvile's order reached the 1st Coldstream Guards, their officers were attacking, and beyond recall. It was unwise to disengage, leaving a Boer force in their rear, and sweeping forward in continuous waves from their left, they carried one 2nd Coldstream Guards Company with them in their charge towards Mount Blanc (Razor Back Ridge) and the Sugar Loaf.

Despite sunrise in their eyes, the 18th Battery Royal Field Artillery opened fire, and pounding the summit with accurate shrapnel fire, enabled the firing line to run towards the base of the hill without loss and take cover in the dead ground. The burghers were forced to climb down the forward slope to fire at the troops sheltering in the dead ground below, and immediately came under heavy fire from those Guardsmen clambering up the northern slopes of Mount Blanc (Razor Back Ridge) and shellfire from the guns. They bolted back over the crest, ran down the reverse slope and, mounting their ponies, galloped off to the East. The 1st Battalion Coldstream Guards crested the deserted summit and fired on the retreating burghers until they galloped out of range. Mount Blanc fell, without a single British fatality, yet not according to plan.[105]

In short, 'The 1st Battalion Coldstream Guards advanced at daylight, but finding their original objective already in our hands, and suffering from

104 Lord P.S. Methuen, *Despatch of Belmont Action*, 26 November 1899, as reproduced in *The True History*, p.6; and Hall, *The Coldstream Guards*, p.33.

105 Hall, *The Coldstream Guards*, pp.33–36. This reference again confirms that this is the correct Mont Blanc, and not that depicted on the post war maps, official histories and subsequent narratives.

enfilade fire from M Blanc, attacked that hill, and assisted by the RF Artillery, cleared it'.[106]

The attack against Sugar Loaf and the ridges to its south was not without loss despite the excellent artillery support put down by the 18th Battery Royal Field Artillery. The infantry fixed bayonets and gained the crest, yet again, found that the burghers rode away to fight another day.[107] Codrington's infantry stumbled down the reverse slopes into the Boer laager. They captured three burghers, drew water from a well and looted the wagons. Thereafter they staggered back to Verner's Hill, almost dropping with exhaustion along the way.

Methuen faced a dilemma. Although Mount Blanc and Sugar Loaf were in British hands, the 9th Brigade had not cleared Table Mountain and were unable to gain the High Ridges and envelope the burghers before they abandoned their southern positions and the laager at Kaffir Kop Farm. His plan lay in tatters and his artillery horses, shattered from exhaustion, poor rations and overwork, incapable of dragging the guns onto the hills to shell the Boer retreat.[108] His cavalry pincers were beyond sight. Numerically weaker than the Boer force they stood little chance of ploughing into them and completing the victory. Portions of Table Mountain were still in Boer hands along with the High Ridges to the East.

Consequently, Methuen ordered Colvile to attack the High Ridges with all available troops. The 75th Battery Royal Field Artillery and the naval guns were to support the attack and reinforcements to link up with and support the 9th Brigade still battling it out on Table Mountain. The attack went in, the burghers gave way and by 6:10 a.m. the burghers were in full retreat.[109] The terrain proved too treacherous for the naval guns to traverse and could not be dragged onto the high ground to shell this retreat, as the crews and mules were exhausted.[110] Nor could the two artillery batteries gain the heights to shell the retreat as their horses were completely finished.

The cavalry pincers proved ineffective. Prior to the action the mounted troops often covered forty miles a day and their horses, like those of the artillery, were done.[111] Gough on the left flank came under fire from parties of burghers who retreated northwards and was forced to pull back. Rimington's column entered the Boer laager only after it was abandoned and some of the 9th Lancers following the Boer retreat were ambushed by a rear guard and fell back under the covering fire of the Fighting 28 who rode to their assistance. After posting sentries along the heights, the Division returned to camp by 10:30 a.m. By 1:00 p.m. all wounded were evacuated off the battlefield.[112]

106 SAL: A 355 31 GRE: (1899), 'Staff Diary of the Guards Brigade', p.26.

107 Hall, *The Coldstream Guards*, pp.34–36.

108 Methuen, Despatch of Belmont Action, pp.6–7; and Methuen, *Minutes of Evidence*, p.120; and Maurice, *History of the War in South Africa*, p.217.

109 Methuen, Despatch of Belmont Action, pp.6–7; Methuen, *Minutes of Evidence*, p.120; and Maurice, *History of the War*, p.217.

110 Prothero, Despatch of Belmont and Graspan Actions, p.24.

111 Anglesey, *A History of the British Cavalry*, p.82.

112 Methuen, Despatch of Belmont Action, p.7.

Spoils of War. British mounted infantrymen with an Orange Free State Republic flag that they captured in the Boer laager. Behind them are some of the wagons, which they burnt before departing. (War Museum of the Boer Republics, with permission)

Rimington's troops looted the Boer laager before setting the wagons and stores alight, on Methuen's instructions. Sixty-four wagons were burnt, along with four large cylinders of gunpowder, 750 shrapnel shells and 5,000 rounds of small arms ammunition. Why the wagons were burnt when they might have been pressed into service by the British forces remains a mystery. Perhaps Methuen realised the potent symbol that the wagon and the laager both held and represented for the Boer people and that these wagons were the private property of the burghers opposing him. Therefore, when word of their destruction spread, the news would strike straight to the core and represent a loss of symbolic protective power, thus undermining Boer morale. Hundreds of cattle and sheep were also captured which topped up the commissariat, well over a hundred horses seized and numerous others killed.[113]

> Before going we collected all the ammunition and heaped it together and made a pile of (kindling) round it which we set ablaze and then drew out into the plain and reined in and looked back. Never shall I forget the view. Our great ammunition fire in the hollow of the hill burned merrily, and by-and-by a furious splutter of Mauser cartridges began, with every now and then the louder report of shells and great smoke balls hanging in the air. But sheer above all, above yellow veldt and ruined Boer laager, rose the hill, the position we had carried, grim and rigid against the sunset and all black. And, with the sudden sense of *seeing* that comes to one now and then, I stared at it for a while and said out loud "Belmont!" And in that aspect it remains photographed in my memory.[114]

113 Methuen, Despatch of Belmont Action, p.7.
114 March Phillips, *With Rimington* (The Project Gutenberg EBook), p.8.

23 November 1899. Treating the wounded, probably wounded soldiers, from the 9th Brigade, at the field hospital set up around the station buildings. (via Author)

Treating the wounded, Belmont railway station. (via Author)

Post battle treatment of the British and captured Boer wounded occurred at two separate points. The Guards Brigade Divisional Hospital located itself at Belmont Farm and the 9th Brigade Divisional Hospital next to and inside the station buildings; 81 wounded were accommodated at the station (59 British and 22 Boers) and 172 at Belmont farm.[115]

Fifteen slightly wounded men remained with their units and were not admitted to hospital and three amputations were performed; two thigh and one through the shoulder joint.[116] Four burghers died of their wounds, being buried on Belmont Farm along with British soldiers, who succumbed to their wounds.[117] One Private of the 2nd Northamptonshire Regiment was buried in the open veld next to the 9th Brigade Field Hospital.[118]

Soldiers killed in action were carried off the battlefield in mule carts and by stretcher-bearers to be buried by the two Brigades in the immediate vicinity of their bivouac. 'In the afternoon we buried poor Fryer and the men who were already dead. It was most harrowing'.[119] 'At 6:00 p.m. we buried the dead and a most painful proceeding it was'.[120] The Guards Brigade cemetery was established immediately south of and in the shadow of Verner's Hill; surmounted by a memorial, which still stands, designed and paid for by Crabbe, with assistance from Russell.

Guards Brigade memorial and burial site at the original bivouac area on Belmont (Thomas's) Farm. (Author's collection)

> My visit to Cape Town (March 1902) will enable me to do some business about these memorials which I have wanted to do for some time. At the beginning of the campaign, Colonel Crabbe agreed to design and erect all the memorials for the whole of the Guards Brigade. When you think how many, alas! have fallen in action, from disease, accidents, and other causes, you can imagine that it has been no light work. I have, of course, assisted him in this, and it has not always been

115 MMK: Burtchaell, *Journal of the Royal Army Medical Corps*, p.305.

116 MMK: Burtchaell, *Journal of the Royal Army Medical Corps*, p.305.

117 Details of British casualties taken by the author in 1999 from the various memorials that were erected at Thomas's Farm and Verner's Hill cemetery and which are now in the Garden of Remembrance, West End Cemetery, Kimberley. Boer details taken from South African War Graves Board Tender Document 1963.

118 Private G Upex of the 2nd Northamptonshire Regiment. Information obtained in 1999 by the author from the South African Heritage Resources Agency War Graves Directorate.

119 Russell, *Letters from South Africa*, p.16.

120 MMK: HG Chandos Pole Gell, Unpublished Diary, p.9.

Moved by his final written words, Eagar's widow and Brine's parents linked their loved one's final sunset and the daybreak of their deaths with the Christian belief of resurrection and inscribed 'Until the Day Break' as their epitaph.* (McGregor Museum, with permission)

* Copy of the diary in the author's collection.

> very easy when we have been on trek, and when the whole trade of the country has been dislocated by the war. I have just completed a somewhat voluminous statement of their present condition, financial and otherwise, of those memorials, and if the C.O. approves of it, I shall send it round to all the other adjutants of the Brigade.[121]

The 9th Brigade buried its casualties in the private cemetery behind Thomas's homestead. The dead of the Northumberland Fusiliers were buried in Thomas's cemetery and Hill officiated over the open graves.[122] For reasons unknown, no memorial was ever erected by the regiment or the 9th Brigade for its casualties. However, Captain Eagar's widow and of Lieutenant Brine's parents erected a joint tombstone above these officers' graves, buried side by side. It includes the names of the rank and file from these officers' regiment, killed during the action. In his diary entry on the night on the 22nd November 1899, Eagar wrote how taken aback he was with the beauty of the sunset over Thomas' Farm. He was shot dead during the dawn attack and never saw a sunset again. His family, which included a widow and four children, later received this diary. [123]

As for officers killed in the action and those who succumbed to their wounds before the hospital train arrived, they were buried in individual graves separate from the mass graves of the non-commissioned officers and men. This elitist practice by the British army was well established at the time of the South African War and reflects the value attached to the lives and status of members of the so-called establishment of that time. In fact, a higher value

121 Russell, *Letters from South Africa*, pp.220–221.
122 Author's collection: Padre Eustace St Claire Hill: Unpublished Diary, 1899.
123 M.G. Dooner, *The Last Post* (Suffolk: JB Haywood & Son, 1980), p.105.

was attached to the lives of officers, drawn from the upper classes of British and colonial society, than that of the rank and file, many of whom joined the army due to rampant unemployment, prevalent in the so called working or lower classes. Whilst en route to Orange River Station on 18 November 1899, Colvile issued the following instruction to the Guards Brigade officers: 'The more senior the officer the more valuable his life'.[124]

The less seriously wounded were railed to Orange River Station and the severe cases to Cape Town on 24 November 1899 at noon, involving 120 British, 40 Boer casualties and 36 unwounded Boer prisoners. Two Guardsmen, Private H. Schultz and Private J. Lynne, died on route, being buried at the Leeuw Gamka railway siding, where their graves stand in the veld today.[125] Shultz was an Australian and reputedly the tallest man in the British army; a plaque being erected in his school at St Arnaud, Australia, to his memory.[126]

Sixteen more Boer prisoners were railed to Orange River Station the following day.[127] Losses vary depending on the sources. British killed were approximately 53, wounded 245 and died of wounds 25. Total fatalities being 78.[128] As a percentage of all troops engaged in the action, this represents 3.4. percent.[129]

As for Boer casualties, Methuen stated that he accounted for 83 burghers killed while 23 wounded were made prisoner and more than 30 captured.[130] Other sources have 45 prisoners taken.[131] Regarding the dead he stated these figures based on reports received from his field commanders. They informed him as to how many Boer dead they buried on 23rd November 1899, and the following day, before the Division recommenced its advance.

In 1962, all four established burial sites at Belmont were exhumed and the human remains and memorials relocated; the British to the West End Cemetery Garden of Remembrance, Kimberley[132] and the burghers to the Magersfontein Burgher Monument.[133] The memorial marking the Boer gravesite on the battlefield, stayed behind and exists to this day.

The centralised burgher burial site at the Magersfontein Burgher Monument lists 25 burghers as formerly buried at Monumentplaas Belmont, the site of a Boer grave memorial in the veld.[134] Also included at Magersfontein Burgher Monument is a tomb for six Unknown Burghers.

124 SAL: A 355 31 GRE: 1899, 'Staff Diary of the Guards Brigade', p.19.
125 Their graves were located at this site by the author during 1991.
126 Wallace, *The Australians at the Boer War*, p.61.
127 MMK: 7654/37A: General Sir J.S. Ewart, Unpublished Autobiography, p.435.
128 Author's 'tally' based on all the sources listed since 1989.
129 MMK: 7654/134: Lieutenant Colonel C.H. Burtchaell, 1912, 'Journal of the Royal Army Medical Corps', United Services Medical Society, Volume XVIII, p.667.
130 Lord P.S. Methuen, Despatch of Belmont Action, 26 November 1899, as reproduced in *The True History of the War*, p.7.
131 W.M. Guest, *With Lord Methuen and the 1st Division* (Klerksdorp: Printer and Publisher, 1902), p.14
132 Located at: Latitude 28°44'4.83"S, Longitude 24°44'10.27"E.
133 Located at: Latitude 28°57'13.22"S and Longitude 24°44'3.53"E.
134 Latitude 28°57'12.84"S, Longitude 24°44'3.76"E. Recorded from the Magersfontein Burgher Monument by the author.

Additional memorials that record the names of burghers killed as a result of the Belmont action are located at Boshof. A memorial at Kroonstad lists the fallen without reference as to where they died and the Jacobsdal memorial merely commemorates the commando. When cross-referencing those names on these three memorials, one arrives at a fatality tally of 39 burghers whose names are recorded on these structures which form a point of reference for public expressions of commemoration. If one adds the 39 burghers' names to those of the six unknown burghers buried at Magersfontein, then some 45 recorded burials are accounted for. Remembering too that Agterryers (African Auxiliaries) could have been killed in action and the British troops on the hills wouldn't have discriminated when counting corpses on the battlefield, this may explain some of the missing identities among the unaccounted-for 38.

So where might the other 38 be buried, assuming that Methuen was correct? Canadian and Australian troops who later camped at Belmont between December 1899 and February 1900, had their outposts on Table Mountain, Gun Hill and Grenadier Hill.[135] They provide the explanation.

> But perhaps their most trying duty was the outpost work on the wide range of Belmont battlefield. It was far from a pleasant duty to have to stumble over the rugged plain and up the steep boulder strewn koppies, where but thirteen days before a bloody battle been fought from ridge to ridge.
>
> Occasionally they would come upon a heap of stones and as the night wind blew across it they knew that beneath lay the dead bodies of some of their enemies. In the cold grey light of dawn, they would sometime catch sight of an arm or a leg protruding from the rough burial mounds–gruesome sights that made a shudder through them as they thought that it might be their turn next.[136]
>
> Some of the Boer dead were indifferently buried on the summits of the kopjes–that is to say, a number of stones were laid on the bodies, which remain partially exposed. In one place I counted five corpses huddled together. Here a swollen head and face protruded, there a blackened hand, a pair of bent up knees in another place, and several pairs of booted feet–a grim and ghastly heap of decaying humanity, all that was left of the Boer warriors who served their country's cause on the heights of Belmont. Huge vultures, those aerial scavengers who do their work so thoroughly, would probably have a change of diet very soon. At that time they were feeding on dead horse, and our pickets on the hill were a temporary guard to the Boer corpses.[137]

These graves were never moved and are still to be found on the battlefield today.

On the afternoon of 23 November 1899, Methuen addressed his troops.

---

135 These hills are strewn with the names of hundreds of Canadian soldiers along with the dates 1899 and 1900 that are carved into the boulders, Observed by the author between 1989–2002.

136 "One of Them", *The 85th King's Light Infantry* (London: Spottiswoode & Co., 1913), pp.130–131.

137 Reay, *Australians in War*, p.50.

While at Belmont Methuen received his first dispatch from Kekewich, smuggled through from Kimberley by Jacob Gout, a black dispatch runner. It took Gout five days to reach the 1st Division, hiding by day and walking through the night. After two days rest, he returned with Methuen's dispatch, reaching Kimberley on the third night. He later made two trips to the camp at Modder River, safely delivering his messages. (From The War Museum of the Boer Republics, *Black Participation And Suffering In The South African War. An Untold History* (Brandfort: Firefly Publications (Pty) Ltd))

A soldier of the Royal Canadian Regiment poses next to a Boer grave on one of the Belmont hills. (Public domain)

> Comrades, I congratulate you on the complete success achieved by you this morning. The ground over which we had to fight presented exceptional difficulties, and we have as an enemy a past master in the tactics of mounted infantry. With troops such as you are, a commander can have no fear of the result. There is a sad side, and you and I are thinking as much of those who have died for the honour of their country and of those who are suffering as we are thinking of our victory.[138]

A number of wounded men died during the course of that day and, at Thomas' farm, their passing was a most unpleasant experience for those who witnessed it. 'Now I hear a poor fellow groaning and dying shot through his chest; he is at last silent, as perhaps God has released him. People congratulate me; the men seem to look on me as their father, but I detest war, the more I see of it'.[139]

138 Wood, *The Northumberland Fusiliers*, p.167.

139 MMK: 7654/194 b: Lord Methuen, Letter to Wife, Unpublished Manuscript, 26 November 1899, p.4.

Lieutenant L. March Phillips succinctly summed up the action.

What happened was the simplest thing in the world. The Boers took up their position in some kopjes in our line of march. The British infantry, without bothering to wait till the hills had been shelled, walked up and kicked the Boers out. There was no attempt at any plan or scheme of action at all; no beastly strategy, or tactics, or outlandish tricks of any sort; nothing but an honest, straightforward British march up to a row of waiting rifles. Our loss was about 250 killed and wounded. The Boer loss, though the extent of it is unknown, was probably comparatively slight, as they got away before our infantry came fairly into touch with them. The action is described as a victory, and so, in a sense, it is; but it is not the sort of victory we should like to have every day of the week. We carried the position, but they hit us hardest. On the whole, probably both sides are fairly satisfied, which must be rare in battles and is very gratifying.[140]

140 Phillips, *With Rimington*, p.8.

5

Battle of Graspan, 25 November 1899

On 25 November 1899, the second battle between the 1st Division and the combined Boer forces of the South African Republic (Transvaal) under De La Rey and the Orange Free State Republic, under Prinsloo, occurred North of Graspan station, 17 kilometres North of Belmont. Known as Graspan by the British forces and Rooilaagte by the Boers, it was tactically identical to the Belmont action.

Shaken by their defeat at Belmont, Prinsloo's commandos retired to Ramdam, 21 kilometres east of Enslin railway station. In his official telegram, He reported that:

> This morning a terrible fight took place, which went against us, as we had to leave the battlefield. There are about 10 killed and 40 wounded on our side. The fight lasted from daybreak to about 11.30am. The battleground was about 12 miles in extent, and in consequence of the great number of cannon of the enemy it was impossible for the center to resist successfully. The enemy loss must be terrible. To restore order among the Burghers I was compelled to retire with my command in the direction of Ramdam. Fighting General de la Rey is in the vicinity. Comdt. Serfontein is a prisoner of war, as he would not leave his wounded son. Ten of our wounded are being well attended by the enemy.[1]

In the Kimberley siege lines, Judge J.B.M. (Barry) Hertzog learnt of this defeat from a despatch rider. He believed the siege to be a failure and proposed that 800 burghers be left to watch the garrison. The rest of the force was then to immediately move South and meet the 1st Division before it arrived at Modder River as the terrain between Belmont and Modder river was waterless. Steyn supported these tactics, yet could not convince Chief Kommandant C. Wessels, commanding the besieging force, to do so.[2]

Meanwhile on 23 November 1899, De La Rey arrived in an area of hills bisecting the railway line four kilometres North of Graspan Station. This was

1 Author's collection: General Prinsloo, War Telegram, 23 November 1899.
2 C.M. van den Heever, *General J.B.M. Hertzog* (Johannesburg: APB Bookstore, 1946), p.68.

General Jacobus Herculaas de la Rey (1847–1914) fought in the Basotho War (1865), Sekhukhune's War (1876), the Transvaal War of Independence and a became a Member of the Transvaal Volksraad in 1883. He opposed Kruger's policies against the uitlanders, and the path to war, yet fought on to the bitter end in 1902. (Public domain)

the first batch of Transvaal reinforcements ordered on, 21 November 1899, by Kruger to this threatened sector. His commando was approximately 600 to 700 strong.[3] The force included Burghers P.J. Bekker and his brother, of the Potchefstroom Commando.[4] De la Rey was aware of the urgency of stopping Methuen's force as far South from Kimberley as possible.[5] These hills formed an ideal position from which to block the British advance North. The veld stretching up towards the hills was a grass plain, devoid of cover.

His forces were not equipped with demolition materials, yet to impede the British advance they tore up approximately 300 metres of railway track just South of their positions. That night he sent a message to Prinsloo urgently requesting him to join forces, which he did the following day. Cronjé's Transvaal forces were also on route, yet had not reached these combined forces by the time of the Graspan action.[6]

The combined Boer force numbered approximately 2,000 men in the defensive positions, with a fairly even numerical split between the Transvaal and Orange Free State forces. Artillery support included a total of three 75 mm Krupp and two 37 mm Pom-Poms and two maxim machine guns.[7] The commandos were from Lichtenburg, Winburg, Bloemfontein, Hoopstad and Fauresmith.[8]

On the morning of 24 November 1899, the 1st Division resupplied itself with ammunition railed up from Orange River Station and prepared to advance. A company of Mounted Infantry and an armoured train were dispatched North to reconnoitre the Boer positions. They were shelled, losing two dead and four wounded,[9] yet reported that about 500 Boers were in position.[10]

In his official telegram de la Rey reported that:

> Yesterday about 10 o clock, an armoured train, accompanied by a number of horsemen, came through to the spot where the rails had been torn up the previous evening. The troops endeavoured to take certain positions on my left. The 4 foremost men, with their horses, were shot dead. The Krupp gun, placed directly in front of the rails, fired three shots, after which the train retired.[11]

3 Breytenbach, *Die Geskiedenis van die Tweede Vryheidsoorlog*), *Vol. II*, p.37.
4 WMBR: Unique ID: 05784/00014: Recollections by Burgher P.J. Bekker.
5 Breytenbach, *Die Geskiedenis van die Tweede Vryheidsoorlog*), *Vol. II*, p.37.
6 Breytenbach, *Die Geskiedenis van die Tweede Vryheidsoorlog*), *Vol. II*, p.38.
7 Breytenbach, *Die Geskiedenis van die Tweede Vryheidsoorlog*), *Vol. II*, p.39.
8 Maurice, *History of the War*, p.234.
9 TNA: WO.108/83: South African Field Force Casualty List, 1899–1902.
10 Maurice, *History of the War*, p.231.
11 Author's collection: General J.H. de la Rey, War Telegram, 25 November 1899.

A 37 mm Pom-Pom of the South African Republic Artillery. At Graspan, the attacking British infantry came under fire from a Pom-Pom for their first time. (Public domain)

Methuen ordered the mounted troops to extend five kilometres on either side of the railway line and the rest of the Division to advance to Swinkpan, where despite insufficient water, they would be in position to attack the following day. This second reconnaissance, which Methuen accompanied, confirmed earlier reports about low Boer numbers. He therefore planned to dislodge them with an artillery bombardment. Under cover of shellfire his infantry would approach the position to mop up survivors, while the mounted troops, positioned across the Boer escape routes, would complete the defeat. Methuen tasked the 9th Brigade and the Naval Battalion with the assault, if required.

On 25 November 1899, at 3:30 a.m. the infantry left their bivouac and, at 6:00 a.m., two naval 12-pounder guns detrained near Graspan Station. Together with the 18th and 75th Royal Field Artillery, they opened fire at 6:15 a.m., immediately coming under return fire from Albrecht's artillery. Methuen realised that he was up against a far stronger force than expected and changed his plan, ordering the 9th Brigade and Naval Battalion to attack the range of kopjes from the East. He deployed the Guards Brigade to secure the eastern flank as reports reached him of a commando hovering nearby.[12]

The attacking infantry advanced towards the Boer position.

12 Maurice, *History of the War*, pp.235–237.

Officers of the Naval Battalion who fought at Graspan. Present too is Dickie, Major J.H. Plumbe's fox terrier who followed him into action. (McGregor Museum, with permission)

> We glanced at the kopies and almost wondered why the guns poured such a tempest of shrapnel over them, rarely did we catch sight of a figure moving among the rocks; and with the exception of the enemy's guns on the right, vigorously replying to our own, the whole position looked harmless and unattended. At 7.45 we were some seven hundred yards from the base of the isolated kopie on the Boer left and the field battery ceased firing.[13]

Describing this intense shellfire, Burgher A. Joubert later wrote to his brother, 'I never got afraid yet I can tell you your throat is dry before you can think about it'.[14] The Boers opened fire. When closing to 550 metres the attacking force returned fire and advanced by rushes 50 to 100 metres at a time. At 9.30 a.m. the final assault went in at bayonet point, supported with artillery fire. The Naval Battalion suffered high losses, as they inadvertently bunched together.

> Advance! Advance! And on we went at the 'quick': the crackling grew fiercer and we looked anxiously to see if anyone was hit. Down dropped three men, falling forward; "Get up!" shouted an officer, but only one rose and he was dazed and bleeding from the back of the neck–a shrapnel had burst overhead. Officers and men quickly grasped the situation and used their rifles independently. The line worked automatically, firing, rushing on and dropping down to fire again.[15]

'The fighting was desperate until 10 when the heights were carried'.[16] Yet again, like Belmont, this was a pyrrhic victory. The Boers rode away, their

13 T.T. Jeans, *Naval Brigades in the S. A. War* (London: RN Sampson Low, Marston & Co. Ltd, 1901), p.27.

14 WMBR: 04220/00034: Letter by Burgher A. Joubert to F. Joubert, 6 December 1899.

15 Jeans, *Naval Brigades*, pp.28–29.

16 MMK: Military History Collection, Letter from Methuen to Buller, 2 December 1899. 25 December 1899.

Commemorative first day cover to commemorate the 75th anniversary of the battle. (Author's collection)

rear guards preventing the British cavalry from closing in on them. The Mounted Infantry and one Squadron 9th Lancers on the Northwest actually got behind and in the line of the Boer retreat, nearly being overwhelmed. Both the Bekker brothers horses were injured during the battle, and mounted on one horse they attempted to retire. Luckily their uncle with his Agterryer saw them and assisted, the Agterryer giving up his horse. 'The Agterryer, a Bushman, had to run alongside' as they managed to escape.[17]

Captain J.V. Forrest of the Royal Army Medical Corps accompanied them. When approximately six kilometres North of and behind the Boer position, they were fired on by a Boer party. He went to aid a Lancer wounded in the thigh and extracted a Martini Henry bullet from his thigh. On looking up Forrest found himself in the direct line of retirement of a Boer commando.

> The advanced party was preparing to do a little snap shooting, when an older warrior shouted out 'Nit schiessen' and in a few minutes I was surrounded by a large crowd examining a 'khaki' at close quarters for the first time. As I explained who I was to the field-cornet, I found the younger bloods were rapidly helping themselves to my spurs and leggings. They were however dropped like hot iron on my appealing to the field-cornet.[18]

These burghers advised Forrest that they had shot a 9th Lancer out to the West and marked the spot by sticking his lance upright into the ground, so that he might be found. Yet, during the withdrawal to Graspan, the casualty

17 WMBR: 05784/00014: Recollections by Burgher P.J. Bekker.

18 MMK: 7654/134: Lieutenant Colonel C.H. Burtchaell, 1912, 'Journal of the Royal Army Medical Corps', United Services Medical Society, Volume XVIII, p.311.

was not brought in, and only found three months later with wounds in the head and abdomen.[19]

The 9th Lancers on the East had the commando hovering on their right flank to be wary of, and like the artillery, their horses were exhausted from a lack of water at their previous bivouac. Pursuit was impossible.[20] Nevertheless, this would not save Gough. Methuen needed scapegoats and, as he was to demonstrate after the Magersfontein action, was not shy in blaming others. He fired Gough immediately after the action and, on 2 December 1899, wrote to Buller stating:

> Twice I had the enemy on toast, but could do nothing because my mounted troops were too weak in number, and I am thankful I sent down Gough CO 9 Lancers, because if such a thing is possible he was more incompetent than his namesake, and I never felt my camp to be in safety. Under (Major) Little the Regiment has done much better.[21]

Of interest is that Methuen acknowledged that his mounted troops were too weak to complete a resounding defeat, yet still chose to scapegoat Gough. The 1st Division fired 50,000 rounds of rifle ammunition and 750 shells.[22]

Casualty figures differ according to the sources. The author's reconstruction of the sources has British losses at 180; which included 29 dead, 148 wounded and 3 missing or taken prisoner.[23] The Royal Army Medical Corps recorded 17 killed, 168 wounded and 10 who died of wounds; fatalities totalling 27 men. As a percentage of the total force engaged, casualties were 4 percent. The Royal Marines lost 47 percent of their strength.[24] Boer casualties were approximately 19 killed, 41 wounded and 43 captured.[25] British accounts have 21 dead Boers buried on the field and 40 seriously wounded being captured in a field hospital behind the Boer positions towards Enslin.[26]

British casualties were interred at four burial sites; one just East of Graspan Station, and the second West of and below the hill that formed the main point of their attack. The third was an isolated grave 4.8 kilometres West of Graspan Station. This was the grave of the 9th Lancer killed in action, that Forrest identified, yet was found three months later and buried in a farm

---

19 MMK: 7654/134: Lieutenant Colonel C.H. Burtchaell, 1912, 'Journal of the Royal Army Medical Corps', United Services Medical Society, Volume XVIII, p.311.

20 Maurice, *History of the War*, pp.238–241.

21 TNA: WO132/15: Methuen–Buller, 2 December 1899. MMK: typed transcript of Letter from Methuen to Buller, 2 December 1899.

22 MMK: Military History Collection, Letter from Methuen to Buller, 2 December 1899. 25 December 1899.

23 See: R. Gurney, *The History of the Northamptonshire Rgt.*, W. Wood, *The Northumberland Fusiliers*; 1st Battalion Loyal North Lancashire Rgt (Devonport: Swiss & Co Army Printers); L. Cooper, *The King's Own Yorkshire Light Infantry* (London: Leo Cooper Ltd, 1970), F.F. Colvin, *Diary of the 9th Lancers* (Kensington: C. Roy, 1904); T.T. Jeans, *Naval Brigades.*

24 Maurice, *History of the War*, p.242.

25 Breytenbach, *Die Geskiedenis van die Tweede Vryheidsoorlog, Vol. II*, p.53.

26 L.S. Amery, *The Times History of the War in South Africa 1899–1902, Vol II* (London: Sampson Low, Marston and Company Ltd, 1902), p.340.

cemetery.[27] Seven burghers, killed in action, were buried North of the British grave, approximately 730 metres away West of the hill of the main attack; yet this grave may relate to the Boer raid on Enslin Station on 7 December 1899, and for which a memorial on top of the hill commemorates the Boer casualties.[28]

While leading the Royal Marines into action, Major Plumb shouted, 'Rush for the hill, men' before being hit and mortally wounded. His last words were, 'Forward! Never mind me'. Dickie watched over him as he died and guarded his body for six hours until the burial parties arrived.* (McGregor Museum, with permission)

* Dooner, *The Last Post*, p.306.

De la Rey's despatches to Bloemfontein on 26 November and 27 November 1899, conveyed something of the Boer experience.

> 26 November 1900.
> The enemy attacked us from opposite sides yesterday. We kept them back until 2 o clock pm, when infantry concentrated in large numbers opposite one point of my commando, which was stationed on a hill where Comdt. Lubbe was also placed. The Burghers defended themselves remarkably well. At the most we had about 10 killed and a few seriously wounded. It is difficult to state all the losses on our side, as the officers of the combined forces have not yet met. We were entirely surrounded, as the English troops were extended about 9 miles, and the only place where we could pass out was occupied by the Lancers. We had thus also to drive them back. Many of our horses were killed and wounded. Comdt. Lubbe was slightly wounded. The enemy suffered severely where Lubbe was stationed. The enemy constantly had 6 guns engaged to one employed by us.
>
> Ignatius Smit, Burgher of Jacobsdal, sent by his Field Cornet to make a verbal report, states that the Free State and Transvaal burghers have again united at Ramdam. The heaviest attack with cannon was on the Jacobsdal men. The names of 7 Jacobsdal burghers who were killed and 7 wounded, including Comdt. Lubbe have been sent in.[29]

27 Author's collection: Report by Lt Colonel A.J. Kenyon and Mr A.C. Long on South African War Graves situated along the railway line from Orange River Station to Magersfontein, 17 October 1962. Probably 4238 Private W. Wilkins. See: WO.108/83: South African Field Force Casualty List, 1899–1902, p.3. The only 9th Lancer Killed in action at Graspan that day.

28 Authors Collection: Report by Lt. Colonel AJ Kenyon and Mr AC Long on South African War Graves situated along the railway line from Orange River Station to Magersfontein, 17 October 1962.

29 Author's collection: General J.H. de la Rey, War Telegrams, 26 and 27 November 1899.

Kommandant D. Lubbe of the Jacobsdal Commando was severely wounded at the Graspan action, losing an eye. (Public domain)

> 27 November 1899
> In addition to the names received yesterday, 41 other Burghers are reported wounded.
> Dr. Ramsbottom reports:- Performed operation yesterday on Botha and Commandant Lubbe; took out an eye from each. Lubbe had his skull broken at left eye, is severely wounded, but progressing favourably.

The officers without exception praise the heroic deeds of the Jacobsdalers, who, during the severest fighting drove back the English several times.

> Field Cornet Venter engaged the lancers and captured 15 horses; 4 Lancers, one of whom who is a corporal. .... Their horses are in miserable condition. Willem Burger, of Smauskraal, has a shot through the shoulder.[30]

The 1st Division bivouacked around Enslin Station where they suffered much from a lack of water. 'They were a lap nearer Kimberley, but they paid a great price for a few koppies in a barren country under a blazing sun'.[31] The following day during a reconnaissance, Verner's horse tripped in an ant bear hole, throwing him off into a serious injury, and ending his military career. The majority of the Boer force withdrew and laagered at Pramberg, south of Jacobsdal on the Riet River, dispirited and not keen on renewing the combat. At midday on 26 November 1899, Cronjé with 300 men, linked up with them. This was the forward element of his forces heading South from Mafeking. That night they left for Modder River in earnest, to stop the British Northern advance, arriving there with 2,100 to 2,200 men, the following morning.[32] On 26 November the British column left Enslin and arrived at Klokfontein, the following day.

30 Author's collection: General J.H. de la Rey, War Telegram, 26 and 27 November 1899.
31 J. Meintjes, *De La Rey: Lion of the West* (Johannesburg: Hugh Keartland Publishers, 1966), p.113.
32 Breytenbach, *Die Geskiedenis van die Tweede Vryheidsoorlog*, *Vol. II*, p.57.

6

Battle of Modder River, 28 November 1899

The Modder River battle is one of the understated yet key battles in this theatre of the conflict, if not during the opening months of the war. This action, also known as the Battle of Two Rivers (Twee Riviere) by the Boers, was fought along the river banks and veld around the Riet and Modder Rivers.[1] The combined Republican forces entrenched themselves along the Riet River banks, where they fired horizontally into the attacking British infantry across the open veld; a precursor to their tactics at Magersfontein. It also saw incompetence on the part of Methuen who, after creating his own intelligence failure, blundered into his third pyrrhic victory.

Although a much better stand was made at Graspan than at Belmont, de la Rey was unsatisfied with the outcome. The British were within striking distance of Modder River and to the last Boer defensive positions at Magersfontein and Scholtz Nek/Spytfontein, before reaching Kimberley.[2] He learnt some valuable lessons from the Graspan battle and from Belmont, although having not been present. The selection of high ground favoured the attacking force, as the hilltops formed an obvious artillery target for the British and, their shells striking hard rocks and ground, they easily detonated, risking the defenders lives and rendering it difficult to withstand the infantry attack. The dead ground at the base of the hills enabled the infantry to assemble, prior their final bayonet attack and, due to plunging fire, the burghers failed to inflict sufficient casualties to render an attack against their positions impossible.[3] However, had they been firing from ground level defences, the outcome at Belmont and Graspan would have been very different. Accordingly, he applied this lesson in the selection of his next position; the confluence of the Riet and Modder Rivers near Modder River Station and the hamlet of Rosmead.

1 It should be noted that the battle of Modder River is a misnomer as the fighting occurred on the banks of the Riet River. As at Belmont and Graspan, the British took the name Modder River, as this was the name of the nearest railway siding and village.

2 J. Meintjes, *De La Rey* (Johannesburg: Hugh Keartland Publishers, 1966), p.113.

3 Breytenbach, *Die Geskiedenis van die Tweede Vryheidsoorlog, Vol. II*, p.58.

General P.A. Cronjé in overall command of the Transvaal and Orange Free State forces. Unfortunate for the Boer cause is that he played a key role in losing them the war in 1900, when surrounded and captured at Paardeberg. (McGregor Museum, with permission)

The surrounding terrain, in particular the northwards approach from the South towards the Riet River near Modder River Station favoured a defensive position. Its riverbanks formed a natural trench system, within which a concealed force could fight from. The ground approach was across a flat glacis. It was summer, dry, and barren of scrub and long grass. Apart from the riverbanks' trees and shrubs, the entire surrounding countryside was devoid of cover, with the river being 8 to 12 metres in width, thus forming a natural moat.[4] His viewpoint was that should an attacking force, which was tied to the railway, be ambushed on this terrain, it could neither advance nor retreat and, exposed, literally be shot to pieces.[5] An ambush it would be – with the aim that fire should not open prematurely. The British force should be allowed to get as close as possible to the Boer positions, so that the burghers' opening salvo be devastating.

During the late afternoon of 27 November 1899, the Boer forces arrived at Modder River. Within 30 minutes, General's Cronjé, de la Rey, and Prinsloo held a Council of War (Krygsraad) to make their final arrangements. Cronjé made the Crown and Royal Hotel his headquarters and General de la Rey his at Rostol's farm.[6] Using the station and damaged railway bridge as their centre positions, the Republicans divided their forces in two. The Transvaal forces, comprising of the Potchefstroom and Lichtenburg Commandos entrenched along the riverbanks East of the railway, which ran along a North–South axis, with elements of the Jacobsdal Commando to the far West. Some 1,000 to 1,100 Orange Free State forces entrenched West of the railway line.[7] Their fox holes and trenches were established some 50 to 100 metres forward of the river edges, were deep enough for protection against shellfire and camouflaged with natural scrub.[8] The farms on the southern bank and the houses of Rosmead and Modder village, yards and kraals, were all prepared for defence.[9]

The soil was hard and chalky and the burghers short of picks and shovels, so work continued late into the night. All that day, men and positions were shuffled about, a cloud of dust moved all the way along the road between Modder River and Jacobsdal as artillery and ammunition wagons were brought up. Dust was also kicked up as the burghers dug themselves in

4 J. Meintjes, *De La Rey*, p.114.
5 Breytenbach, *Die Geskiedenis van die Tweede Vryheidsoorlog, Vol. II*, pp.58-59.
6 J.H. Meyer, *Kommando-Jare 'n Oud-stryder se persoonlike relaas van die Tweede Vryheidsoorlog* (Cape Town and Pretoria: Human & Rousseau, 1971), p.45.
7 Breytenbach, *Die Geskiedenis van die Tweede Vryheidsoorlog, Vol. II*, p.60.
8 Meyer, *Kommando-Jare*, p.43.
9 J. Meintjes, *De La Rey*, p.118

Although taken after the battle, these two photographs depict the Boer trenches, which were a series of fox holes, and the fortified buildings at Rostel's Farm, in the centre of their positions. (McGregor Museum, with permission)

This photograph depicts the open ground over which the British had to advance and the improvised nature of the Boer trenches. (via Author)

General James Barry Munnik Hertzog K.C., better known as Barry Hertzog (1866–1942), served throughout the war and later became Prime Minister of the Union of South Africa from 1924 to 1939. (Public Domain)

and horseman rode about.[10] This activity and dust did not pass unnoticed by the British scouts, yet Methuen later failed to accept what it heralded.

Total Boer numbers were between 3,500 and 4,000 men with four 75 mm Krupp field guns and one 37 mm Pom-Pom machine gun.[11] The artillery was positioned in two sectors. Two 75 mm Krupp guns East of the railway line, commanded by Gun Commanders Lamprecht and Raubenheimer and two West of the railway line under Albrecht, Lieutenant Stockenberg and Gun Commanders van Rensburg and Sergeant W. du Plessis.[12] All these guns were manoeuvred around the terrain during the subsequent battle, resulting in overstated numbers of Boer guns in all the source accounts.

The end of the Western defences anchored around a mud brick farm house and kraal and a low rocky ridge which protected the only viable crossing point – a drift across the Riet River just forward of Rosmead village (now Ritchie), defended by the Fauresmith Commando.[13] These 70 burghers, led by Kommandant B. Greyling were isolated and deserted by at least half of their commando.[14]

However, the Achilles heel in the Boer defence was that this crossing point was defended by demoralised Orange Free State burghers who had already experienced defeat twice within the same week. On 27 November 1899, just after sunset, Judge Hertzog arrived at the scene to find that of the 1,600 Orange Free State forces, only about 1,000 were in position. He immediately sent Kommandant Viviers to force them back into position and set off to find Prinsloo to rectify this. He found Albrecht with his two guns, who informed him that there were no burghers North of him to defend his guns, saying that, 'the English would be fools if they do not cross the river there tonight,' pointing to a position to the right of Prinsloo's forces. 'They will take my guns before I can fire a shot. But come what may, I stay by my guns until my head is blown off'.[15]

10 J. Meintjes, *De La Rey*, pp.117-118.

11 J.H. Breytenbach has artillery strength being 4 or 5 Krupp's, 2 Pom-Poms and 2 Maxim machine guns, yet on balance, after consulting all the sources, the author has arrived at the number stated in the narrative, because many of the same guns were moved around during the action, creating the impression that there were more. See: Breytenbach, *Die Geskiedenis van die Tweede Vryheidsoorlog, Vol. II*, p.61.

12 MMK: 7654/12a: Sergeant Willie du Plessis, p.4.

13 F. Conradie, *Met Cronjé Aan Die Wesfront (1899–1900)* (Cape Town: Nasionale Pers Beperk, 1943), p.42.

14 van den Heever, *General Hertzog*, p.70.

15 van den Heever, *General Hertzog*, pp.70–71.

Hertzog set off to find Prinsloo and at 11:00 p.m. found him at the drift opposite Rosmead Village. Hertzog pointed out that the ridge on the South bank and immediately West of the farmhouse was undefended and that should the British force gain this they would then cross the river. Hertzog insisted that the defences be further extended Westwards. He argued fruitlessly with Prinsloo for over an hour, who seemed despondent, yet could receive no action from him other than the comment that there were too few burghers to extend the line. They were still talking when splashing in the Riet River told them more burghers were abandoning their Southern bank positions. A Winburg Commando Veldkornet told them that 'his men could not be held back any longer', as they believed their right flank to be dangerous.[16] Prinsloo ordered them back, yet the Veldkornet refused to obey the order. Hertzog stepped forward and threatened to arrest him and have him court martialled, whereupon they returned to their positions. He again urged Prinsloo to extend the positions, yet to no avail.[17]

Methuen planned an eastward flank march for the next morning, taking five days' provisions with him. His plan was to mask the Modder River bridge by a reconnaissance in force, while he marched to Jacobsdal, and thence by Brown's Drift across the Modder River to Abon's Dam, located 26 kilometres Northeast of Jacobsdal. There he would turn the Boer position at Spytfontein where he was convinced they intended to offer battle.[18] Worth noting is that despite evidence materialising to the contrary, Methuen never shifted from this view. Despite all the information he later received, he dismissed it as a Boer rear-guard ahead of him on the Modder and Riet Rivers. Furthermore, his map of the Modder River Station vicinity was completely inaccurate. It reflected that the Modder River was fordable in most places, when in fact it was not. Nor did it depict the Riet River flowing across his path.

On 27 November 1899, the British force arrived at Witkop Farm (a point almost 18 kilometres North of Graspan). Methuen established his headquarters at Klokfontein railway siding, some seven kilometres South of Modder River Station.[19] Additional reinforcements were on route; the 1st Argyll and Sutherland Highlanders had entrained for Klokfontein from Orange River Station and the 62nd Battery Royal Field Artillery by road from Orange River Station, where half of the 2nd Black Watch Regiment had arrived.[20] Back at Orange River Station, Gough met with Wauchope and, 'poured all his grievances against Methuen into Wauchope's ear'.[21] Dissatisfaction with Methuen's tactics and his choice of frontal attacks during the last two actions were being expressed down the line.

From Klokfontein, Methuen 'proceeded to reconnoitre to Modder River. He later testified before the Royal Commission that, 'from the information I had received, came to the conclusion that the entire force of the enemy had

16 van den Heever, *General Hertzog*, p.71.
17 van den Heever, *General Hertzog*, p.71.
18 Maurice, *War in South Africa*, vol. 1, pp.245–246.
19 SAL: OCLC Number:101723531: J.A. Glegg Collection.
20 MMK: 7654/37A: General Sir J.S. Stewart, Unpublished Autobiography, p.436.
21 MMK: 7654/37A: General Sir J.S. Stewart, Unpublished Autobiography, p.437.

assembled at Spytfontein and that I should not meet with any determined resistance on the Modder'.[22] Despite what unfolded, he clung obstinately to this view, even after the action. Writing on 2 December 1899 to Buller, Methuen expressed his view then that:

> People talk of making a detour, or sending one Brigade round a flank; there is no talking in that way with 8000 horsemen in front of you, a river and a position not to be turned. The job has to be done, and we have taken an infernal position with less loss than I expected, for many casualties are light. No credit due to me, for I believed the bulk of the 8000 were at Spytfontein, and I never expected Kronje, de la Rey with their hosts to be hidden in the river. There was not a sign of them.[23]

Yet was this in fact the case?

That afternoon, a reconnaissance patrol probed close enough to the Boer positions to draw rifle fire. Trooper E.M. le Seur of Rimington's Guides being shot through the stomach. He died that night in the field hospital at Klokfontein.[24] The patrol reported that the Boer forces were holding Modder River. Major Little, 9th Lancers, estimated Boer numbers as high as 4,000.[25] Major Rimington ascertained that the Boers expected reinforcements, and were entrenching on the South bank near Modder River bridge.[26] Yet Methuen concluded 'that the entire force of the enemy had assembled at Spytfontein, and that I should not meet with any determined resistance on the Modder'.[27]

This information of a strong Boer force ahead was officially accepted and entered into writing that night. A photocopy of a handwritten diary, which appears to be a Divisional diary in the McGregor Museum collection, for which there is no accession number, refers. Dated 27 November 1899, and being a daily diary, the entry was presumably written in the late evening. 'Received news that the force of enemy at the Modder River have been reinforced'.[28]

There is no doubt that Methuen received sufficient eye witness information alerting him to the dire threat facing his Division, by an entrenched Boer force along the banks of the Riet and Modder rivers. Yet he ignored this, believing that they were entrenched on the hills at Spytfontein, as at Belmont and Graspan, and remained tactically inflexible.

On the morning of 28 November 1899, additional information reached Methuen, 'through a native that that Modder River village was strongly

---

22 TNA: WO 132/15.

23 TNA: WO132/15: Methuen–Buller, 2 December 1899. MMK: typed transcript of Letter from Methuen to Buller, 2 December 1899.

24 In a horrific twist of fate, Eustace Monroe le Seur was from Klerksdorp where he was well known, owning a store and being great footballer and cricketer. He was shot by a friend of his serving with the Boer forces. J. Lane, *The War Diary of Burgher Jack Lane 1899–1902* (Cape Town: Van Riebeeck Society, 2001), p.20.

25 War Office Library London: Secret South Africa Despatches, Methuen, pp.45–46.

26 Maurice, *War in South Africa*, Volume 1, p.246.

27 TNA: WO 132/15: Methuen Despatch on the operations at Modder River.

28 MMK: Military history collection.

occupied'. The station master at Modder River, at great personal risk, sent a note with this African runner to Methuen that the Boers, 'were digging themselves in to the river like rabbits'.[29] and 'that Modder River village was strongly occupied'.[30] Major General R. Pole-Carew recollected that the African runner's message was received the night of 27 November 1899, which was more likely, given the impossibility of crossing the Boer lines and the open veld in daylight.[31]

Methuen decided to crush this pocket of resistance before continuing with his original plan to bypass Spytfontein via Jacobsdal, and 'establish myself on Modder River before proceeding any further'.[32] Yet he never, for a moment contemplated nor realised the reality confronting him. According to J.A. Glegg, who served under Methuen, and writing later, 'It was not his most lucid moment'.[33]

On 28 November 1899, at 4.00 a.m. the British force left its bivouac for Modder River Station, yet many troops were not fed in the haste to reach the objective. 'In the hurry of turning out, some battalions got no breakfast and started on empty stomachs'.[34] 'But in some cases, regiments did not give their men that cup of hot comfort which is so necessary, and the want of which afterwards reduced the men nearly to pulp'.[35] A blunder indeed. For the 1st Argyll and Sutherland Highlanders this would compound their ordeal. They stumbled into the bivouac the night before, 'many of them so dead beat from hunger on their journey from Orange River and from their march from railhead to the bivouac, in which they lost their way, that they did not eat the food which other battalions had prepared for them'.[36] When their Colonel remonstrated that his men had not yet eaten breakfast, an excitable Staff Officer replied. 'Don't worry about breakfast, you can get breakfast when you get to Modder

Major General R. Pole Carew entered the Coldstream Guards in 1869, and served as a Staff Officer to Lord Roberts in the Second Anglo-Afghan War in 1878. He later commanded the 11th Division of the South Africa Field Force, before becoming General Officer Commanding 8th Division in Southern Ireland in 1903. (From M. Menpes, *War Impressions Being A Record In Colour* (London: Adam & Charles Black, 1901))

29 MMK: 7654/183: Notes of conversation with Major General Sir Reginald Pole-Carew on 25th February 1903; and Pakenham, *The Boer War*, p.189.

30 TNA: WO 132/15: Methuen, Despatch on the operations at Modder River.

31 MMK: 7654/183: Notes of conversation with Major General Sir Reginald Pole-Carew on 25th February 1903.

32 TNA: WO 132/15: Methuen Despatch on the operations at Modder River.

33 SAL: OCLC Number:101723531: J.A. Glegg Collection.

34 MMK: 7654/183: Notes of conversation with Major General Sir Reginald Pole-Carew on 25th February 1903.

35 MMK: 7654/182c: Letter by Major General Sir Reginald Pole-Carew, Modder River, 2 December 1899.

36 MMK: 7654/183: Notes of conversation with Major General Sir Reginald Pole-Carew on 25th February 1903.

River. There's Modder River, just walk on down there'.[37] Yet a major brunt of the fighting would befall them that day.

Hunger and deprivation were also true for Cronjé and De la Rey's burghers. Their commissariat arrived amongst their central positions, literally after the British force was sighted.

> The men, however, soon had the cart empty, some had made fires others not, some just letting the meat get warm, others eating it raw, to get something into their stomachs to satisfy their hunger. Most, I should say, got nothing at all. As for myself, I never smelt a piece of bread or meat. The cry is the British are coming on in thousands.[38]

Whilst driving this ration cart into the Boer defence lines, Burgher J. Lane observed the Boer mobile reserve, which later played a key role.

> Going down the incline, you get a large, we call it a 'sluit'. It is now dry, but when the river is full, it flows in it, and beyond is a long island, which, when river is full, would be about the middle of river, which now being low flows on other side of this island. In this dry sluit, which is about twenty yards broad and about a mile long, I saw about three hundred horses hidden away so as to be out of sight of British, all saddled, and tied with the reins in lots of twelve. I got orders to bring cart and all into this place.[39]

Burgher Jack Lane refused to bear arms when conscripted by the Boer forces and was seconded to the Commissariat. His diary, written during the events he described, is a first-hand witness account of the combats that he experienced. (Courtesy of Van Riebeeck Society, Cape Town)

At daybreak Hertzog decided to visit the Fauresmith Commando to urge the unwilling men back into line. When he reached the drift he found a group of deserting burghers just crossing, saying that they were going to fetch fodder for their horses. While ordering them back another group of 80 burghers approached the drift. He drew his pistol and threatened to shoot the first man who attempted to cross the drift. This had the desired effect; the burghers reluctantly turned back.[40]

From the advancing British perspective, up ahead, across the veld, 'In the village itself we could not see any sign of men, guns or wagons, but to the East of the village

37 Author's collection: Midge Carter, 'Lieutenant Colonel B Lang, Interview: "The Boer War", Durban (9 March 1970).

38 Lane, *The War Diary*, p.23.

39 Lane, *The War Diary*, p.23.

40 van den Heever, *General Hertzog*, p.72.

we found the enemy in strong force, and aggressive'.[41] At around 5:30 a.m. the 9th Lancers and Mounted Infantry to the East and ahead of the infantry were shelled by three Boer guns, which fired with great accuracy. Cronjé saw them as an emerging threat to the Boer left flank, while de la Rey recalled this movement such that, 'before the battle began, [Cronjé] took two guns out of their positions and advanced upstream along the Modder river and was the last time that I heard from him that day'.[42] He was horrified by this action, believing that by doing so, Cronjé shirked his duty and left him in the lurch.[43] Soon after 07:00 a.m. the infantry began arriving on the impending battlefield.[44] The 75th and 18th Battery's Royal Field Artillery eventually disabled one of these Boer guns.[45]

Even at this stage Methuen deluded himself about the Boer forces. 'The enemy appeared to be retiring, and there were no signs that the village was held in strength. We all believed that the force in our front was fighting a retiring action, and had no idea that 8,000 Boers had been brought from Spytfontein to oppose us.'[46]

In the Boer trenches and foxholes, the 'shout went up. "Daar kom de Britische."'[47] Burgher I. Meyer lay on the northern bank of the Riet River, just West of its confluence with the Modder River, concealed amongst the riverside bamboo and reeds, anxiously staring across the open veld before him.

> Left and right of me, amongst the other burghers, lay a group of my friends, such as Kalfie Beukes, Coenraad Meintjes and Kobus Minaar. Right before me, towards the South, stretched the open plain over which the enemy must cross. A little to my right, was the railway line and main road over which the English are expected.[48] I lay with my Mauser in my hand and my heart restlessly bouncing inside me. Because the report had arrived: Methuen was on route!
>
> The clock ticked. It's already a quarter past seven and the sun began to bake. Today it's going to be hot. Dead still we lay and waited. And then, suddenly, I saw them, thousands of them. Like a swarm of locusts, they poured over the ridge. A broad solid mass of marching infantry and horse sections. Methuen's ten thousand men. The morning sun flickering on a huge sea of glistering rifle barrels. Beautifully in line, they marched and rode, these ten thousand men. Gripping and terrifying.[49]
>
> What an awesome face: a line over 5 miles long, ten thousand men in full force! With the precision of a machine they march. And yet not like a machine, for there is pride in their step, a determination in the swing of their arms that involuntarily

41 TNA: WO 132/15: Methuen, Despatch on the operations at Modder River.
42 MMK: 7654/24: General J. de la Rey, Unpublished Manuscript, p.12.
43 J. Meintjes, *De La Rey*, p.119.
44 C.H. Burtchaell, *Journal of the Royal Army Medical Corps Vol. XV111* (United Services Medical Society, January to June 1912), p.419.
45 TNA: WO 132/15: Methuen, Despatch on the operations at Modder River.
46 TNA: WO 132/15: Methuen, Despatch on the operations at Modder River.
47 Lane, *The War Diary*, p.23.
48 Burgher I Meyer was laying in the centre of the Boer position.
49 Meyer, *Kommando-Jare*, p.47.

> bring you to admiration. It's the cream of the British infantry, the proud brigades of the mighty Empire. My friends and I are amazed at the spectacle and gaped at it.[50]

Methuen ordered the Guards Brigade to attack East of the destroyed railway bridge which, unbeknown to him, formed the approximate centre of the Boer position. The Guards Brigade were 'to develop their attack first, which they did with the 1st Scots Guards on the far right who were to swing their right well around to take the Boers in the flank. The 2nd Coldstream and 3rd Grenadier Guards making the frontal attack, the former on the left to keep in touch with the 9th Brigade, the 1st Coldstream in reserve in the right rear.'[51] The left flank of the 2nd Coldstream Guards were to keep touch with the 9th Brigade to their left (West).[52]

Their explicit written orders were:

> Brigade Morning Orders
> 2 Miles S of Modder river
> 28/11/99
> Attack on Modder river
>
> 7 a.m.–The Brigade will attack from the east. The Scots Guards, Grenadier Guards and the 2nd Battalion Coldstream Guards in 1st Line. The latter Battalion keeping 4 Companies in reserve, and connecting with the IX Brigade. In reserve 1st Battalion Coldstream Guards. Objective, the three tall poplars. The Scots Guards will direct. The IX Brigade will attack the village as soon as the flank attack of the Guards Brigade has developed from the east.[53]

The 9th Brigade under Pole-Carew were to advance to the West of the railway line and maintain its line with the Guards. As indicated in the Guards Brigade Morning Orders, the 9th Brigade were to capture Modder River village, a fact that escapes the established narratives of the Battle of Modder River. Fate would have them capturing another village, that of Rosmead. For it was Pole-Carew's troop deployments and use of topography that later determined the final outcome. He:

> Received written orders to make a frontal attack on the broken railway bridge, i.e. my centre was to be opposite it, but I was to conform to the Guards who were then in process of extending to the right of the railway, at the same time a verbal message from Lord Methuen reached me to the effect that he believed there were no Boers at the river at all except possibly about 400 who might be holding the broken railway bridge.
>
> When I saw that the extension of the Guards would bring their left close to the railway line and overlapping would inevitably occur, I changed my direction left to get to what I then believed to be the enemy's right, in order to overlap it

---

50 Meyer, *Kommando-Jare*, p.49.
51 TNA: WO 132/15: Methuen, Despatch on the operations at Modder River, 29 November 1899.
52 TNA: WO 132/15: Colvile, Despatch to CSO 1st Division, 30 November 1899.
53 SAL: A 355 31 GRE: 1899, 'Staff Diary of the Guards Brigade', p.59.

> and get round their right flank if possible. I did not inform Lord Methuen of my intention.
>
> I had therefore to march across the enemy's front, about 2000 yards south of the river bank, but my movement was more or less concealed from the enemy by the formation of the ground. I kept touch with the Guards and prolonged their line to the left by extending each of my battalions in succession who then moved up practically in line with the Guards to where the ground suddenly slipped down towards the river at distances varying from 1750 to 1200 yards. I had to extend myself widely because I felt it essential to turn the Boer right if possible.[54]

The deployment of the 9th Brigade, in succession, was the 1st Northumberland Fusiliers on the right flank in touch with the 2nd Coldstream Guards to their right flank and, from their left in a westerly direction, the 2nd King's Own Yorkshire Light Infantry, then the 1st Argyll and Sutherland Highlanders and the half battalion 1st Loyal North Lancashire Regiment. The 2nd Northamptonshire Regiment remained at Klokfontein, guarding the baggage.

Lieutenant March Phillips with Rimington's Guides wrote entries into his notebook while in the saddle, and offer insights into the build up to the battle, during that early fateful morning.

> One can see a vast distance over the surface. Along the north horizon there is a ripple of small hills and kopjes, looking blue, with the white grass-land running up to them. It is a comparatively cool morning with a few light clouds in the sky and a pleasant breeze. On our left is the railway, and all along on our right, extending far in front and far behind, advances the army. The river flows somewhere across the landscape yonder in the plains. One cannot see it, but a few belts of bushes indicate its course. It is just that awkward moment before one gets touch of the enemy. They, no doubt, can see us (I wonder how they like the look of us), but we cannot see them. They must be somewhere along the river among those bushes, and probably in trenches. But where does their main strength lie? Where are their guns? It was three minutes to eight when the first shot was fired. "This will be a bit more history for the kiddies to learn," yawns the next man to me, leaning idly over his pony.[55]

Watching this British infantry deployment before him, Burgher Meyer lay, shaking with fear.

> "Wait until four hundred paces is the order", whispered my friend Jerry Basson, who lay next to me. Four hundred paces from this terrifying mass of soldiery. It's crazy, completely crazy, the thought ground through my brain. I shook like a reed and the sweat poured from my forehead. It was a terrifying view. Ten thousand men advancing directly towards you. I lay, with my trembling finger on the trigger, but didn't know where to aim. There was too many of them. They

54 MMK: 7654/183: Notes of conversation with Major General Sir Reginald Pole-Carew on 25th February 1903.

55 Lieutenant March Phillips, *With Rimington*, Letter IV, MODDER RIVER CAMP, 1 December 1899.

> advanced to within eight hundred paces, seven hundred, six hundred. I wiped the sweat out of my eyes. The tension was unbearable.[56]

In the British line, Colvile watched, 'the Scots Guards moving ahead to the right, when Lord Methuen said to me, "They're not here". "They are sitting uncommonly tight if they are sir", I answered; and as if they had heard him, the Boers,' opened fire'.[57]

'And suddenly, slap, there was a shot, five, six shots', as the Fauresmith Commando, defending the drift, started shooting. 'Then the earth began to shake'.[58] Immediately thereafter, the entire Boer line opened fire, their rifle fire initially crackling along their line, followed by a crescendo.

> Colvile recorded that: 'At 08:10 a.m. a sudden and very heavy fire was opened by the enemy concealed in the bushes on the river banks, which besides causing many casualties all along the line, completely wiped out the 1st Scots Guards machine gun detachment and nearly 20 percent of their detached company'.[59] For the 9th Brigade, 'as the leading battalion crossed the railway line the Boer guns opened on them and shortly afterwards the whole river bank was alive with rifle fire'.[60]

In his position Burgher Meyer, fired as rapidly as he could.

> This is war. Now I am the outright murderer who is a man on the battlefield: deliberate, coldblooded. Gone is the tension, the terrible fear that clutched me. I am dead calm now, and dead calm I seek out my man, one by one, I seek him out, my Mauser level, my left eye closes, I take him in the sights and my Mauser barks. The Englishman stumbled, released his rifle, grabbed his chest, staggers, stumbles forward, drops to his knees, tilts over, stays down. I shoot them flat, one after the other, one after the other. But they come and they come.
>
> Soon the battlefield is sprinkled on their side with wounded, dying and dead. As sheaves on an oat field they lay. But still they come, without hesitation, death-defying. These are brave men. They storm, stumble down, struggle again, storm again, fall, stay flat. But still they come like rolling waves, the back one's over the foremost. No longer the close, orderly line of just now, but they come.[61]

Also facing the Guards Brigade lay Burgher Lane.

> Boom, Boom, came two shells, bursting about forty yards above us on the bank. I said to myself, 'Oh God I am in for it now, my baptism from cannon fire.' I can assure you, I don't relish it much, feel a sort of emptiness about the stomach. Now the cry is to get into some sort of cover, but there is not much of that, everyone

56 Meyer, *Kommando-Jare*, p.50.
57 Colvile, *The Work of the Ninth Division*, p.6.
58 Meyer, *Kommando-Jare*, pp.50-51.
59 TNA: WO 132/15: Colvile, Despatch to CSO 1st Division, 30 November 1899.
60 MMK: 7654/183: Notes of conversation with Major General Sir Reginald Pole-Carew on 25th February 1903.
61 Meyer, *Kommando-Jare*, p.51.

Pinned down in the open, the infantry lay under intense fire all day, suffering from thirst and hunger. (Public domain)

> looking out for himself, no order or discipline. With my glasses I could then see them, looked like a swarm of locusts, all over the veld. The fire is incessant. Artillery and small arms, from both sides, it is simply 'hell let loose'. I could never have realised, or one who is not here, what it is like. For two hours I laid in one position on my stomach making myself as small as possible. Maxim shrapnel bullets hitting to within two inches of me.[62]

During the initial phase of the action East of the railway line, the 1st Scots Guards machine gun section, while setting itself up in an empty reservoir near the banks of the Riet River, attracted Boer Pom-Pom fire, killing or wounding its crew, all except one, the Native Driver.[63] Attempts to rush forward came to naught, immediately stopped by Boer rifle fire, as was efforts to evacuate wounded or to supply ammunition and water to the firing line. The Guards Brigade attack came to a complete stop, with the Guardsmen pinned down in their positions for the entire day.

Some 1st Coldstream Guards under Codrington managed to cross the Riet River, yet had to return, for the crossing proved too treacherous.[64] Like

---

62 Lane, *The War Diary*, p.24.

63 Maurice, *History of the War* p.249. The Pom-Pom was a large belt fed machine gun that fired 37 mm calibre high explosive shells singularly or in bursts.

64 Maurice, *War in South Africa*, pp.249–250.

the rest of the Guards Brigade, the 2nd Coldstream Guards lay prone on the open veld under heavy Boer fire. In returning fire, these soldiers depleted their ammunition, and re-supply became a critical tactical issue. Were the infantry to run out of ammunition, their situation would rapidly collapse. An officer from the 2nd Coldstream Guards recalled that, 'We were out of ammunition by 09:00 a.m. except what we had in the magazines'.[65] Ammunition supply, or the lack of it, certainly influenced the tactical outcome of the battle in this sector; as borne out by what followed, and by Methuen's reference in his despatch of a Warrant Officer serving with the Coldstream Guards. 'Sergeant-Major S Wright, Coldstream Guards, showed great coolness when a change of ammunition carts was being made, and was of great value at a critical time'.[66] These carts were all driven by Native Drivers, under direct fire across the coverless terrain.

The ammunition and other cart transport was located behind the fighting troops yet was driven, at slow speed across a bullet swept veld, to the infantry up ahead. Native Driver Matthew Thomas, attached to the 2nd Coldstream Guards, at great personal risk, drove a mule cart into the firing line and replenished this battalion with ammunition. This enabled the 2nd Coldstream Guards to maintain their positions throughout the action and hold the firing line between themselves and the 9th Brigade to their left flank, who were about to launch the decisive strike against the Boer positions.

When the Boers opened fire, the 9th Brigade immediately extended westwards across the railway line, and by 8:30 a.m. they too were pinned down by heavy and accurate shooting from the burghers. The Fauresmith Commando, guarding the weir crossing on the South bank, were anchored on a low rise to the 9th Brigade's extreme left and the mud brick farmhouse and kraal on a slight eminence, approximately to the left-centre position of the Brigade. These two positions enabled the commando to bring a cross fire on any attempt to cross the Riet River. It was here that the outcome of the battle would occur.

Pole-Carew:

> Began to suspect, and so did my Brigade Major, now Lieutenant Colonel Bulfin, that the farm and kraal were a tete du pont, covering some ford over the river. I attempted to storm it, but failed in my first attempt. Next I tried with the Battalion of North Lancashire's to turn the Boers out of the stony rises, still further to the west but without success.[67]

March Phillips recorded in his notebook at 9:30 a.m. that,

> All the time the subdued rumble of Maxims and rifles goes on, like a rumble of cart-wheels over a stony road. Now it increases to one continuous roar, now

65 MMK: 7654/291: H.G. Chandos Pole Gell, 2nd Battalion Coldstream Guards, Unpublished Diary, pp.10–11.

66 TNA: WO 108/74 X/K 696: Despatch by Lieutenant General Lord P. Methuen.

67 MMK: 7654/183: Notes of conversation with Major General Sir Reginald Pole-Carew on 25th February 1903.

The Guards Brigade attack quickly became a day-long lay down; unable to advance nor retire, due to the relentless Boer fire from their camouflaged positions along the tree-lined riverbank up ahead. (Public domain)

> slackens till the reports separate. Now, after one and a half hours, the fight seems to be concentrating towards the village opposite. A haze of smoke hangs over the place. The guns thunder. Now the under-current of rifle fire becomes horrible in its rapidity. Can anything in that hell down there be left alive? 10 A.M.—Both sides are sticking to the business desperately. The rattle of rifle-fire is one low roar. The air shudders and vibrates under it.[68]

Thirst became an ordeal as sun temperature reached 110 degrees Fahrenheit (43.3 °C) by midday and the soldiers' water bottles emptied.[69] For the prone Highlanders, their exposed backs of their knees blistered and burnt, injuring many, as 'The backs of our legs were being burnt to a cinder'.[70] An unknown Native Driver, attached to one of the infantry battalions fighting in this sector drove a water cart into the firing line, being killed by a direct shell strike to his cart. As witnessed by Private F. Stakes of the 2nd Battalion King's Own Yorkshire Light Infantry, who wounded during the action, recalled:

> At the last fight at Modder River we had nothing to eat for two days. Some of us were dying for water. A water cart came in sight and some dozen [men] rushed forward for a drink, right in the midst of heavy fire. A shell was fired at them, killing the driver, and most of the men and smashing the cart to pieces.[71]

---

68 Phillips, *With Rimington*, Letter IV, 1 December 1899.

69 Guest, *With Lord Methuen*, p.32.

70 Author's collection: Midge Carter, 'Lieutenant Colonel B Lang, Interview: "The Boer War"', Durban (9 March 1970).

71 Wallace, *The Australians at the Boer War*, p.67.

Dying of thirst. Numerous desperate dashes towards the water carts often met with fatal consequences.
(McGregor Museum, with permission)

The infantry attacked the farmhouse and kraal, clearing the way to crossing the Riet River and rolling up the Boer right flank. (McGregor Museum, with permission)

After the first attempt failed, Pole-Carew was:

> Lying to the East of the farm in the firing line of the battalion of the Argyll and Sutherland Highlanders which was containing the enemy in the river; and I noticed a depression in the ground, a sort of donga leading to the river. It occurred to me that men might get down into the trees on the river bank and so get behind the Kraal-farm. I accordingly sent 2 officers, both youngsters–and about 20 men of the A&S Highlanders rushing down into the bush with which the bank and bed of the river were thickly lined. They got there without the loss of a man'.[72]

Those Boers entrenched along the southern banks of the Riet River dared not fire at these troops, for risk of hitting their own forces around the farmhouse and kraal. It was then that Methuen appeared and informed Pole-Carew that the Guards Brigade attack had failed and asked what could be done as the men were starving from want of water and that the overall position was very serious. Pole-Carew described to Methuen what he had done with the small party of Highlanders, that his plan was to reinforce them and to again attack the farmhouse and kraal and to get across the river. Methuen agreed, charged down with them, before walking back unhurt.

Pole-Carew then directed a party of the 2nd King's Own Yorkshire Light Infantry to assemble in the hollow. At 9:00 a.m. a second assault was

72 MMK: 7654/183: Notes of conversation with Major General Sir Reginald Pole-Carew on 25th February 1903.

launched on the farmhouse positions, led by Lieutenant R.M.D. Fox of the 2nd King's Own Yorkshire light Infantry with a mixed party of Highlanders and 1st Northumberland Fusiliers. Fox was severely wounded, his arm shattered by a bullet, yet they seized the position by 9:00 a.m.[73] The Boers holding the farm-kraal bolted, the defenders of the stony rise followed suit and also retired with great rapidity.[74] Under continual Boer fire, a party of about 150 infantrymen started crossing the river at about 10:30 a.m., just East of an island downstream from the weir.[75] In places, the water came up to their elbows and armpits. Then, 'we sat down and tried to drink the river dry. I don't think I was ever so done or so thirsty, or so frightened in my life'.[76] All this was achieved without direct artillery support, for two guns only moved to support them from the vicinity of the captured farmhouse a little after midday.[77]

Joined by the 1st Loyal North Lancashire Regiment, who crossed the Riet River about 400 metres downstream and West of the stony rise, the bridgehead was seized by 11:00 a.m. They cleared the burghers from the buildings and bungalows of Rosmead Village and took up position in some furrows and held these with grim tenacity.[78] Another 300 to 400 men from various units reinforced Pole-Carew, including Sappers from the 17th Field Company Royal Engineers, one of whom was hit by a Mauser bullet.

> There were only two of us got shot out of the 17th Field Company, RE. The Boers had a 40 Pounder playing on us all the time, and if their shells had exploded as they should have done, there would not have been one of the 7th Black Horse spared to have told the tale. Our Naval Guns and Brigade did some splendid service. When our troops crossed the river they found the Boer trenches full of dead.[79]

After preparing to repulse any attempt by the burghers to recapture the position, Pole-Carew advanced this force upstream through the brushwood, supported by rifle fire from across the river. Boer shell fire inflicted casualties, as did misdirected British artillery fire from the South bank of the river, by two guns of the 18th Battery Royal Field Artillery which moved into position near the captured mud brick farmhouse and kraal, and from the naval guns at Klokfontein. They concentrated on the two Boer guns in this area, subjecting them to intense shellfire; killing Lieutenant Stockenberg and wounding four

73 MMK: 7654/182c: Letter by Major General Sir Reginald Pole-Carew, Modder River, 2 December 1899.

74 MMK: 7654/183: Notes of conversation with Major General Sir Reginald Pole-Carew on 25th February 1903.

75 MMK: 7654/189: Letter by Major General Sir Reginald Pole-Carew to one of his officers, 16 January 1903.

76 MMK: 7654/182c: Letter by Major General Sir Reginald Pole-Carew, Modder River, 2 December 1899.

77 MMK: 7654/189: Letter by Major General Sir Reginald Pole-Carew to one of his officers, 16 January 1903.

78 Guest, *With Lord Methuen*, p.33.

79 Author's collection: Sapper Charles Gwilliam, 17 Field Company Royal Engineers, Letter to his Mother from Station Hospital Wynberg, 4 December 1899.

Various units of infantry and engineers, crossed the Riet River under fire and secured a bridgehead in Rosmead village.
(McGregor Museum, with permission)

Sergeant W. du Plessis before the war. (J. Wolvaardt, with permission)

artillerists, namely van Niekerk, J.A. Serfontein, Delport, and Schoeman.[80] Sergeant W. du Plessis continued operating his gun on his own.

When the infantry reached the neighbourhood of Fraser's Farm, the two Boer guns were at direct risk of being captured. Gun Commander van Rensburg and Sergeant W. du Plessis waited until the infantry were within 100 paces, endeavouring to cross long hedges of prickly pear, and through strong wire fences, before opening fire with canister shot, adding to the Boer artillery firing from near the railway station.[81] The burghers in the trenches on the South side of the river, turned their aim from the right and centre of the 9th Brigade, pouring in rifle fire.[82] The infantry started collapsing from exhaustion and dehydration, having not eaten, before going into battle.[83]

At 02:00 p.m. the 62nd Battery Royal Field Artillery arrived on the battlefield, having marched up from Orange River Station, and came straight into action, their fire supporting the British attack across the river. Hunger, thirst, and British shellfire caused wavering in the ranks and, due to this 'friendly fire' some of the soldiers refused to advance further. Others pressed on, and their attack soon threatened to roll up the Boer right flank, and capture Albrecht's guns.

De la Rey then led his mobile reserve, the Lichtenburg, Bloemhof, and Wolmaransstad Commandos,[84] in a counterattack against this British wedge, successfully forcing the infantry back into Rosmead. The infantry were so closely pursued that, in order to cover their retreat, two groups, of about a dozen men from the 1st Loyal North Lancashire Regiment and 1st Argyll and Sutherland Highlanders, threw themselves into some farmhouses, and stubbornly defended their position for many hours, despite losses.[85] Major General Pole-Carew consolidated the position, being reinforced by some 300 Royal Engineers.[86]

> When I got to the furthest point you could get. A little tiny farmhouse I suppose it was, probably a native dwelling. I don't know what it was, and there I found Major Irvine of my regiment quite immobile, he was completely exhausted, dehydrated he really was. Absolutely done in, he couldn't move hand or foot. And there was another man in the kitchen. He was on the dining room table.

---

80 MMK: 7654/12a: Sergeant Willie du Plessis, p.5.

81 MMK: 7654/12a: Sergeant Willie du Plessis, p.5. See also: War Museum of the Boer Republics, Bloemfontein: WMBR: 02005/00001: War Memories by P.J. Horak, Bloemfontein, p.19.

82 Maurice, *War in South Africa*, pp.256–257.

83 MMK: 7654/183: Notes of conversation with Major General Sir Reginald Pole-Carew on 25th February 1903.

84 MMK: 7654/24: General J. de la Rey, Unpublished Manuscript, p.12.

85 Maurice, *War in South Africa*, pp.255–256.

86 MMK: 7654/183: Notes of conversation with Major General Sir Reginald Pole-Carew on 25th February 1903.

In the nick of time, four guns of the 62nd Battery Royal Field Artillery unlimbered and opened fire at 2:00 p.m., joined by another two guns at 6:00 p.m. This enabled two guns of the 18th Battery Field Artillery to move closer to the river just West of the farmhouse captured by the 9th Brigade and support its attack along the North bank of the Riet River. (Author's collection)

> He was dying. He was dying on the table. Another fellow wounded there. Two men who weren't wounded. I heard the Boers you see. In the trees, firing the other way. I sent back word twice. Runners, I used these men as runners to go back to any force they could find and report. If they only sent a couple of companies over, we would have got them absolutely sitting. There we were, we were right behind them. They never turned up. If they had sent half that battalion [the 1st Highland Light Infantry, who had detrained at Klokfontein], there would have been no Magersfontein, cause they would have bagged a whole lot of guns.[87]

At around 2:00 p.m. during the counterattack against the British wedge around Rosmead, De la Rey was wounded by a shell splinter in his right shoulder yet continued directing his forces. His son Adriaan, who remained at his side throughout the battle, soon thereafter had a shell fragment rip open his left abdomen, mortally wounding him. De la Rey carried his son to a protected area to await an ambulance and asked him, "Are you in pain my son"? "Yes Father", he replied. "Do you think you will die from this"? "Yes father".[88] A shocking experience to hear, yet while awaiting the ambulance, the General left to relay additional commands before returning to his son. In the absence of any ambulance, de la Rey did as any father would do. 'I was obliged to

87 Author's collection: Midge Carter, 'Lieutenant Colonel B Lang, Interview: "The Boer War"', Durban (9 March 1970).

88 Breytenbach, *Die Geskiedenis van die Tweede Vryheidsoorlog, Vol. II, p.82.*

Lieutenant Colonel H.P. Northcott. 'He never left me. He rode my horse to take a message asking for reinforcements, and was shot through the stomach. I was wounded sitting behind an artillery wagon dead beat'.* (McGregor Museum, with permission)

* MMK 7654/207: Letter by Lord Methuen to wife, 10 December 1899.

take my son to Jacobsdal approximately nine miles away'.[89] Due to the nature of his wound, Adriaan de la Rey was carried in a blanket, his wounded father walking beside him.[90]

It was around this time that in the centre of the line, Methuen, assisted by Lieutenant Colonel H.P. Northcott, attempted to redirect troops from the Guards Brigade sector, both being wounded by Boer rifle fire.[91] Northcott died later that evening and, with these two officers carried off the battlefield, communication between the Brigades on either side of the railway line broke down.

The overall command devolved to Colvile, who ordered a bombardment of the entire Boer position until dusk when the Guards Brigade would launch a bayonet attack. The bombardment commenced and at 3:00 p.m. Colvile wisely later cancelled the attack, instead ordering more troops to reinforce Pole-Carew's force.[92] Two fires were lit at the Riet River crossing and, under cover of darkness, the remainder of the 9th Brigade and the 1st Highland Light Infantry, who had just arrived on the battlefield, with a company of the 2nd Coldstream Guards, crossed the weir reinforcing the wedge along the northern bank.[93]

At 3:00 p.m. a Boer counterattack launched from the direction of Jacobsdal, supported by machine gun and artillery fire, and delivered along the Guards Brigade eastern right flank, threatened to outflank the infantry and stampede their ammunition carts. However, Native Driver Matthew Thomas stopped the Native Drivers attached to these ammunition carts from falling back and, by strength of personality, forced them to stay in position. This Boer counterattack was thwarted by machine gun fire, delivered by the 1st Scots Guards and 3rd Grenadier Guards Maxim machine guns, and eventually petered out. Methuen later recommended Native Driver M. Thomas for a Distinguished Conduct Medal (DCM) for bravery,[94] possibly the only African in the war to receive such a recommendation, which was never awarded.

At sunset, the firing spluttered out.

89 MMK: 7654/24: General J. de la Rey, Unpublished Manuscript, p.13. He was not present at the Krygsraad later that night when General P.A. Cronjé opted to abandon the position and fall back to Spytfontein.

90 J. Meintjes, *De La Rey*, p.122.

91 Maurice, *War in South Africa*, p.257.

92 MMK: 7654/183: Notes of conversation with Major General Sir Reginald Pole-Carew on 25th February 1903.

93 Maurice, *War in South Africa*, p.259.

94 TNA: WO 132/15. 112981: Lt General Lord P. Methuen, Despatch.

Full of dead and dying men. Blood, broken rifles, cartridges all littered about giving a ghastly scene in the flickering firelight. The banks too were lined with wounded who were food and waterless and with no covering of coats or blankets. Luckily a Doctor arrived in a Cape cart with medical comforts and before long we had Bovril brewed which I was asked to distribute; to my joy man after man refused a gulp and only after much persuasion would consent to take a sip, the excuse being his pal was more seriously wounded than he. The mist rising from the river was cold and the wounded were still uncovered.* Author's collection.
* Author's collection: Padre Eustace St Claire Hill: Unpublished Diary, 1899, p.28.

> Although the Boers had supreme command on the battle towards the evening of 28 November 1899 a false report was spread that the British had received fresh reinforcements and were fighting back and towards dark, the commandos had to fall back. Towards dark that evening a false report was spread in our lines that the British had fought back and taken our positions and we were ordered to fall back with the result that Cronjé retreated and left our guns behind because all the horses were killed.[95]

The threatened Orange Free State Artillery Corps two guns near Rosmead lay vulnerable. Albrecht had asked Cronjé for horses, as theirs were all dead or wounded. By 9:00 p.m. none had arrived. They struggled with wounded horses and without manual labour, yet the artillerymen retrieved their guns, within earshot of the British force holding the buildings around Rosmead, a remarkable feat.[96] Having heard that the British had not seized them and were laying on the ground exhausted nearby, a party went in to hook them up.[97] However, the risk to the artillery was not yet over.

It was past midnight that 'I personally that night heard the guns being taken away. I heard the guns and men shouting to each other. The Boers, taking the guns away'.[98]

95 MMK: 7654/14: Letter by Colonel Meyer to Julian, 9 July 1970.
96 MMK: 7654/12a: Sergeant Willie du Plessis, p.6
97 JG Maydon, *French's Cavalry Campaign* (London: C. Arthur Pearson Ltd, 1902), pp.49–50.
98 Author's collection: Midge Carter, 'Lieutenant Colonel B Lang, Interview: "The Boer War"', Durban (9 March 1970).

As for the farmhouse which was captured on the South bank after a bitter fight, it was on a lighter note that, just after dark, a soldier was ordered to the river to collect water for the wounded. 'He returned in a great fright saying, "Please, sir, I can't go near it, there's a crocodile there and he's lashing his tail". It turned out to be a wounded Boer pony.'[99]

Opinion amongst the Boer forces as to continue fighting or to withdraw was divided. Generals Cronjé and Prinsloo wished to abandon the position, while de la Rey's forces not. The tension amongst the burghers unbearable, while their officers deliberated. 'At approximately 10:00 p.m. came the order:

> Get ready. We are going to withdrawal. What I then saw was panic, unashamed panic. It was chaos. Here at the drift, just above the hotel where the Jacobsdal road crosses over the Modder River road, came Prinsloo's Free Stater's with a bunch of Transvaaler's who stormed through from the other side. They displaced each other, tramped over each other like a bunch of sheep packed into a small kraal, crossing the small drift, they cursed and swore each other. With a thunderous noise, they rushed off into the night. I look around me. It's just me and about thirty of my friends. In silence we raised our horses and rode at a gallop in the direction of the fugitive commando.[100]

However, Burgher Meyer and his group had not gone far when they came across one 75 mm Krupp and two Pom-Poms, abandoned by the bolting forces. Although helpless, the artillerymen stood by their guns. All the gun team horses lay dead, some distance away under a tree, where they were tethered. A single shell had killed them. This prized artillery they hooked up to their horses. About 5 km further on, they came across another abandoned 75 mm Krupp and Pom-Pom, which they too hooked up.[101] Meyer recalled that, 'it was only the next afternoon that we reached our commando. I went straight to the nearest Commandant and told him that I, with my friends had brought all the guns out. I had the audacity to ask him why they fled leaving the guns behind. The Commandant was very annoyed at me for asking him all that.[102]

On that road, that night de la Rey and those assisting him to evacuate his dying son heard the sound of approaching horsemen. Cronjé and his Staff rode up. The party laid Adriaan to the ground and de la Rey faced his Commanding Officer, seated on his horse above him, silhouetted by the moonlight. "Well Veggeneraal," said Cronjé, "how did the battle go?" De la Rey replied in a blaze of fury, "You as Commandant General ought to know without having to ask me. You have shirked your duty. What on earth made you leave me in the lurch? How is it that the whole day we saw or heard nothing of you?" "I was at a certain place," replied Cronjé coolly. "Anyone

---

99 MMK: 7654/134: Lieutenant Colonel CH Burtchaell, 1912, 'Journal of the Royal Army Medical Corps', United Services Medical Society, Volume XVIII, p.427.

100 Meyer, *Kommando-Jare*, pp.54-55.

101 Meyer, *Kommando-Jare*, p.55.

102 MMK: 7654/14: Letter by Colonel Meyer to Julian, 9 July 1970. This saga of the abandoned Boer artillery suggests that the guns were jettisoned by the fleeing forces, after some of the guns were initially retrieved from near Rosmead.

who wants to know more can come and ask me. Come along men". And with that, they spurred their horses and rode off into the night.[103]

Adriaan was picked up and they continued into the night, until a mule cart arrived from Modder River. Driven by Veldcornet Coetzee with his son, Hansic inside, his throat shot away. Both these father's sons were at school together. Adriaan was loaded in and, the two fathers with their two sons at death's door, made it to Jacobsdal hospital. Adriaan died soon thereafter in his father's arms. Followed by Hansie Coetzee, who perished in dreadful agony.[104]

Lane recalled this retirement. 'We are passing through' hundreds of men, some on foot, some on horseback, horses laying dead, which have succumbed to their wounds. Men with sour looks, lots of them wounded, wounds unattended to. Our ambulance and Doctors cannot be found, believed to have fallen into the hands of the British'.[105] These doctors, with their ambulances, were taken prisoner by the British forces, the day before and spent a miserable night locked up in a barn without blankets. They were then sent to Cape Town, under arrest, accused to have breached the Geneva Convention.[106]

At first light the British artillery opened fire on the Boer positions, yet soon realised that the Division had won the day. Pursuit was impossible, due to the limited cavalry and mounted troops and exhaustion of the entire force. Although claimed by the British army as a victory, the Modder River action saw the commandos successfully retire for the third time in a week, with their fighting formations and artillery intact.

Methuen's undoing was his lack of proper reconnaissance and adherence to inaccurate information. In short, he blundered into the Boer ambush because of a complete intelligence failure, something he would soon be again punished for at Magersfontein. What saved his force from higher losses, or outright defeat, was his dominance of artillery, soon to be repeated at Magersfontein. The 18th Royal Field Artillery fired 1,029 rounds, the 62nd Royal Field Artillery 247, the 75th Royal Field Artillery 1,008 and the naval guns 260.[107]

By the afternoon, the entire Division crossed the Riet River, and concentrated on its northern bank.

> The scene on both sides of the river was a fearful demonstration of the effect of shell fire. All the houses were simply riddled with shrapnel, and bodies of dead Boers were found in them. The trenches on the south side were strewn with shrapnel and numbers of dead Boers were found in them, hundreds of thousands of Mauser cartridge cases were heaped in miles of the trenches.[108]

103 J. Meintjes, *De La Rey*, p.122.
104 J. Meintjes, *De La Rey*, p.122.
105 Lane, *The War Diary*, p.28
106 Breytenbach, *Die Geskiedenis van die Tweede Vryheidsoorlog*, *Vol. II*, p.86.
107 Maurice, *War in South Africa*, p.259.
108 Guest, *With Lord Methuen and the 1st Division*, p.14.

British troops and African auxiliaries crossing the Riet River after the battle. (McGregor Museum, with permission)

This same crossing point over the Riet River in 1996. (Author's collection)

> These shelters, a long line of them, are littered thick with empty cartridge cases, hundreds in each; one thinks involuntary of grouse driving. Bodies still unburied lay about when I was there. Such odours! Such sights! The unimaginable things that the force of shot and shell can do to poor, soft human flesh. I saw soldiers who had helped to do the work turn from those trenches shaking.[109]

Casualty accounts vary based on sources. British losses were at least 71 killed in action and more than 400 wounded. The Royal Army Medical Corps recorded 69 killed, 414 wounded and 30 who died of wounds; total fatalities being 99 dead. As a percentage of the total force engaged, casualties were 4.7 percent.[110] However it is possible to determine with accuracy how many were killed in action and, buried on the South side of the battlefield, a total of 77 killed, which is the most accurate account.[111]

Regarding Boer losses, the Red Cross of the South African Republic recorded these as 16 killed and 66 wounded.[112] An average that the author has established from all the sources consulted is least 37 Boer killed and 45 wounded. An unknown number of unidentified Agterryers would have been killed or wounded that day.[113] At least one African auxiliary serving with the 9th Brigade was killed in action.

On the note of Auxiliaries serving with the 2nd Coldstream Guards:

> We went on to the river and buried the poor Colonel on the way then got across the river and went to our camp and lay down to get a bit of sleep.[114] Here Henniker thanked Matthews in charge of the ammunition cart for his gallant conduct at the Modder River fight.[115]
>
> The Highlanders suffered terribly from the sun striking the inside of their knees which the kilts failed to cover. Sun blisters, as big as hen's eggs and as full, afflicted numbers of them. There was great criticism of the kilt. – the OC snorted at this and said it was all rot his men limping about like cats on ice and ordered them to go to hospital for treatment. I was there as a lugubrious line of Scotties filed in. The treatment was quick and drastic. The afflicted had to file past a tin of grease and a big handed Cockney. "Come on Jock", I heard him shout and the leader shuffled up with a wistful look on his face. Cockney raised the tail of his kilt with his left hand and sock, sock, went his right, bursting the blisters and slapping in a wad of grease. "Next please" he shouted, drowning the "Hoots"! of the victim. I heard no more criticism of this and any subsequent blisters got home treatment I fancy.[116]

---

109 March Phillips, *With Rimington*, p.29.

110 MMK: 7654/134: Lieutenant Colonel CH Burtchaell, 1912, 'Journal of the Royal Army Medical Corps', United Services Medical Society, Volume XVIII, p.667.

111 Author's collection: Modder River, Graves of those fallen during Anglo Boer War 1899–1900–1–2, Colonel. DE Lines of Communication, September 1902.

112 Breytenbach, *Die Geskiedenis van die Tweede Vryheidsoorlog*, *Vol. II*, p.89.

113 Casualty accounts vary dependent on sources. This is an average that the author arrived at in particular with Boer losses as these were always understated.

114 Colonel HR Stopford, 2nd Coldstream Guards, was killed by a shell fragment and AH Henniker-Major thereafter took command.

115 MMK: D 7654/291: HG Chandos Pole Gell, Unpublished Diary, p.14.

116 Author's collection: Padre Eustace St Claire Hill: Unpublished Diary, 1899, p.30.

The following day Methuen issued his Divisional Orders.

> The Lieutenant General congratulates the Division on having secured the Modder River after one of the hardest fights in the annals of the army. It is not possible with so mobile a foe to get around a flank, and therefore one had to accept the inevitable, and attack the position in front, trusting to the courage and stubbornness of our troops to gain the day. The casualties, though heavy, are not so great in proportion as those suffered at Belmont.
>
> The Division will rest for one week, in order that the bridge may be repaired, and the Highland Brigade will replace the IX Brigade, which has done more than its fair share of the hard work of the past week.[117]

This statement by Methuen is not accurate. According to the Royal Army Medical Corps, at Belmont, as a percentage of all troops engaged in the action, casualties were 3.4 percent.[118] At Modder River, as a percentage of the total force engaged, these were 4.7 percent.[119]

These statements by Methuen reveal his incompetence, based on a rigid and inadequate tactical thinking. He learned nothing from virtually being defeated. Nor from his third frontal attack. The Boers had adapted their tactics, fighting from horizontal positions. Yet he bludgeoned on towards Magersfontein. It is important to note that for most of his career Methuen served as a Staff Officer, the only occasion he commanded troops in the field was during the bloodless 1882 Bechuanaland Campaign. He had never commanded as much as a battalion until Belmont. Hertzog found it unusual that Methuen claimed a victory when in fact it was Cronjé who handed him the position, noting at the time that 'My faith in British history has been shaken by this war'.[120]

Burying the dead

'It was heartrending, one's friends being maimed and wounded, killed one after the other'.[121]

Ten burial sites were established on the battlefield, all on the southern side of the Modder and Riet Rivers. Three other burial sites were later established on the northern bank for post battle burials. These included some officers who, killed at Magersfontein, were removed from the battlefield and buried there; soldiers who died of wounds received at Magersfontein and from an action fought at Koedoesberg Hill by the Highland Brigade during 5-8 February 1900, during the build up to the Relief of Kimberley. However,

117 SAL: A 355 31 GRE: 1899, 'Staff Diary of the Guards Brigade', pp.59–60.

118 MMK: 7654/134: Lieutenant Colonel CH Burtchaell, 1912, 'Journal of the Royal Army Medical Corps', United Services Medical Society, Volume XVIII, p.667.

119 MMK: 7654/134: Lieutenant Colonel CH Burtchaell, 1912, 'Journal of the Royal Army Medical Corps', United Services Medical Society, Volume XVIII, p.667.

120 van den Heever, *General Hertzog*, pp.73–74.

121 Russell, *Letters From South Africa* p.20.

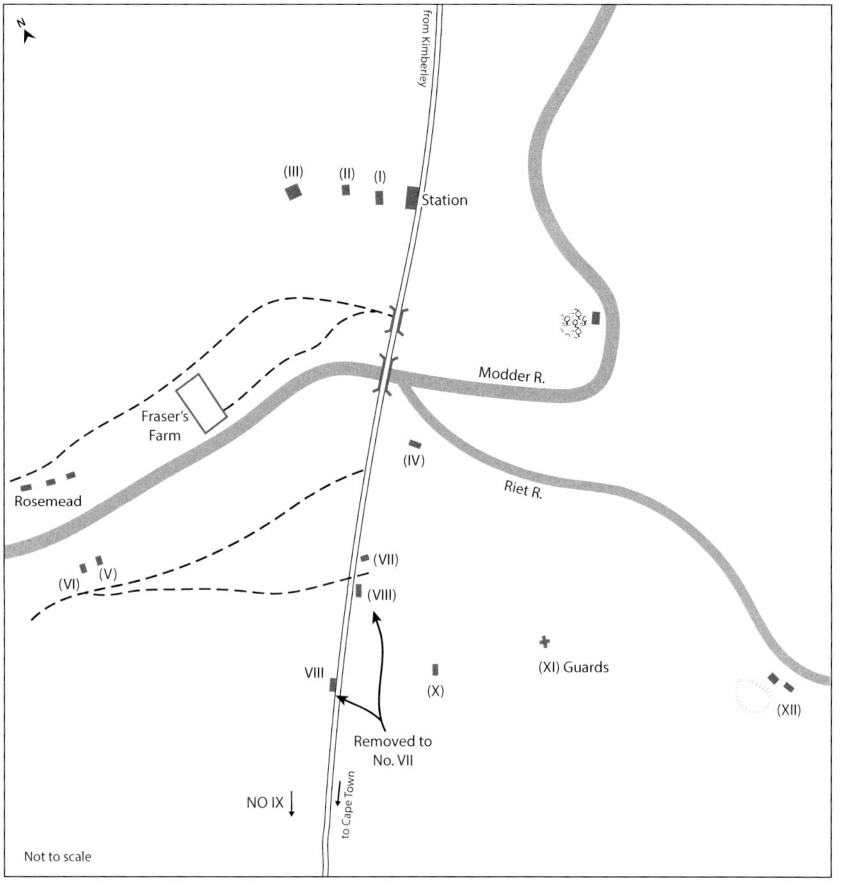

Map of all grave sites in the Modder River vicinity, compiled by Draughtsman A.J. Bailey for the District Engineer, Lines of Communication, as of September 1902. (Author's collection)

the majority of casualties were from disease in the subsequent garrison and troops stationed in the vicinity until the end of the war.[122]

On the South bank, casualties were buried where they fell, and provides an indication of where the unit positions were. In the Eastern sector, Grave XII near the reservoir was the Scots Guards burial site and before September 1902, was moved to Cemetery IX.[123] Incidentally Cemetery IX was the first cemetery created, at the site of the camping ground at Klokfontein; its first casualty being Trooper le Seur, who died during the night of 27 November 1899.

In the Western sector were two burial sites.

Buried at Cemetery VI were three casualties from the 1st Loyal North Lancashire Regiment, established by Padre Hill. However, there was more than the obvious to this site. After the infantry crossed the river on 29 November 1899, Hill stayed with the wounded and dead. Yet, 'The dead seemed to be endangering the wounded as this sun acts so quickly on corpses'[124] and, there was no burial detail available, Hill located a deep empty well into which he

122 Author's collection: Modder River, Graves of those fallen during Anglo Boer War 1899–1900–1–2, Colonel. DE Lines of Communication, September 1902.

123 Author's collection: Modder River, Graves of those fallen during Anglo Boer War 1899–1900–1–2, Colonel. DE Lines of Communication, September 1902.

124 Author's collection: Padre Eustace St Claire Hill: Unpublished Diary, 1899, p.29.

Trooper le Seur's grave on the veld at Klokfontein. The surrounding terrain depicts the barrenness and lack of cover for the attacking British force. (McGregor Museum, with permission)

Cemetery X marked the site of the 75th Battery Royal Field Artillery and, containing two burials, was relocated to Cemetery IX. These were Gunner F.J. Thomas and Driver J. Humpage graves in Cemetery X. (McGregor Museum, with permission)

Cemetery VII. Cemeteries VIIIa and VIIIb had soldiers from the 1st Northumberland Fusiliers, later relocated to Cemetery VII, containing 1st Argyll and Sutherland Highlanders, killed in this area of the battlefield, before the move in support of the 9th Brigades assault on the Boer positions defending the crossing point on the Riet River. (McGregor Museum, with permission)

Cemetery IV contained Lieutenant Colonel Northcott and Lieutenant Colonel. Stopford and two other burials.* The structure visible behind them was part of Rostel's Farm, while the open veld beyond was open ground over which the attacking infantry attempted to traverse. (McGregor Museum, with permission)

* Author's collection: Modder River, Graves of those fallen during Anglo Boer War 1899–1900–1–2, Colonel D.E. Lines of Communication, September 1902.

had the bodies lowered of: Lance Sergeant H. Wigston and Private A. McNeil (1st Argyll and Sutherland Highlanders); Private J. Brown and Private J. Griffiths (King's Own Yorkshire Light Infantry); and Sergeant J. Radford (Northumberland Fusiliers) . After reading the funeral service, the well was partly covered in. Later he interred a dead horse and, after filling that in, was asked to bury another four corpses. These were Sergeant Richardson, Sergeant F. Wilson and Private H. Bell, (1st Loyal North Lancashire Regiment); and Sergeant A.K. Smith (1st Argyll and Sutherland Highlanders).[125]

This well burial site was reopened before September 1902, as some of those interred there were then moved to other cemeteries. Lance Sergeant H. Wigston and Private A. McNeil were moved to Cemetery VII, Private J. Brown, and Private J. Griffiths to Cemetery V, while Sergeant Richardson, Sergeant F. Wilson and Private H. Bell remained in Cemetery VI.[126] Sergeant J. Radford's final resting place remains unaccounted for. Nor is he recorded

125 Author's collection: Padre Eustace St Claire Hill: Unpublished Diary, 1899, p.29.

126 Author's collection: Modder River, Graves of those fallen during Anglo Boer War 1899–1900–1–2, Colonel D.E. Lines of Communication, September 1902.

Cemetery V contained the 2nd King's Own Yorkshire Light Infantry casualties. (McGregor Museum, with permission)

Cemetery V was later marked with the 2nd King's Own Yorkshire Light Infantry South African Campaign memorial, which still stands and is identical to a previous memorial erected by the regiment in Afghanistan. (Author's photograph)

on the central memorial erected in Cemetery I, during 1999, by the War Graves Division of the South African National Monuments Council.[127]

All these Modder River grave sites, with the exception of Cemetery VI, were relocated in 1962 into the Garden of Remembrance, West End Cemetery, Kimberley,[128] through a misguided policy, which destroyed this military heritage.

In 1999, three black granite memorials were erected, two in Cemetery I and one in Cemetery III.

Only one casualty is known to remain buried in Cemetery 1; a soldier of the Cape Town Highlanders who committed suicide in 1901, and whose grave was not moved in 1962. Cemetery II contained six burials; one who died of wounds after Magersfontein and the remainder from disease. This cemetery was moved after September 1902 into Cemetery III, which central memorial commemorates casualties who died of disease and wounds received at Koedoesberg.[129]

127 TNA: WO.108/83: South African Field Force Casualty List, 1899–1902 for Sergeant J. Radford, 1st Northumberland Fusiliers, whose name is omitted from the memorial.

128 Located at Latitude 28°44'4.89" S: Longitude: 24°44'10.24" E.

129 Cemeteries I and III are today locally known as Doorns A (Cemetery I) and Doorns B (Cemetery III).

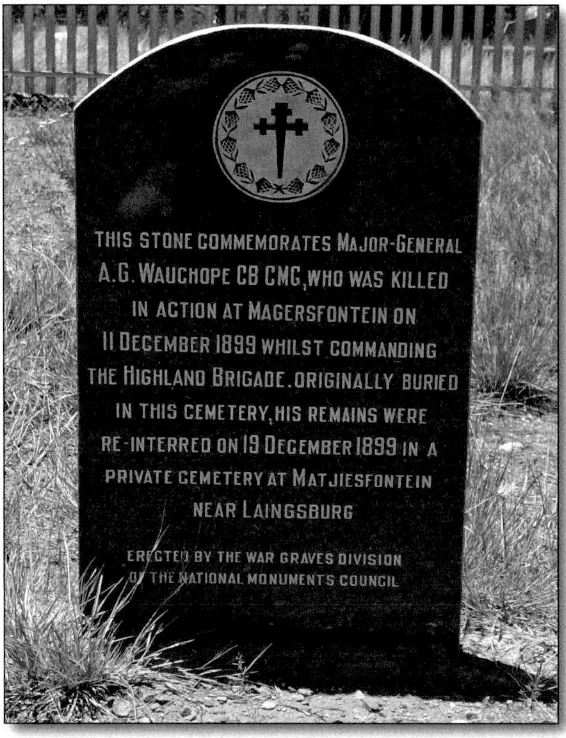

A headstone marks the approximate original burial site of Major General A.G. Wauchope. (Author's photograph)

South African War campaign memorial erected by the 1st Argyll and Sutherland Highlanders on 28 November 2002. (Author's photograph)

Left: Many of the Boer dead were buried where they fell, in their trenches and fox holes. 'I saw a Boer trench with a splendidly built Boer dead on the piled sandbags – I cut the contents loose and said a prayer over him.'*

* Author's collection: Padre Eustace St Claire Hill: Unpublished Diary, 1899, p.29.

Right: Medical personnel searching the Boer defences for dead and wounded. Many of the Boer dead were covered in where they fell and remain buried in unmarked graves on the battlefield.

7

The Boers prepare and entrench at Magersfontein

Methuen's exhausted army, having fought three battles within a week, spent the period of 28 November 1899 to 9 December 1899 replenishing their supplies and awaiting reinforcements, while the Royal Engineers established a deviation bridge adjacent to the damaged Modder River bridge.

Their main camp, on the sandy, featureless and open veld East and West of the railway station, lay in full view of the Boers, who had observers atop the Magersfontein and Langberg hills. Methuen, recovering from his wound, established his headquarters in the Crown and Royal Hotel, alongside Modder River railway station.[1]

The Boer forces, having abandoned their positions around Modder River, fell back through the night of 28 November 1899, towards Jacobsdal. The following morning, they regrouped at Rolfontein Farm, in the vicinity of Brown's Drift. There they were reinforced with additional commando's ordered down from Mafeking and also from Edenburg in the Orange Free State. During the day a Council of War was held, from which de la Rey was absent, as he was in Jacobsdal burying his deceased son. Their main concern was that Methuen would rapidly follow up his success and strike rapidly for Kimberley. Therefore, they urgently needed to take steps to stop this. With this in mind they decided to immediately occupy the heights around Scholtznek and Spytfontein which also bisected the railway line. That day most of these commandos left for Scholtznek and Spytfontein, approximately 15 kilometres North of Modder River Station and began preparing gun emplacements and sangers along the hilltops. On 30 November 1899, the mounted commandos still at, or arriving at Brown's Drift, joined them.[2]

---

1 Built in 1897, the Crown and Royal Hotel was popular as a weekend retreat amongst the Kimberley socialites. After 28 November 1899 and until 15 February 1900 (Relief of Kimberley) this hotel was used as the headquarters for the Kimberley Relief Column. After the Magersfontein action, it accommodated many of the British wounded. Some well–known British officers such as Field Marshal Lord Roberts, Lord Kitchener, Major General French, Colonel Douglas Haig (later Field Marshal) stayed here along with Rudyard Kipling, a renowned author then serving as a military journalist.

2 Breytenbach, *Die Geskiedenis van die Tweede Vryheidsoorlog*, *Vol. II*, p.96.

The deviation bridge over the Modder River. The rock piles supporting the bridge still existed until heavy flooding swept them away in the early 1990s. (McGregor Museum, with permission)

On his return to Scholtznek on 30 November 1899, General de a Rey found numerous burghers without horses avoiding the front by staying behind in the rear echelon laagers. These he hurried forward, believing that, as flight without horses would be infinitely more difficult than at Modder River and Graspan, there was a stronger likelihood that they would stand and fight. As for the mounted burghers these he would position on the flanks to protect the central positions and, using them as a mobile reserve, could reinforce the static defences at threatened points when required.

In the Boer laagers there was much recrimination about the abandonment of the Modder River/Riet River positions. Cronjé, in his official despatch to Steyn, stated that the Orange Free State forces had abandoned their positions in a cowardly manner. He further informed Steyn that there was little he could use the demoralised Orange Free State forces for and requested that the President arrange for additional reinforcements from elsewhere. De la Rey also reported to Steyn that while the Transvaal forces had held back the British forces attacking their sector, the Orange Free State forces, as at Graspan, had abandoned their positions. Kruger requested Steyn to personally go to the front and impress upon the Orange Free State Commandos' officers and burghers the need to conduct themselves as they should.[3]

3 Breytenbach, *Die Geskiedenis van die Tweede Vryheidsoorlog*, *Vol. II*, pp.90-91.

On his arrival at Scholtznek, de la Rey telegrammed Steyn to advise that he would impress upon Cronjé and Prinsloo his ideas for a static defence line in turn supported with a mobile reserve. In a separate telegram he made a heartfelt appeal to the President to visit the frontline positions. He was not in agreement with the Council of War decision made in his absence and needed political support to override that decision in favour of adopting his tactics. He further advocated that they should seize the initiative and harass the Modder River camp. With this in mind he pushed for a force 500 strong to attack the railway logistics in the Enslin area.[4]

After a personal reconnaissance on 2 December 1899, de la Rey advocated that Magersfontein should form their next position from which to block Methuen; not where they were currently entrenching.[5] If the British forces occupied Magersfontein they could use it as an artillery position to dominate the Boer positions. However, at Magersfontein, as at Modder River, the use of ground level defences could repel a further British advance. However, if forced to withdrawal, then they had strong fall back positions already established in the Scholtznek/Spytfontein area.

It became a heated argument between these two Boer generals. 'And now, once again, there was division among our leaders. Cronjé – stubborn, hard-headed, refused to move to Magersfontein. De la Rey – a man who also knows what he wants – refused to commit to Spytfontein and Scholtznek. And Prinsloo-never really, a man with convinced convictions – does not know who he should support.[6]

Cronjé would hear nothing of the ideas proposed by de la Rey. An angry telegram from Steyn was read out where he referred to the Modder River positions being abandoned despite the battle already being won by the Boer forces and that Cronjé had not attacked Methuen's camp at Witkop Farm before the Modder River battle. He abandoned perfectly good positions, opting instead to occupy Spytfontein, which had no water for his forces and where he was busy building defences on the hills. He was not alone. Hertzog saw this as a blunder.[7]

Cronjé replied that the only reason that de la Rey was angry about the abandonment of the Modder River positions was because his son had died defending them.[8] De la Rey later said that:

> My son was killed there yet what caused me to shed the greatest tears is the giving away of the prize of the Tweerivier positions. If we stayed there then the English would have been forced to withdraw to Orange River Station, because between Modder River Station and the Orange River there is not enough water for so many men and animals. With them that far back we could have linked up with the forces under Grobler and Hendrik Schoeman at Colesberg.[9]

---

4 Breytenbach, *Die Geskiedenis van die Tweede Vryheidsoorlog*, *Vol. II*, pp.98-99.
5 Amery, *The Times history*, p.386.
6 Meyer, *Kommando-Jare*, p.58.
7 van den Heever, *General Hertzog*, p.73.
8 Sergeant Willie du Plessis, p.6.
9 F Conradie, *Met* Cronjé *Aan Die Wesfront (1899–1900)*, p.43.

An infantryman of The Black Watch (Royal Highlanders) drawn by Giorgio Albertini (Helion & Company)

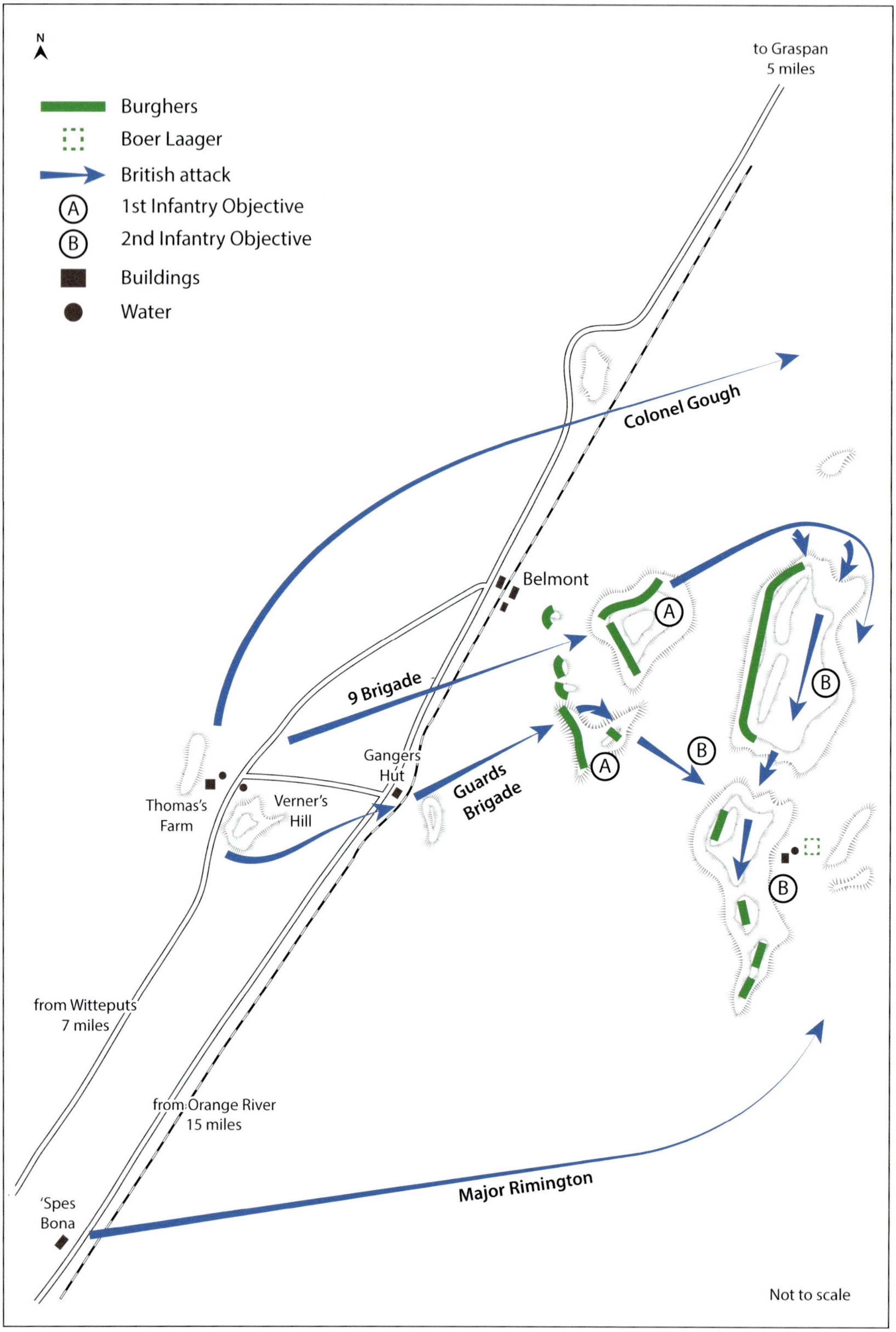

British plan of attack, devised on 22 November 1899. Methuen planned to crush the Boer force between his two infantry Brigades, but his ignorance of the topography would see a very different result.

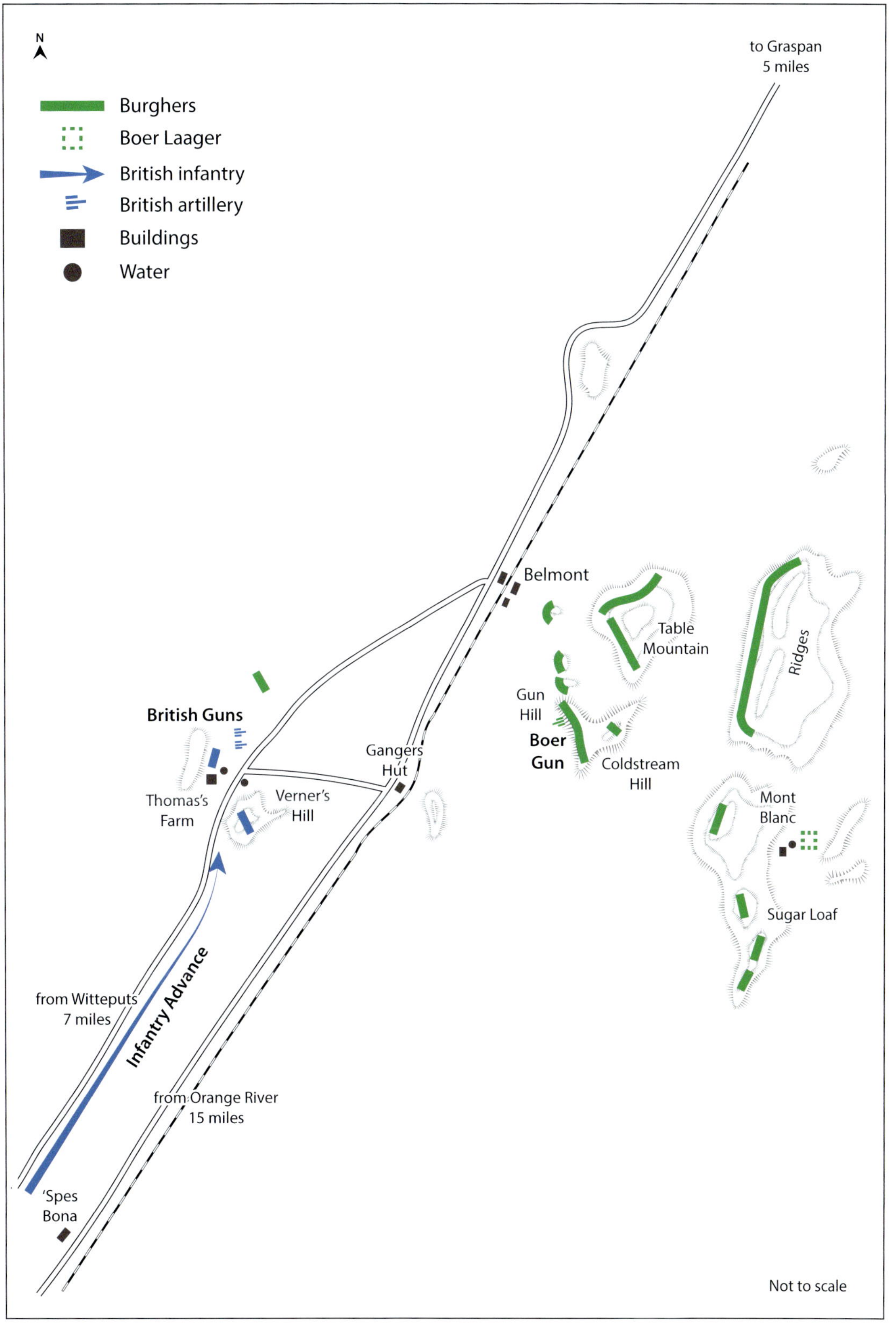

Battle of Belmont. Advance to contact. The situation between 1600-1800hrs, 22 November 1899.

Rhodes commissioned Sir Herbert Baker to design a memorial which commemorates those who fell during the Kimberley Siege. Rhodes sent Baker to Greece to study ancient memorials – the Nereid Monument at Xanthus greatly influenced his design. The monument is built of sandstone quarried in the Matopo Hills in Zimbabwe (Rhodesia) and is the tomb of 27 soldiers. It's written dedication, engraved on an exterior wall, Rhodes specifically commissioned Rudyard Kipling to write. The Long Cecil gun that was designed and manufactured by Labram in the workshops of De Beers Consolidated Mines during the siege is mounted on its stylobate. It is surrounded by shells from the Boer Long Tom Creusot gun. The memorial was dedicated on 28 November 1904. (From https://www.kimberley.co.za/places/kimberley/free/the-honoured-dead-memorial/, accessed 16 May 2020. (Author's photograph 2022))

Burgher Monument Magersfontein. Burials occurred at this monument on three different occasions. Those who died of wounds at the Boer field hospital located 390 metres Southeast of it and those killed in action; those reinterred here during the late 1920s and those reinterred during the 1960s from graves within a radius of about 100 km thereof. (Author's photograph 2021)

Grenadier Hill, 1999. The ground over which the 3rd Grenadier Guards attacked the Boer position. Gun Hill is to the far left of the picture. (Author's photograph 2001)

Boer fortifications on top of Coldstream (Grenadier Hill). 1 marks the Gangers Hut, 2 marks Verner's Hill and 3 marks Belmont (Thomas') Farm. The open terrain is over which the night advance and dawn attack unfolded. (Author's photograph 2001)

Table Mountain is centre of the photograph and the veld over which the 9th Brigade attacked. (Author's photograph 2001)

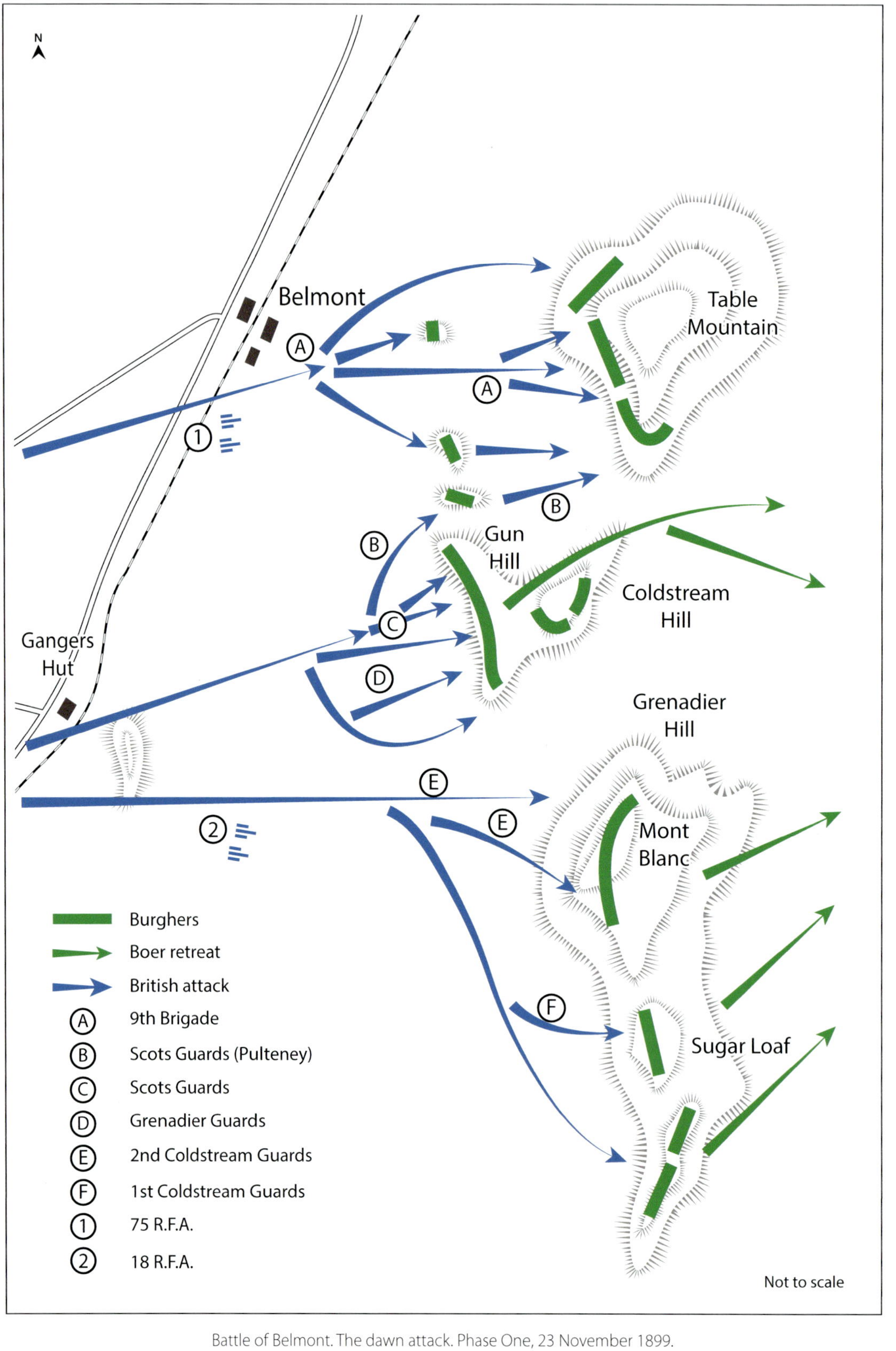

Battle of Belmont. The dawn attack. Phase One, 23 November 1899.

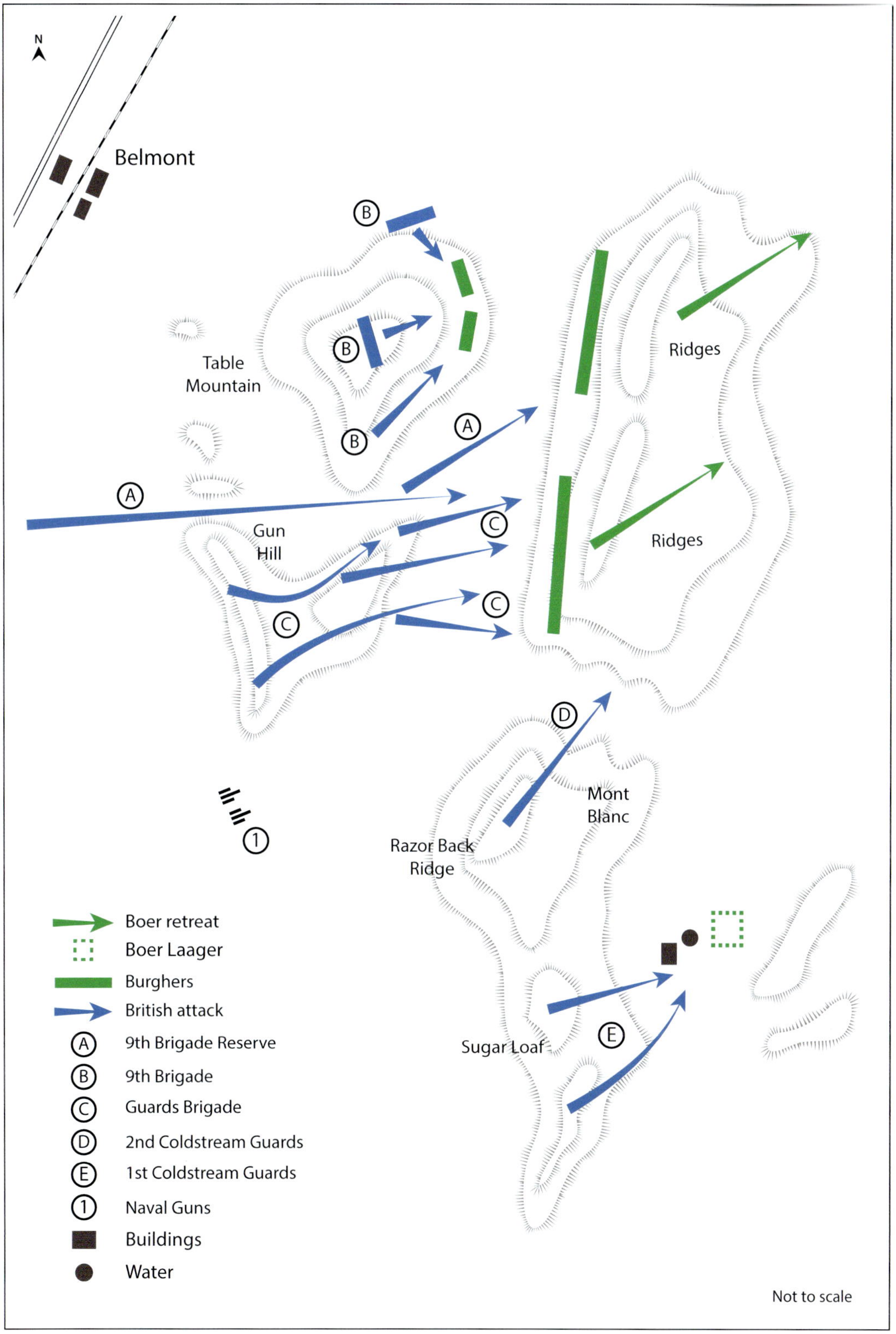

Daylight attach phase Two, 23 November 1899. Confused objectives resulted in a British attack that failed to close like a nutcracker around the Boer defences. The commandos fell back to fight another day.

The Burgher Monument atop Gun Hill, looking West towards Verner's Hill and Belmont (Thomas' Farm). (Author's photograph 1993)

Boer grave RIP on Table Mountain. (Author's photograph 1993)

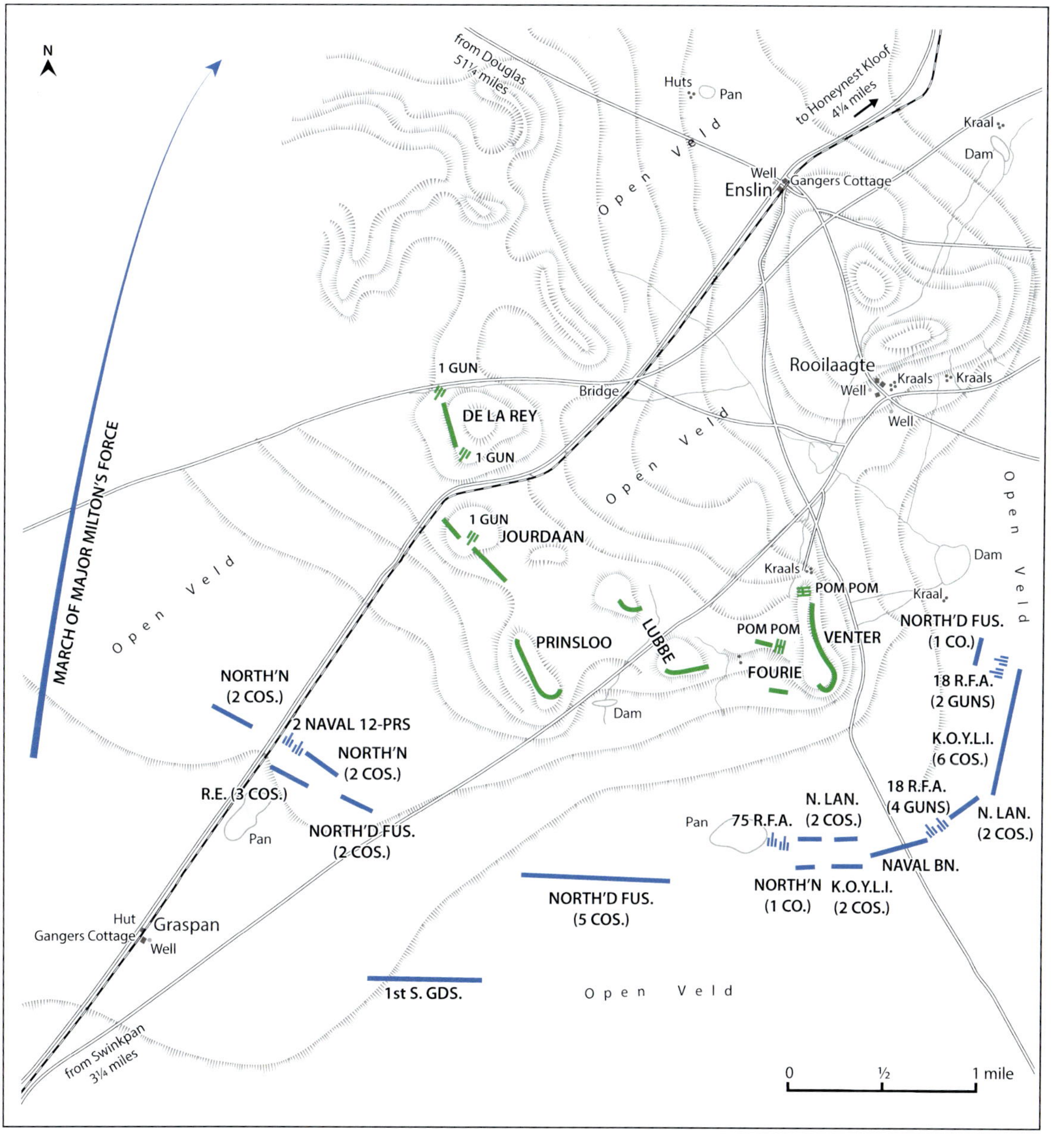

Battle of Graspan, 25 November 1899.

Cemetery XI was the Guards Brigade burial site, and marked with the Brigade memorial, which still stands on the spot. The memorial was paid for by Colonel E.M.S. Crabbe, with assistance from Lieutenant A.V.F.V. Russell. See: Russell, *Letters from South Africa*, pp.220–221. (Author's photograph 2022)

In Cemetery I, the central memorial lists casualties who died of wounds received at Magersfontein. (Author's photograph 2022)

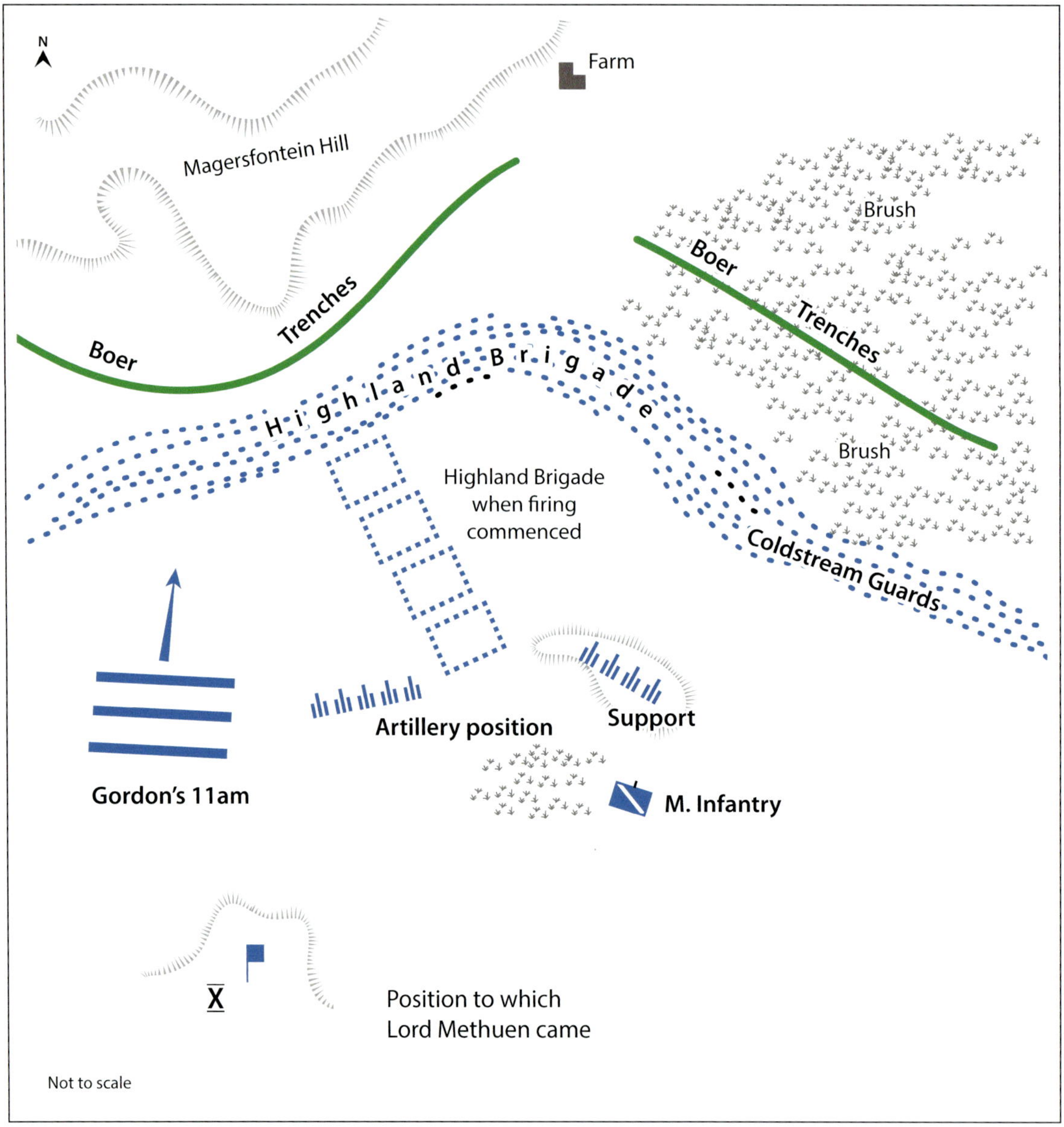

Map drawn by Ewart depicting the Highland Brigade in mass of quarter column and in the act of deploying when the Boers opened fire. (McGregor Museum, with permission)

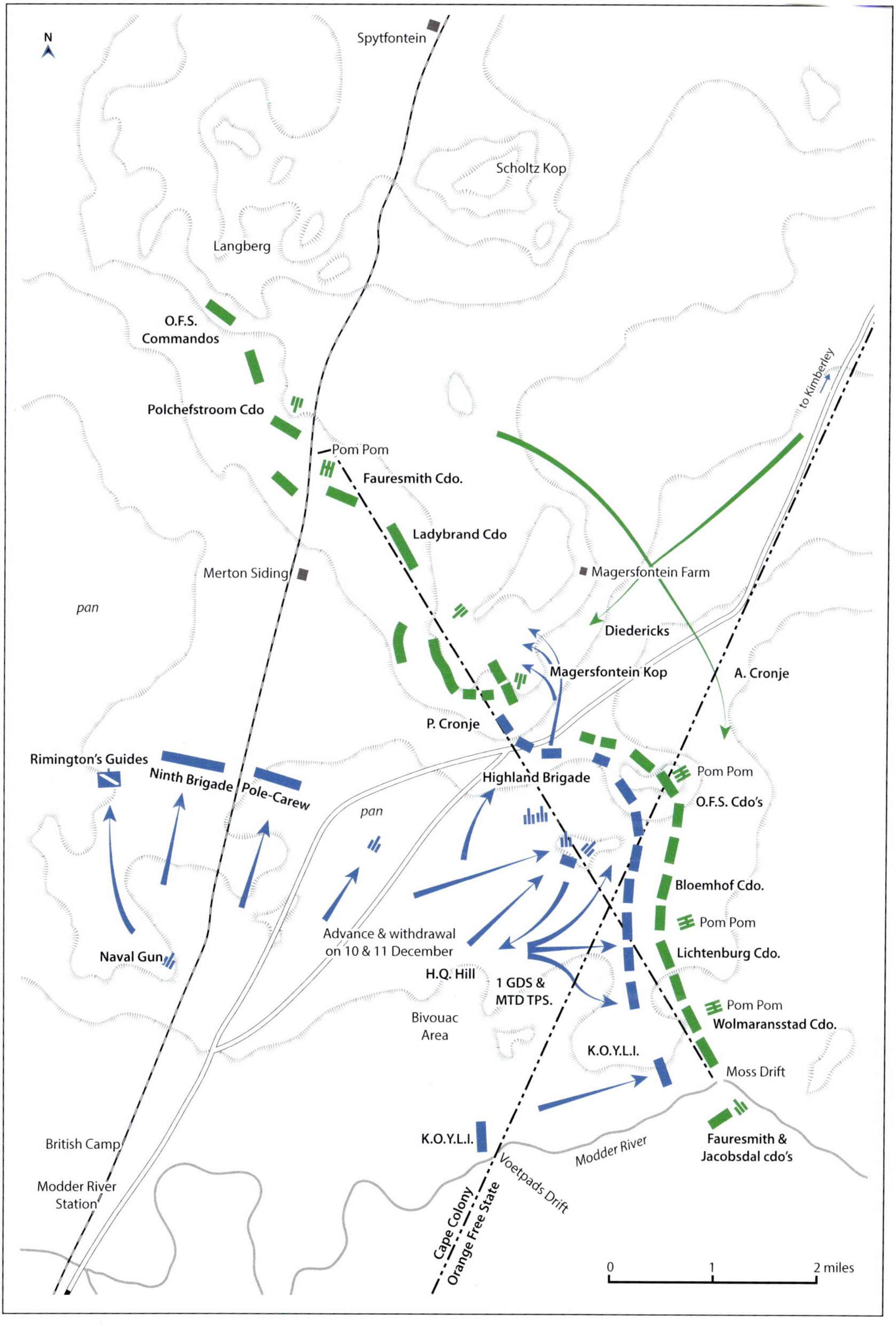

Battle of Magersfontein. 11 December 1899.

Also erected in 1902 was the Black Watch Memorial, a white marble obelisk, approximately in the centre of the Highland Brigade position, when the battle started, and at one of the three grave sites established by Lieutenant Colonel Ewart. Located at: Latitude 28°58′29.18″S and Longitude: 24°42′3.14″E. (Author's photograph 2019)

British Forces Garden of Remembrance, West End Cemetery, Kimberley. (Author's photograph 2022)

Immediately after the Modder River action, Steyn resolved to visit the front as de la Rey's telegrams reinforced a sense of urgency. So much so that Steyn forwarded these telegrams to Kruger, who agreed that horseless burghers should fight as infantry from prepared ground level defences, with mounted commandos on the flanks, forming a mobile reserve. On 3 December 1899, Steyn arrived at Scholtznek, with an objective of unifying the two Republican forces.[10]

It took the President to break the deadlock between these two generals during a Krygsraad, held on 4 December 1899. This Council of War comprised eight members, chaired by, three generals and five Kommandants, four from each Republic.[11] Steyn was accompanied by his counsellor, Abraham Fischer, and personally inspected the Boer positions, and those proposed by de la Rey at Magersfontein.[12] It did not take much to convince the President. The decision made was to immediately entrench Magersfontein and, separately, attack the British logistics at Enslin, thus interdicting their supplies to Modder River, then being railed up for the next advance North.

Despite the scarcity of water at Magersfontein, this could be obtained from Magersfontein (Bissett's) farm just under 2 km North of the main Magersfontein position; in any event water was also scarce in the Scholtznek and Spytfontein area. Once the arrangements were agreed to, Cronjé supported the move and, on 5 December 1899, telegrammed Kruger that these new positions were tactically better suited.[13] That he supported this realignment of both Republican forces stands to his credit, as with the outcome of the battle of Magersfontein, soon to unfold itself, under his command. While much praise has been heaped on de la Rey for his choice of defences, it must be recognised that he would not be present during the battle, as he would return to the main laager outside Kimberley to recover from his wound which troubled him greatly.[14] Cronjé would later win the battle.

The total number of Burghers serving with the commandos on the day of the battle is difficult to conclusively establish. According to Steyn and Fischer, Cronjé had 6,000 burghers under his immediate command at Magersfontein. However, there would have been a number of men left in the laagers, approximately 2,200. Thus the total was 8,200 strong[15] comprising of the following commandos and detachments from commandos serving elsewhere: Bethlehem, Bloemfontein, Bloemhof, Fauresmith, Ficksburg, Heilbron, Hoopstad, Jacobsdal, Kroonstad, Ladybrand, Lichtenburg, Potchefstroom, Soutpansburg and Wolmaransstad Commandos and the Skandinaviskå-kåren (the Scandinavian Corps).

---

10 Breytenbach, *Die Geskiedenis van die Tweede Vryheidsoorlog*, *Vol. II*, p.99.

11 MMK: 7654/24: General J de la Rey, Unpublished Manuscript, p.15.

12 Abraham Fischer (1850–1913), was a Prime Minister of the Orange River Colony after the South African War, and later a member of the Cabinet of the Union of South Africa in 1910. His grandson Abraham Louis Fischer (23 April 1908–8 May 1975) was a South African lawyer, notable for anti-apartheid activism, a member of the South African Communist Party, and for the legal defence of Nelson Mandela and his co-accused at the Rivonia Trial. Following the trial, he was himself trialled, accused of furthering communism, and sentenced to life imprisonment.

13 Breytenbach, *Die Geskiedenis van die Tweede Vryheidsoorlog*, *Vol. II*, pp.99-101.

14 Breytenbach, *Die Geskiedenis van die Tweede Vryheidsoorlog*, *Vol. II*, p.121.

15 Breytenbach, *Die Geskiedenis van die Tweede Vryheidsoorlog*, *Vol. II*, pp.114-115.

The Skandinaviskå-kåren comprised of 57 Danes, Finns, Swedes and Norwegian immigrants who, although exempt from war service, volunteered to fight for the Boer cause.* Commanded by Veld Kornet J. Flygare (centre row, eight from left), they were from Johannesburg and Pretoria, many having worked on the gold mines.** (McGregor Museum, with permission)

* G. Benneyworth, 'Scandinavia's Magersfontein Dead – Their Final Resting Place?, *South African Archaeological Bulletin*, 72' (206): 142–147, (2017), p.142.

** S. Bojerud, 2009, 'Scandinavian volunteers in the Anglo Boer War, 1899–1902', *Military History Journal* 14 (2009), pp.169–171.

On 4 December 1899, the Boer forces then moved into an area incorporating what became their Western, Central and Eastern Defensive Clusters, then fortified and entrenched.[16] Their positions were based around these three core defensive clusters, versus a single 14 kilometre line of defence works. All three Defensive Clusters could only be approached over open ground, devoid of significant natural cover, much as at the Riet and Modder Rivers.

Their main laager moved itself to Brown's Drift.[17] Other Headquarters points included Langberg Farm (Western Defensive Cluster) and Magersfontein Farm (Bissett's) which became the Headquarters and field hospital for the Central and Eastern Defensive Clusters. Jacobsdal continued

16 The concept of the Central, Western and Eastern Defensive Clusters is the authors' original concept and interpretation of the archival and terrain evidence, since a first visit to Magersfontein in 1978 unto the present, and is not taken from any literature. This is an original claim by the author.

17 Amery, *The Times history*, p.386.

as the main supply depot, despite the risk of a hostile force moving between that town and the Boer commandos preparing their three Defensive Clusters.

Burgher Meyer recalled this decision:

> I did not actually overhear what was going on in the War Council but it was generally accepted that the British would advance along the railway line to Kimberley and had it not been for Genl de la Rey and President Steyn who insisted that the trenches had to be built at the foot of the hill slopes instead of on the hill slopes as suggested by Cronjé the fight at Magersfontein should have been different.[18]

The Boer positions were laid out from the West of the railway at Langberg Farm, and ran East through the Magersfontein hills which lay approximately in the centre of their defence line, ending Southeast on the Modder River at Moss Drift. Some of these defence works were sited on the heights, notably at Langberg and, as at Belmont and Graspan, comprised of rock works. However, the majority were trenches, earthworks and sangars – small protected structures used for observing or firing from – built up from ground level, running along the Scrub Ridge East of Magersfontein to Moss Drift on the Modder River, approximately five kilometres from the main hills at Magersfontein. The positions were all camouflaged with bushes, grass, and sand.[19]

Their right or western flank incorporated Langberg and the railway approach, occupied by the Orange Free State commandos, the Soutpansburg Commando, with a section of the Potchefstroom Commando placed in a forward position dominating the railway line.[20] Artillery support included one 75 mm Krupp under Artillerist Thuynsma[21] and one 37 mm Pom-Pom.[22] Cronjé was certain that the British attack would be against the Western Defensive Cluster, so he kept the bulk of his mounted strength in this Defensive Cluster, to protect his horses from potential shellfire on the Magersfontein hills and thus enable him to use these mounted burghers as a mobile reserve.[23]

The Central Defensive Cluster included the Magersfontein hills approximately two kilometres in width, running along an East to West axis. Part of the Potchefstroom Commando occupied the Western part of the hills and, directly below the main hill, 30 metres forward of it, the main Boer trench was defended by the Hoopstad, Kroonstad and Bloemfontein Commandos under General Kolbe and Kommandant P. Fourie.[24] Other sources have this trench defended by approximately 1,000 burghers, namely 250 Transvaalers

18 MMK: 7654/14: Letter by Colonel Meyer to Julian, 9 July 1970.

19 Breytenbach, *Die Geskiedenis van die Tweede Vryheidsoorlog*, *Vol. II*, p.105.

20 Breytenbach, *Die Geskiedenis van die Tweede Vryheidsoorlog*, *Vol. II*, p.117.

21 Latitude 28°55’55.78”S. Longitude 24°39’39.26”E.

22 The 75 mm Krupp was from the Orange Free State Artillery Corps and the 37 mm Pom-Pom from the South African Republic. See: MMK: 7654/12a: Sergeant Willie du Plessis. No page number on typed document.

23 Breytenbach, *Die Geskiedenis van die Tweede Vryheidsoorlog*, *Vol. II*, p.105.

24 Breytenbach, *Die Geskiedenis van die Tweede Vryheidsoorlog*, *Vol. II*, p.117.

under Veld Kornet van Graan and 750 Free Staters.[25] British sources have the Bloemhof and Boshof Commandos in the trench.[26] Meyer recalled that he, and elements of the Potchefstroom Commando, took up their 'place of honour', occupying the trench where it ended just South and South-east of the hill, against the Kimberley road.[27] These burghers were selected, as being unmounted, would fight as infantry, defending this trench One 75 mm Krupp gun, emplaced on the main summit on 6 December 1899, offered artillery support.[28]

This trench was forward from the hills behind it, as de la Rey insisted it should be, convinced that the British would, as at Belmont and Graspan, believe that the Boer forces would be on the hills, and target the heights. Decoy emplacements were also built during broad daylight along the slopes of the hills to distract from the ground level defences. Groups of burghers, armed with Martini Henry rifles firing black powder, were placed in these dummy positions. Their role, to fire on any British scouting patrols, again reinforcing the ruse that the Boers occupied the heights.[29] As for the main trench, being forward of the hill, this had a dual purpose. With the hill behind them and the British artillery shelling the hills, the dismounted burghers defending the trench could not retire and would stand fast in their positions.[30]

However, was it in fact a trench, excavated during this period from virgin soil? It was not, despite what every written account on this matter has previously stated.

Rather, it was an improvement to a pre-existing gulley created by millennia of rain water runoff from the hills above it. As with the Modder River battle, Boer versatility played a role, adapting local circumstances to their advantage. Using this gulley, they burrowed in, deepening it where required, or merely creating a parapet, if already deep enough. Which is why, although approximately 450-500 metres long,[31] it was not one consistent excavation; rather a series of sections with gaps in between, later joined together after the battle into one single length.[32] Depths varied from 0.80 metres to 1.25 metres deep with an earth parapet in front and skilfully camouflaged with scrub and bushes.[33] This entrenching occurred at night, undertaken by labourers and Agterryers attached to the commandos. By 9 December 1899, this trench stopped short by 150 to 200 paces from the Kimberley dirt road, yet was soon to be extended.[34]

---

25 MMK: 7654/12a: Sergeant Willie du Plessis. No page number on typed document.

26 Maurice, *History of the War*, p.307.

27 Meyer, *Kommando-Jare*, p.61.

28 MMK: 7654/12a: Sergeant Willie du Plessis, p.12. Latitude: 28°58'6.57"S. Longitude: 24°41'49.37"E.

29 Meyer, *Kommando-Jare*, pp.59-60.

30 Breytenbach, *Die Geskiedenis van die Tweede Vryheidsoorlog*, *Vol. II*, pp.103-104.

31 MMK: 7654/12c: Unnamed Witness Account. The battlefield at the foot of the ridge on Magersfontein on 11 December 1899.

32 This theory, by the author, was developed over 30 years of walking the ground. It is the first known theory of its kind that a pre-existing water runoff gulley was adapted into the main Boer trench/entrenchment and stands as original work.

33 MMK: 7654/12a: Sergeant Willie du Plessis, p.12.

34 F Conradie, *Met* Cronjé *Aan Die Wesfront (1899–1900)*, p.78.

An eye witness account supports the fact that this defensive work was an improvised pre-existing gulley. N. Hofmeyr, a Boer historian who visited Magersfontein in mid-January 1900, and who was given a personal tour of the battlefield by Cronjé wrote in 1903 that:

> Before that hill [Magersfontein] there was a sloot that had been occupied by a number of Kroonstad, Hoopstad and Potchefstroom men, but the Scotsmen in the vanguard had marched past that dangerous position in the dark without realising it. Had their officers known where they were finding themselves early that morning, they could have taken the Magersfontein Hills from the eastern side by swerving to the left and in this way come behind our centre."[35]

The sloot, or ditch referred to, is none other than the main Boer trench adapted from nature. Another myth for debunking is that of wire entanglements or obstacles. The Boers made no use of wire entanglements as part of their defensive work prior to and during the battle. What is correct is that farm fences enclosing various paddocks did exist, as too fencing along both sides of the road to Kimberley. These fences posed some obstacle during the action, particularly during the early morning fighting behind the Northern slopes of Magersfontein Hill, and in the vicinity of the Scandinavian positions. Yet in no way did they impede movements, as evidenced by this not being mentioned in any of the primary sources used for this work.

The Boer left flank or Eastern Defensive Cluster comprised Scrub Ridge to Moss Drift, defended by the following commandos: Lichtenburg under Kommandant H.C.W. Vermaas, Wolmaransstad under Kommandant F.J. Potgieter, and Bloemhof under Kommandant T. de Beer. To their Eastern flank a section of the Fauresmith Commando under Kommandant P. Jacobs closed the gap between them and Moss Drift.[36] They were also bolstered by sections of the Ficksburg, Ladybrand, Bethlehem and Heilbron Commandos.[37]

Artillery support included one 75 mm Krupp, positioned on the southern bank of the Modder River near Moss Drift, in a position that could fire on an approach by a British force along the eastern side of the course of the Modder River.[38] This Krupp was supported by the Jacobsdal Commando.[39] At least three Pom-Poms provided additional fire support to this Eastern Defensive Cluster. Positioned along Scrub Ridge and between Moss Drift, this indicated the importance that the eastern flank played for the Boer generals during their planning of defensive positions and their risk analysis.

The Boer officers kept the British camp under surveillance from the heights, clearly visible through their telescopes. An elite reconnaissance corps comprising a section of Danie Theron's Reconnaissance Corps, commanded by Lieutenant K. Jooste, and a section of Orange Free State Scouts under

35 N. Hofmeyr, *Zes Maanden bij de Commando's* (Gravenhage: W.P. van Stockum & Zoon, 1903), p.259.

36 Breytenbach, *Die Geskiedenis van die Tweede Vryheidsoorlog, Vol. II*, p.116.

37 Breytenbach, *Die Geskiedenis van die Tweede Vryheidsoorlog, Vol. II*, p.117.

38 To the author's knowledge this position has never been identified on the ground.

39 MMK: 7654/12a: Sergeant Willie du Plessis. No page number on typed document.

Photograph taken after the Boers abandoned Magersfontein in February 1900, this image depicts, how the position was strengthened with sandbags after the battle. The Boer trench was a series of excavations and not one continuous line, which was later the case. The gaps in the line were because the trench was, at that stage, a reinforced and improved upon rain water run off gulley. Were it not, and instead a trench excavated into virgin soil, it would have eroded differently over the last century, with areas of pooling rain water runoff and different erosion issues. Yet, with any current rains, the trench runs off neatly along the gulley to a spilling out area, supporting this point that it was an adapted rain water runoff gulley. (With permission, National Archives of South Africa)

Point A being where a windmill stood. Points B to B was the first trench dated 9 December 1899 and C to C being a subsequent entrenchment created by 11 December 1899.* (F. Conradie, *Met Cronjé Aan Die Wesfront (1899–1900)*, Nasionale Pers Beperk, Kaapstad, 1943))

* F. Conradie, *Met* Cronjé *Aan Die Wesfront* ***(1899–1900)***, p.61.

Although taken post battle the photograph gives a good indication of the trench extension made immediately after the bombardment during the afternoon of 10 December 1899. A raised embankment on the veld topped with sandbags, it was used in the battle and then later extended further into the gap between the Central and Eastern Defensive Clusters. On the far left is Kommandant A.J. Naudé of the Winburg Commando, later killed in action at Driefontein on 10 March 1900. (Western Cape Archives and Records Service, with permission)

The exact position in November 2021. Author's photograph.

Taken after the battle, another view of the trench looking towards the Modder River Kimberley road and the open veld devoid of cover, over which the Highland Brigade launched its attack. (McGregor Museum, with permission)

Captain Fichardt, kept the British force under close surveillance. On 5 December 1899, they reported that trains from Belmont were arriving with reinforcements and supplies at the British camp and that the resumption of their advance was being finalised.[40]

Kruger was adamant that the British force should not be allowed to replenish and recuperate unhindered. On 6 December 1899, he instructed Cronjé to attack the Modder River camp and destroy it. However, Cronjé hesitated doing so, believing that the attacking force always incurred a higher ratio of casualties. However, he reported back to the President that, based on the Council of War decisions on 4 December 1899, Prinsloo was on route to attack Enslin. As for Prinsloo, he left groups of burghers in the Eastern vicinity of the British camp to watch it closely, and screen his movements, while proceeding forwards with his raiding party. On 6 December 1899, one of these groups intercepted six members of a scouting party from the 12th Lancers, capturing four of them.[41]

British force movements

Methuen could expect reinforcements, including Wauchope's Highland Brigade, additional artillery, and cavalry. On 28 November 1899, just before and during the Modder River battle, he received the 1st Argyll and Sutherland

40 Breytenbach, *Die Geskiedenis van die Tweede Vryheidsoorlog, Vol. II*, pp.107-108.
41 Breytenbach, *Die Geskiedenis van die Tweede Vryheidsoorlog, Vol. II*, pp.106-107.

Major General Andrew Gilbert Wauchope (1846–1899)*
(McGregor Museum, with permission)

* Major General A.G. Wauchope joined the Royal Navy as a Midshipman in 1860. Five years later he re-joined the army, being commissioned in the 2nd Battalion Royal Highlanders (Black Watch). He saw active service in the Ashanti War (1873) and was severely wounded. He then served in Cypress, followed by Egypt where he saw action at the battle of Tel el-Kebir (1882) and the Sudan (1884) and was again severely wounded. He married and had twin boys, yet his wife and one child died, the other child being severely mentally impaired. In 1898 he commanded a Brigade in the Sudan, seeing action at the Omdurman battle and remarried that year. Promoted to Major General he commanded the Highland Brigade, being killed in action at Magersfontein.

Highlanders and the 1st Highland Light Infantry. However, he displayed no aggressive action, and this would force him to conform to the Boer actions, and not the other way around. He made no attempt to interrupt their plans.

A question is could he have? Some aggressive patrolling would have revealed the Boer preparations then underway, thus mitigating the disaster, soon to unfold at Magersfontein. Reconnaissance being a key component of military operations, yet it was never pushed through with fervour, during this interlude at Modder River. With a dominance in artillery, he could have interdicted the Boer preparations and continually harassed them, which in turn would have revealed something of their force dispositions and positions. The entire mounted forces could have escorted the artillery, which might have then shelled the supply wagons moving between Jacobsdal and Magersfontein, in turn revealing something. Yet none of this was attempted.

In vain Major General Pole-Carew implored that he might be allowed to make a dash on Jacobsdal, which lay at the British force's mercy, yet to no avail. Unchecked, the Boers supplies continued to Magersfontein.[42] By 7 December 1899, unbeknownst to Methuen, Lieutenant Colonel J.S. Ewart was well aware that there, 'was the burning discontent in every camp and bivouac against him; his tactics at Modder river had deprived him of the confidence of his troops'.[43] Wauchope had serious doubts about Methuen's capability to command and control, maintaining until his death at Magersfontein, that the key to the relief of Kimberley was to outflank and outmanoeuvre the Boer forces from their defensive positions. Not to attack frontally as the three prior actions saw. The path to Kimberley lay via Brown's Drift to the East, not North along the railway line. Wauchope's concern is vital to understanding Methuen's failure at Magersfontein, as there were alternatives, and this information has remained dormant for almost 123 years.[44]

42 Maydon, *French's Cavalry Campaign*, pp.55–56.
43 MMK: 7654/40b: MMK: 7654/40b: General Sir J.S. Ewart, Unpublished Manuscript.
44 At the time of writing this work.

The unpublished autobiography of Brigade Major Lieutenant Colonel Ewart offers much insight into Methuen's actions and thinking on the eve of Magersfontein, and into the views of his senior Generals, that of Wauchope, and the battle itself.[45]

On the day of the Modder River Action, Wauchope, then at Orange River Station:

> Now engaged a man as Guide for the Highland Brigade, who said that he knew the road into Kimberley via Browns Drift perfectly and that he could take us in that way. Wauchope promised to pay him well out of his own pocket and told me that he thought it all important to secure the services of a guide who could take us by the only road by which Kimberley could be relieved. Wauchope was very strong about this and repeatedly reiterated his conviction to me that the road by Jacobsdal and Browns Drift was the only one by which the relief of Kimberley should be attempted. Even at this period my poor doomed General was greatly concerned about Lord Methuen's tactics which revealed he thought great want of military skill, he said he deplored his "bludgeon tactics" more than he could say. All his, Wauchope's, views appeared to be thoroughly shrewd and sound.[46]

Back at Orange River Station the wounded from Modder River spoke freely of their ordeal. 'The tactics at the Modder had been worse than those adopted at Belmont and Graspan as far as I could make out the troops had simply banged on to the top of the Boers'.[47] Reinforcements continued to be railed up to Methuen, who ordered the Highland Brigade to concentrate at Modder River Station. 'Everyone seemed to anticipate some sharp fighting and the hope was generally expressed that, after the experiences of the engagement on the Modder, Methuen would abandon his habit of making frontal attacks and instead manoeuvre the Boers out of their position by a turning movement via Jacobsdal and Brown's Drift'.[48]

On 3 December 1899, at Orange River Station, Wauchope tasked Ewart to travel up with the Brigade Staff and use the opportunity to meet with Methuen. He impressed upon him that:

> "For heaven's sake, try to put him off these wretched frontal attacks". I told him that it would be very difficult in my position and rank, to remonstrate with Lord Methuen but, if I got the chance of saying anything I would. Poor Wauchope–the hand of death seemed to be on him already, and he constantly adverted to the folly of the tactics which were being employed, and yet, as he had not yet personally come under the direction of Methuen himself, he felt, I know, some delicacy in saying anything to his Chief until he actually reached his headquarters.

On 4 December 1899, when Ewart reached Modder River, he learned that Methuen wished to see him. He went over to His Lordship's room off a

---

45 Hence this work by Lieutenant Colonel J.S. Ewart is extensively referred to.
46 MMK: 7654/37A: General Sir J.S. Ewart, Unpublished Autobiography, p.438.
47 MMK: 7654/37A: General Sir J.S. Ewart, Unpublished Autobiography, p.440.
48 MMK: 7654/37A: General Sir J.S. Ewart, Unpublished Autobiography, p.441.

Sir John Spencer Ewart, (1861–1930)* (McGregor Museum, with permission)

* Sir J. Spencer Ewart was commissioned into the Queen's Own Cameron Highlanders in 1881, served in Egypt and fought at the Battle of Tel el-Kebir (1882). He was involved in the Nile Expedition in 1884, and served with the Sudan Frontier Field Force from 1885 to 1886. During the South African War, he worked as a staff officer and in 1902 was promoted to Colonel; in 1904 appointed as Military Secretary and in 1906 moved on to be Director of Military Operations at the War Office. In 1910, he was appointed Adjutant-General to the Forces, and later appointed General Officer Commanding Scottish Command in 1914, a post he held until 1918. S. Ewart was an Aide-de-Camp General to King George V from 1910 to 1914, and retired in 1920.

courtyard in the Crown and Royal Hotel, was greeted most cordially and asked to take a chair next to his bedside.[49] Methuen made several enquiries about Wauchope and his brigade expressing pleasure at its arrival, as he felt he had a tough job ahead of him. He then asked, 'And what are they saying in the Army about my fights'?

> Well Sir, I replied, "everyone is delighted at your success but I feel bound to say that people doubt the advisability of these frontal attacks on the Boers. He replied, "Yes that is all very well, but what are you to do when you can't get at their flanks? I can assure you that on the Modder River, they held such a long line that I could not outflank their position. Moreover, I cannot leave the railway. I am tied to it, because I have not been given transport enough to undertake a wide turning movement". There was such force, I saw, in this last argument and I said no more, I felt that perhaps, I had already said too much and I should not have said what I did, had it not been for Wauchope's parting injunction on the platform of Orange River Station.[50]

Methuen's comments reflect an utter lack of alternative thinking and rigid inflexibility to adapt to changing circumstances. The Boers had adapted their tactics to the terrain at Modder River after Belmont and Graspan, and were doing such at Magersfontein, while he spoke with Ewart, yet he showed no sign of doing so. His rationale about his lack of transport, thus tying him to the railway is disingenuous, considering he burnt the Boer laager at Belmont, when those wagons could have been pressed into service.

After his discussion with Methuen, Ewart met with Generals Colvile and Pole-Carew, the A.A.G. Colonel A.E. Mainwaring and Major G.E. Benson D.A.A.G.

> No one seemed in a very happy frame of mind and a distinguished officer who shall be nameless remarked to me: "It is lucky that you fellows have arrived, for the Guards or the 9th Brigade will not stand much more of Methuen. His frontal

49 Lord P.S. Methuen was recovering from his thigh wound.

50 MMK: 7654/37A: General Sir J.S. Ewart, Unpublished Autobiography, p.443.

> attacks are downright butchery". I was told that, at the Modder, he, Methuen, stumbled right on to the top of the Boers entrenched in the river bed, while he was discussing with his Staff which house he would occupy on the opposite bank. A heavy fire suddenly opened from the front, put an end to these conversations, and ushered in the commencement of a battle in which no skill of any kind was shown.[51]

Attempts by British mounted troops to scout towards Magersfontein were thwarted. On 6 December 1899, 'The enemy fired on our patrols on N and NE front.'[52] The Boers clearly occupied the area.

Attack at Enslin, 7 December 1899

Daylight on 7 December 1899 saw the only Boer attempt against the British supply lines during the Western Campaign. Prinsloo led approximately 800 burghers into an attack against Enslin Station;[53] having moved into the area from Scholtznek undetected. However, this was his last active command, for he was dismissed immediately afterwards; coming after his lacklustre leadership during the Belmont, Graspan and Modder River actions.

The British defences consisted of two positions; the first 'an outpost of 35 men were on a kopje some 1,200 yards from the station',[54] this being the main position. It consisted of the station building, a small four roomed masonry house with a garden enclosed by a 1.2-metre-high wall which formed a square, approximately 15 to 18 metres in length. Defended by two companies of the 2nd Northamptonshire Regiment, commanded by Captain H. Godley, they had dug internal trenches and banked up the walls with earth. The combat lasted nearly eight hours, yet the Boers did not press home their attack. Had they done so, and inflicted more damage to the railway infrastructure, they might have disrupted and delayed Methuen's plans for Magersfontein. Instead, they opened fire on the station with at least one 75 mm Krupp gun, first from a koppie north of the station and then from another koppie South of the station. Some seventy shells were fired into the position, one went through the roof of the house and wounded 11 men.[55]

They also destroyed two military telegraph huts North and South of the station, demolished with explosives a railway culvert about five to six kilometres South towards Belmont, and tore up 180 metres of rail track. The garrison was in a parlous state until the 62nd Royal Field Artillery and 12th Lancers arrived, along with Wauchope and the 2nd Seaforth Highlanders

51 MMK: 7654/37A: General Sir J.S. Ewart, Unpublished Autobiography, p.443.

52 Copy of a handwritten diary, which appears to be a divisional diary in the McGregor Museum collection, for which there is no accession number. A copy of this copy in the authors' collection.

53 MMK: 7654/12a: Sergeant Willie du Plessis, p.12.

54 Guest, *With Lord Methuen*, p.44.

55 MMK: 7654/7B: Brigadier General H.R. Kelham, The First Battalion H.L.I. South Africa 1899–1901, Unpublished Manuscript, p.39. Captain H. Godley received the Distinguished Serve Order for his handling of the defence.

who, having just arrived in Modder River Station that morning at 7:00 a.m. had to about turn where they disembarked at Enslin at 1:00 p.m. 'The Boers decamped in the direction of Jacobsdal',[56] leaving behind 13 dead and one severely wounded burgher.[57] Cronjé ordered Prinsloo to return as fast as possible, as he had received information that Methuen planned to break through to Kimberley on 11 December 1899.[58] Unbeknownst to them then, this commandos' return would play a critical role in the battle and determine the outcome of the action. Kommandant I.S. Ferreira replaced Prinsloo as General.[59]

On 7 December 1899, during the late afternoon and, in the absence of Wauchope who was at Enslin, Ewart was asked to accompany Methuen (who rode in a cart due to his wound), Generals Colvile, Pole-Carew and J.M. Babington, Colonel C.W. Douglas, who replaced A.E. Mainwaring as A.A.G., and Majors G.E. Benson and Rimington, to reconnoitre the Boer position towards Magersfontein. After riding for some distance, Methuen alighted and explained that he planned to make a night march to occupy a prominent hill to their right front, about eight miles away called Magersfontein (12.8 kilometres). He further announced that he intended to deploy the Highland Brigade to do this. Ewart understood that the bulk of the Boer force was at Spytfontein, yet some of the party declared that they could see shelter trenches and gun pits at Magersfontein, yet others said they could see nothing. Yet it did not appear certain to Ewart if the Boers occupied Magersfontein. 'We were really not near enough and it was a thousand pities, in the light of the subsequent disaster that no proper reconnaissance in force was pushed home to clear up the situation and obtain some definite information.'[60]

Ewart gathered that in the very near future that the Highland Brigade, guided by Benson, would undertake a night march to occupy Magersfontein to then make it a base of operations against Spytfontein. 'I greatly regretted this decision, for like my dear General Wauchope, I had set my heart on a forced march by the Highland Brigade, lightly equipped, clean around the Boer position, via Jacobsdal and Brown's Drift.'[61]

While riding back alone to Modder River, Ewart was overtaken by one of Methuen's *aides-de-camp*, who told him not to say anything about what he had heard, as Methuen had already changed his mind and did not intend to undertake a night march. He saw this as an attempt to silence him, as Methuen realised that he had spoken openly about his plans and did not want word of this to leak out.[62]

56 TNA: WO108/237: Major General A.G. Wauchope, Report called for in regard to the attack on Enslin, 7th December 1899, p.44.

57 Maydon, *French's Cavalry Campaign*, p.59.

58 J Van Rensburg, *My Persoonlike Ondervinding Magersfontein Slag*, 24 November 1949. It would be fascinating to know where General PA Cronjé obtained this accurate information from.

59 Amery, *The Times history*, p.389.

60 MMK: 7654/37A: General Sir J.S. Ewart, Unpublished Autobiography, p.445.

61 MMK: 7654/37A: General Sir J.S. Ewart, Unpublished Autobiography, p.446.

62 MMK: 7654/37A: General Sir J.S. Ewart, Unpublished Autobiography, p.446.

The 4.7-inch naval gun opens fire on Magersfontein. (McGregor Museum, with permission)

On 8 December 1899, Wauchope arrived at Modder River camp where Ewart at once told him about Methuen's reconnaissance and apparent change of mind. Wauchope was aghast.

'The next thing Ewart is that I will be sent to Cape Town for I shall feel it my duty to protest against the conduct of this campaign. I don't mind for myself, but I don't think the men should be sacrificed in these frontal attacks'.[63] Wauchope reiterated his stance about a turning movement being the option and said he would consult Pole-Carew to ascertain his views. Ewart gathered from this discussion that Wauchope would consult both Pole-Carew and Colvile and, should they agree with him, then he would remonstrate with Methuen.

On 8 December 1899, the two forces exchanged fire. The following day a reconnaissance by the cavalry, one Battery of Royal Horse Artillery and an infantry regiment, together with the 4.7-inch naval gun, christened Joe Chamberlain, probed North of the camp towards Langberg. The gun, dragged into position near the Ganger's Hut by two teams of oxen, just North of the camp, proceeded to fire 12 shells with much precision at a range of

63 MMK: 7654/40b: General Sir J.S. Ewart, Unpublished Manuscript.

5.5 kilometres from the Boer position.[64] The Boers did not reply. However a mounted patrol moving North East towards Magersfontein drew rifle fire.[65] One Boer, Burgher J. van Tonder was killed by this shellfire, whilst looking after horses behind the hills.[66] Killed too was an Agterryer, name unknown.[67]

Lieutenant Colonel D.S.W. Ogilvy, 10th Earl of Airlie, and some of his 12th Lancers cavalry officers observed, 'a stream of wagons and carts, and mounted men, shifting ground to strengthen the Boer left wing, which our gunfire had revealed as the point of our attack'.[68]

In the Boer laager on 9 December 1899:

> "There is a rumour in laager this morning, it is the intention of the British to force their way through' to Kimberley in a day or two. I hear the General has got information to that effect, from where I cannot tell. I imagine there is communication carried on by some Colonials. If we are tackled by a flanking movement, it will be all up with the Boers. But a frontal attack will be fatal to the British, as the Boers are too well entrenched. It won't be so easy to make the wily Boer 'break cover.' In a trench with these Mausers they are devils to shoot, and having cartridges ad lib, he makes them fly".[69]

On 9 December 1899, Wauchope and Ewart accompanied a reconnaissance towards Magersfontein, comprising the 9th Lancers, a Horse Battery, the naval gun and some infantry and mounted infantry. Ewart repeated his discussion with Methuen yet remained uncertain if the Boers occupied Magersfontein. Wauchope could see the folly of Methuen's thinking and on their return to camp, sought out Colvile and Pole-Carew. He later exclaimed to Ewart:

> "Well it's no go. I have seen Colvile and he tells me that, although he was of my opinion at the time about a turning movement, he now thinks that Methuen is right to stick to the railway. Pole Carew quite agrees with me; but, as Colvile takes up this attitude, I shall say and do nothing. We must just do our duty, whatever happens".[70]

And with that, the die was cast.

The British force had three axis of advance to relieve Kimberley. North along the railway (as before) towards Langberg and through these positions

---

64 The Ganger's Hut was located at Latitude 29° 0'12.83"S, Longitude 24°38'40.72"E. Gangers were railway employees who maintained a section of track. Also known as platelayers.

65 Copy of a handwritten diary, which appears to be a divisional diary in the McGregor Museum collection, for which there is no accession number. A copy of this copy in the author's collection.

66 Dr Arnold van Dyk Collection, Bloemfontein. Telegrams and letters to J. van Tonder's father, who was a Member of the Orange Free State Parliament. J. van Tonder, a former pupil of Greys College Bloemfontein, was initially buried at Jacobsdal and later reinterred on the family farm Vaalbank, just north of Bloemfontein.

67 Lane, *The War Diary*, p.38.

68 Maydon, *French's Cavalry Campaign*, p.63.

69 Lane, *The War Diary*, p.38.

70 MMK: 7654/37A: General Sir J.S. Stewart, Unpublished Autobiography, p.447.

on to Spytfontein and then Kimberley, which based on the Belmont and Graspan experience might have actually succeeded, given the weight of British artillery and force strengths.

The second option was to follow the main Modder River to Kimberley dirt road, which runs immediately adjacent to the eastern edge of the main Magersfontein hill. This presented potential for the British and high risk for the Boers. It would sever the Magersfontein central positions from the Scrub Ridge positions, which started approximately one and a half kilometres to the East. This gap between these two positions presented a weakness in this area.

The third option, along the course of the Modder River, would outflank the Boer position, sever them from their supply bases at Jacobsdal and the water resources from the river; or go so far as to capture Jacobsdal. This option would collapse their defensive positions between the river, westwards through their central Magersfontein positions and up to their western flank at Langberg. This was the tactical and most obvious option for the British forces, and the core weakness in the Boer defences.

Yet it would be a night march followed by frontal attack; just as at Belmont, Graspan and Modder River. No turning movement, no options, just a rigid adherence to outdated, redundant tactical thinking and folly, created by a general unfit to command.

That afternoon Wauchope conversed with Methuen in the Crown and Royal Hotel. When he left, he said to Colonel Douglas, 'I do not like the idea of this night march'. Douglas urged him to see Methuen again and frankly tell him, yet Wauchope left without doing so.[71] He also conversed with Colvile, who said to him that as the Guards Brigade were to be in reserve, he supposed that they would not see much of the fight. Wauchope shook his head and said, 'Things do not always go as expected; you may not be in reserve for long'.[72]

Lord Methuen's battle plan

'After Modder River it took a long time to build up the forces again. He couldn't have gone on at once. Things were damn slow in those days'.[73]

Reinforcements increased Methuen's army to approximately 15,000 men, of which about 12,000 were combat troops, supported with 35 guns. The Guards Brigade and 9th Brigade were reinforced with the 3,488 strong Highland Brigade. Cavalry included the 12th Lancers, additional mounted infantry, and artillery increments included G Battery Royal Horse Artillery, the 65th Howitzer Battery Royal Field Artillery, a 4.7-inch naval gun which had already opened fire, an observation balloon section of the Royal Engineers and medical detachments.

---

71 Maurice, *History of the War*, p.311.

72 Colvile, H.E, *The Work of the Ninth Division*, p.14.

73 Author's collection: Midge Carter, 'Lieutenant Colonel B Lang, Interview: "The Boer War"', Durban (9 March 1970).

Methuen's tactics at Magersfontein were, as Wauchope lamented, 'bludgeon tactics',[74] no different than those used at Belmont and at Graspan and Modder River. At 3:00 p.m. on 10 December 1899, the attacking infantry would assemble in Modder River Camp and then march 6.5 kilometres to the reverse slope of a low rise which formed their forward assembly area, designated Headquarters Hill. The artillery would shell the Magersfontein hills. On 11 December 1899, at 02:00 a.m. the Highland Brigade would advance under cover of darkness, deploy, and at dawn attack the southern end of the main Magersfontein Hill to overrun the Boers' Central Defensive Cluster. It was not absolutely certain if the Boers held the ground of their Eastern Defensive Cluster, yet was assumed so.

The 9th Brigade would follow the railway line and be a containing force and diversion for those Boers in position around Langberg. The Guards Brigade would initially remain in reserve at Headquarters Hill, and then, if required, move off to secure the Highlanders' right flank. The 12th Lancers, a company of Royal Engineers, plus the ammunition column and medical units were attached to the Guards Brigade. The 2nd King's Own Yorkshire Light Infantry would leave the forward assembly area, proceed along the North bank of the Modder river to Voetpads Drift where they were to entrench and secure the far right flank. The Half Battalion of the Loyal North Lancashire Regiment would guard Modder River camp, along with five companies of the 2nd Northamptonshire Regiment, two companies of the 1st Royal Munster Fusiliers and the four 12 pounder naval guns, with the Naval Battalion.[75]

Having captured the Central Defensive Cluster, a force 1,200 strong with two guns would entrench there and, holding Moss and Brown's Drift, secure the supply lines while the force pushed on to Abon's Dam to attack Sholtz Nek.[76]

Orders for the attack on Magersfontein Ridge[77]

[1] Enemy in occupation of koppies to north and north east of camp and also high round between Modder and Riet rivers.

[2] Intention of GOC to hold enemy on the north and to deliver an attack on the southern end of Magersfontein ridge. On the afternoon of Dec 10th the position will be bombarded; it will be assaulted on the 11th. With this end in view three columns will be formed.

[3] No 1 Column will assemble on ground NE of 9th brigade camp at 3pm on Dec 10th in the following formation: -
9th Lancers

74 MMK: 7654/37A: General Sir J.S. Ewart, Unpublished Autobiography, p.438.

75 Maurice, *History of the War*, p.311.

76 Amery, *The Times history*, p.393.

77 Maurice, *History of the War*, pp.312-315.

Mounted Infantry
G battery RHA
Brigade Division RFA, 18th, 62nd, 75th and 65th Howitzer battery
Highland Brigade (in mass)
Bearer company, Highland Brigade
2nd Yorkshire Light Infantry
Sec. TB.,RE
Balloon Sec RE
The CRA will arrange for a portion of the ammunition column to accompany this force.

[4] The advance will be directed on the southern end of Magersfontein Ridge.

[5] At 3pm the RHA, cavalry and mounted infantry will advance covering the front from railway to Modder river: the mounted infantry forming escort to RHA. After reconnaissance the cavalry will withdraw to the right flank of the Highland brigade and protect that flank leaving a party to watch the left of the artillery.

[6] At 3.10pm the remainder of the column will advance on the southern edge of Magersfontein ridge keeping well under shelter of Outpost Ridge (concealed from view of enemy) in the following order: -
Advance guard-half battalion; followed at 2.30 by half battalion RFA; remainder of force (except 2 Yorkshire LI) in the order of parade.

[7] The RFA will when within range open fire on the ridge applying to GOC Highland brigade for an escort.

[8] The remainder of column will form up concealed to right rear of artillery in action.

[9] 2nd Yorkshire LI will proceed, from place of assembly, along the N bank of Modder River (under the guidance of Rimington's Guides), to Bridle's Drift or as it was known Voetpads Drift, 4 miles up river, where they will entrench themselves against attack from all sides- especially from northeast to south.

[10] Half rations for 11th Dec will be carried in haversacks. One blanket per man will be carried.

[11] Tents will not be struck.

[12] No. 2 Column, under Major-Gen. Pole-Carew, composed of 1 battalion, 9th Brigade, Naval brigade (with 4.7 inch gun) and Rimington's Guides will assemble at such hour and place as may be fixed by him, so that the column will be in position at 4pm, to co-operate with No.1 column, making a diversion against Magersfontein ridge, along the railway.

This force will remain in position on the night of the 10th and will recommence the bombardment on the morning of the 11th; but the fire is on no account to be directed on the southern end of the ridge which the Infantry will be assaulting.

[13] No.3 column will consist of 12th lancers, No.7 Field Company RE, Guards Brigade; Bearer Company Guards brigade, Field hospitals Guards' and Highland brigades and divisional troops, ammunition column. This column commanded by Major-Gen. Sir H Colvile, will assemble on the same ground as No.1 column, at such hour, so as to enable it to reach 500 yards to the left rear of the RFA brigade division of No.1 column, by 3am on the 11th. A staff officer of No.3 column will accompany No.1 column to ascertain

[14] The supply column, with 5 days rations, escorted by half Gordon Highlanders, will assemble at the place of assembly of No.1 column, at 4am on the 11th, and will follow its route for two miles and await orders.

8

The Battle of Magersfontein, 10 December 1899 to 12 December 1899

On 10 December 1899, at 7:00 a.m. Wauchope assembled all the Highland Brigade battalion commanding officers in his tent and explained his views and intentions. These officers included: Brigade Major Lieutenant Colonel S. Ewart, Lieutenant Colonel J. Coode (2nd Black Watch), Lieutenant Colonel J. Hughes-Hallet (2nd Seaforth Highlanders), Lieutenant Colonel G. Goff (1st Argyll and Sutherland Highlanders), and Lieutenant Colonel H.R. Kelham (1st Highland Light Infantry).

A veteran of Tel el Kebir (as was Ewart), Wauchope would adopt a similar attacking formation as used in that 1882 attack. The Highland Brigade would advance in mass of quarter column with the 2nd Black Watch leading, and the 2nd Seaforth Highlanders, 1st Argyll and Sutherland Highlanders and 1st Highland Light Infantry following in succession.[1] After deploying, the attacking formation would be the 1st Argyll and Sutherland Highlanders on the left, the 2nd Seaforth Highlanders in centre, the 2nd Black Watch on the right flank, with the 1st Highland Light Infantry as reserve. Each battalion would have four companies in the front line and four in the second.[2]

What is critical to understanding what subsequently transpired and how Wauchope planned to deliver a successful attack after receiving orders that he knew had every probability of floundering, is what were his intentions, and were these conveyed?

He left nothing to chance and explained his plan in detail. To avoid a south-north axis frontal attack on the main hill, he remarked that he wanted to get well round the main Magersfontein Hill and outflank it from the North.

> He impressed on all present that, having got well round the hill under cover of darkness, he should deploy and then lie down, not advancing until he had light

1 Maurice, *History of the War*, p.312.

2 MMK: 7654/37A: General Sir J.S. Ewart, Unpublished Autobiography, p.449.

> enough to see his way clearly.[3] He impressed this on me personally several times and added, "I am not going bungling on when not knowing where I am going". This point is important and it makes it clear that Wauchope never had any idea of a bayonet charge at the end of his march upon a fixed position as at Tel-el-Kebir. The fact is we did not know if the Boers held the hill at all, and if they did, whether they were entrenched on its slopes, or on the flat ground around its base. We literally knew nothing when we started from Modder River, nor was any intelligence memorandum issued for our enlightenment and guidance. At my suggestion, in case it was a dark wet night the battalions, over unknown ground, would only be able to move in close column instead of the double line that Wauchope hoped to be able to adopt if we had clear weather and found the going good.[4]
>
> Just before we started, about 1 pm, we, of the brigade staff took a hurried lunch at a gangers hut on the railway line. Poor Wauchope seemed sad and depressed and I recollect him saying:- "My heart has been in my mouth ever since I heard of this mad scheme however whatever happens we can but do our duty". To me personally he expressed his fear that our enterprise might end in failure. He thought we were courting disaster.[5]

Wauchope was correct. Methuen's plan was tactically unsound. On 10 December 1899, after the last voluntary church service at 2:30 p.m. the troops paraded in pouring rain and a thunderstorm, their last meal was at noon that day'.[6] They were issued with 450 grams of tinned meat between two men, 100 rounds of ammunition per man, had to leave behind their greatcoats and carry their blankets on their waists.[7]

To compound his poorly thought out plan, Methuen then threw away any element of surprise.

> To make it quite certain (throwing away any element of surprise) we paraded at 2 p.m. in the open, in full view of Magersfontein from whose heights the Boers could have, with telescopes, counted the regiments, for we stood on parade for quite half an hour. Lord Methuen remarked to me on the fine appearance of my battalion (Highland Light Infantry), in which his father had served in former years, and after riding round the ranks of the Brigade, we moved off.[8]

At 3:15 p.m. the Highland Brigade marched out of camp in drizzling rain. After proceeding approximately 4.8 kilometres they reached some high ground from where, at 4:00 p.m. the artillery opened fire on the Magersfontein hill.[9] The bombardment lasted until 6:40 p.m. and for the last half an hour,

---

3 The underlined text is original as made by J.S. Ewart.

4 MMK: 7654/37A: General Sir J.S. Ewart, Unpublished Autobiography, p.449.

5 MMK: 7654/37A: General Sir J.S. Ewart, Unpublished Autobiography, p.449.

6 MMK: 7654/30: Extract of C.E. Stewart's Boer War diary – an account of the battle of Magersfontein and of Boer and British casualties.

7 MMK: 7654/22: C.E. Stewart: an account of what occurred on 10 & 11 December 1899.

8 MMK: 7654/7B: Brigadier General H.R. Kelham, The First Battalion HLI I South Africa 1899–1901, Unpublished manuscript, p.42.

9 MMK: 7654/37A: General Sir J.S. Ewart, Unpublished Autobiography, p.450. The approximate area is: Latitude 28°59'40.59"S. Longitude 24°40'18.09"E.

A Royal Artillery gun section opens fire. (Author's collection)

the fire was concentrated on the right (East) portion of the hills. A number of the airburst shells malfunctioned due to faulty fuses, although the percussion shells detonated satisfactorily.[10]

These batteries were the 65th Battery (Howitzer), and the 18th, 62nd and 75th Royal Field Artillery, firing from positions East of the howitzers. 18th Battery Royal Field Artillery fired at a range of 2,537 metres, 62nd Battery Royal Field Artillery at 3,200 metres and G Battery Royal Horse Artillery, to the northeast of the three batteries, at a range of 1,372 metres.[11] G Battery Royal Horse Artillery fired nearly 200 rounds per gun, approximating to 1,200 shells.[12] The naval gun also opened fire. 'You could have sworn there was not a Boer left in the place'.[13] Assuming that the Boers were atop Magersfontein hills, which they were not. 'We could see vast volumes of earth rise high into the air where the 4.7 Lyddite shells exploded. One thing this heavy firing certainly did. It plainly warned the enemy we were about to attack.'[14] It 'only warned them to clear out while it was going on'.[15]

The shelling killed one burgher and wounded three and did not intimidate the Burghers in the least.[16] An unidentified Burgher from Bloemfontein was unimpressed:

> When a fearful bombardment of lyddite, shrapnel and other shell of the most infernal kind failed to frighten us out of our senses. The lyddite shells make a terrible noise by their explosion-the very ground around you seems to shake; but it is just like the usual explosive. When it drops among a dense crowd it may kill 30 or 50 but dense crowds are seldom found for targets among the wary Boers.[17]

---

10 TNA: WO132/16: Lieutenant Colonel FH Hall, Despatch on the Magersfontein Action, 13 December 1899.

11 GR Duxbury, *Magersfontein 11 December 1899*, p.22.

12 TNA: WO132/16: Lord P.S. Methuen Unpublished Despatch on the Magersfontein Action, 13 December 1899.

13 MMK: 764/32: Black Watch – copy of a letter dated 17 December 1899 at Modder River supplying information concerning the battle of Magersfontein.

14 MMK: 7654/7B: Brigadier General H.R. Kelham, The First Battalion H.L.I. in South Africa 1899–1901, Unpublished Manuscript, p.42.

15 MMK: 7654/30: CE Stewart, Unpublished Diary.

16 Breytenbach, *Die Geskiedenis van die Tweede Vryheidsoorlog*, *Vol. II*, p.120.

17 E.M. Spiers, *Letters from Kimberley Eyewitness Accounts from the South African War* (London: Frontline Books, 2014), pp.84-85.

Howitzers in action. (McGregor Museum, with permission)

The shelling continued until dusk, leaving the Boers in no doubt as to the exact point of the intended attack. Burgher Meyer recalled his experience of this artillery attack:

> Terrified as a child you involuntarily press your body into the deepest corner in the ground. After a while I lifted myself up and looked over the lip of the trench. It was an astonishing, scary view that greeted me. The entire Magersfontein Hill, slightly behind us shone in a strange light. The hailstorm of explosive and the shot up ground and ironstone boulders, flung up fifty feet into the air by the bursting lyddite shells, made it appear as if the entire hill was converted into an inferno. A deathly silence descended on the plains and ridges of Magersfontein, a silence of tension, of uncertainty. I quickly glanced left and right of me down the trench. Every eye is pointed in front. The faces tense. The rifle in hand, finger on the trigger. We wait and we wait.[18]

Methuen was optimistic. In a letter to his wife that afternoon he wrote:

> Darling – My reinforcements were complete this morning, so I begin fighting this afternoon, and anticipate 3 days hard work, and then the relief of Kimberley a gigantic job. That said that any civilians who remain in Kimberley unless he has some valid reason will be turned out by me, and have to find food and transport, which means death. I have now 13000 men and 30 guns, so the Boers must suffer. I fired long range gun with Lydite at their position 4 miles off at daybreak yesterday. T(?) about 5 hours 2 niggers came here having bolted from the Boers – They said the Boers were in bed when the first shell came; they got 16 of them, could not tell where they came from. Loathsome (?) men, cleared away, or got into trenches.
>
> Anticipate having to fight 10000 or 12000, because the Transvaal have sent half from Natal, and they are determined to destroy my force: however am in a stronger position than I have been yet, and hope to deal a heavy blow on Wednesday.

18 Meyer, *Kommando-Jare*, pp.62-63.

> I have an interesting, but most anxious campaign, for I am afraid of having my communications cut, being held in front, and being locked up here, but I think they are frightened to death of me from all I hear, and not likely to come near me than they can avoid doing. We have ended a splendid voluntary church service, and the best chaplain I have met in the army.[19]

The reference by Methuen to Boer trenches, prior to the attack, is of interest. As soon as the shelling stopped, Cronjé and his officers who were in the laager at Brown's Drift galloped over to the summit of Magersfontein Hill, then walked down to the main trench and held a Council of War with his leading Kommandants.[20]

Lieutenant C.M. Hore-Ruthven believed that:

> This action has been much criticised and I think rightly. It entirely destroyed any hope of surprise–if the Boers, who could watch all our movements from their commanding hill top, required any further warning of impending attack they must have been much stupider than they ever showed themselves to be, either before or after. Subsequent information and events both show that they were expecting exactly what happened.[21]

Wauchope far surpassed his commander in tactics and generalship. He then attempted to prematurely force the Boers into revealing their positions, despite having no orders to do so. This would allow him to adapt his attack to new information, considering the complete intelligence failure to date. He led the Brigade past the right (East) of the artillery positions and continued its advance for some distance along a low laying depression of the ground.

Wauchope told Ewart that:

> He wanted to push on some way to the front with a view to trying to get some idea as to the whereabouts of the enemy's entrenchments. He desired me to follow the Black Watch, at a reasonable interval with the other three battalions. We pushed on thus rapidly to the front and sniping had commenced freely in the thick bushes,[22] when an order was brought by Colonel Mainwaring from Lord Methuen directing us to return immediately. Mainwaring remarked to me, as he rode up, "You have spoilt everything by going so far", but I could not follow the point of his remark, saying that the Highland Brigade must have been visible to the Boers and that the Artillery was engaged in what was obviously a heavy preparatory bombardment of Magersfontein hill. The enemy could have been in no doubt as to the meaning of our proceeding or our objective. Wauchope seemed very vexed when he returned exclaiming as he rode up to me. "If I had only been allowed to go a bit further I should have found out if they have got a position".[23]

19 MMK 7654/207: Letter by Lord Methuen to wife, 10 December 1899.
20 Maurice, *History of the War*, p.395.
21 MMK: 7654/41a: Colonel C.M. Hore-Ruthven, A personal account of the battle of Magersfontein, 1933.
22 The firing was from the Boer positions on Scrub Ridge.
23 MMK: 7654/37A: General Sir J.S. Ewart, Unpublished Autobiography, p.450.

In the main trench Burgher Izak Meyer with two of friends, Bertie Strauss and Driesie Lemmer watched this unfold, through a set of Meyer's binoculars.

> Clearly we could observe every movement and manoeuvre. By this time, we were well familiar with the different regiments and sections of the British infantry. In the middle of the enemy line we perceived the Highland Brigade. On the [British] left flank the famous Black Watch. On the right flank were the cavalry sections. Myself and Bertie and Dries looked at each other. We knew what this in front of us meant. Instinctively we pulled our rifles closer, fingers drumming above the trigger.
>
> At about 4.30pm the long kakie-line advanced towards us. Slowly, carefully they felt their way. It almost looked as if the Englishmen were suddenly trying to intimidate us. And then, suddenly the unexpected happened. The enemy fell back. Slowly, but steadily the kakie-line fell back about four to five hundred paces. Then they came to a halt. The troops standing as if awaiting something.[24]

The Boers had no doubt that they faced an imminent attack the following dawn on the main Magersfontein position. After the initial shelling on 9 December 1899, they identified that their Central Defensive Cluster would be the point of attack, and, in all likelihood, their Eastern Defensive Cluster, with its one-kilometre-long gap between these two defensive clusters. Immediately after the initial shelling on 9 December 1899, they started to reinforce these two Defensive Clusters. The burghers extended their main trench another 150 to 200 paces East towards the Kimberley road, which in one account was referred to as 'this trench or gulley'.[25]

> A little after sundown we could see the stuff as if the troops are trekking out. So tomorrow, there is certain to be a big fight. Commandants and officers going the rounds, seeing everything is right, telling burghers to keep steady in the trenches, be in no hurry until enemy comes within range. Then not to spare ammunition. Wonder where we will be this time tomorrow evening. No chance of sleep tonight, all sorts of reports flying in the air.[26]

That night they put out their outposts, one of them being The Skandinaviskå-kåren who occupied a forward observation position on a low ridge later known as Horse Artillery Hill, in order to detect any British advance towards Scrub Ridge in the dark. Their selection of this position indicates that the Boer officers recognised that this position was of importance to the British force, as the Highland Brigade had advanced into this area during the afternoon's reconnaissance.

Their left edge of the main trench below the hill ended on the Modder River to Kimberley dirt road. They immediately set to work after dark, extending this trench across the road to plug this gap. The question stands, how much of an extension was made that night?

---

24 Meyer, *Kommando-Jare*, pp.61-62.

25 F. Conradie, *Met Cronjé Aan Die Wesfront (1899-1900)*, p.78.

26 Lane, *The War Diary*, p.40.

On 11 December 1991, the author identified on the terrain that an earthwork continued from the road and into this gap for approximately 130 metres. Thereafter, extending further towards Scrub Ridge, terrain evidence revealed that an earthwork existed for another 300 to 400 metres. It has always been presumed that this was constructed after the battle.[27] It is possible that part of this line was post battle, however, had the trench extension and a portion of this earthwork not existed, then there would have been no obstacle facing the axis of the Highland Brigades' attack and nothing to prevent them from breaking through. In the 1990s the author identified on the surface numerous Martini Henry cartridge cases and that of Mauser and Gueddes, along with Mauser charger clips. However, the key archaeological evidence was a few remaining .303 bullet heads in the soil spill. The only occasion that .303 ammunition was fired into this position was during the battle by Highlanders, pinned down before it. Sadly, since the 1990s identification of this defensive line, the archaeological evidence was looted.

For the Lichtenberg Commando on Scrub Ridge, they took up their positions during early evening while the bombardment was underway. The burghers built their firing positions beneath the trees and scrub bushes. This was ideal for both shade and camouflage in the shadows. Before them lay a grass plain, broken by an occasional tree. During the night their officers went around their lines, speaking words of encouragement and emphasising that the attack would come during dawn the following day.[28]

At dusk, as the shelling petered out, the Highland Brigade returned to a rising knoll to the right East of the artillery, called Headquarters Hill. There they remained until midnight, spending a rain drenched hungry night, laying down in mass of battalion quarter columns. No light was to be lit and 'no smoking permitted from 07:00 p.m. on 10th to 04:00 a.m. on 11th'.[29] Adding to their misery, half rations for the following day were to be carried in haversacks, yet ordered not to be eaten until the morrow. The terrain in the early 1990s bore evidence to their hunger that night, and the night of 11 December 1899, the veld littered with empty beef and emergency ration tins. And a boot heel, which broke off a soldiers' boot, leaving him limping into action. This along with a .303 rifle bolt and firing pin; which slid out in the dark, leaving a Highlander with a useless weapon with which to go into battle.[30]

The Guards Brigade arrived at around 09:00 p.m. yet rest was impossible. 'Imagine lying down on sopping wet ground in pouring rain, merely in thin and sodden khaki, with nothing to cover one at all; and the cold was cruel'.[31] For the Boers in their positions, it was a miserable night. In the main trench, Meyer stood:

27 Conversations with former employees of the McGregor Museum during the 1990s.

28 MMK: Military History Collection: A.C. Schulenburg, *My Ondervindinge in Die Boere-Oorlog*, Unpublished Diary, p.11.

29 Maurice, *History of the War*, p.315.

30 Observed by the author on the terrain in 1993.

31 Russell, *Letters From South Africa* p.24.

> Enchanted by the majestic, overwhelming spectacle. It began to rain, heavy rain. The heavenly taps opened. It bucketed down. We stood unprotected from the wild night. Rapidly our trench turned into a liquid stream from two to three feet deep. Trembling we stood and waited the entire night for Methuen.[32]

Before the Highland Brigade assembled, their Commanding Officers briefed all the officers as to their orders. 'On Dec 11th, a few minutes past midnight, we fell in silently' Ewart approached his commander and, 'I asked General Wauchope in what formation he wanted to move. He replied, "I see no alternative but to advance as we are", ie in mass. Neither did I.'[33]

This formation was in mass of quarter column, involving 30 companies of approximately 3,500 men advancing one behind the other, each holding on to the man in front, in compact column with a front of about 38 metres and a length of 155 metres. There was a six pace interval between companies and eight paces between battalions.[34] Benson and two soldiers from Rimington's Guides led. To their left was Major General A.G. Wauchope, with his *aides-de-camp*, Captain Rennie and Lieutenant Arthur Grenville Wauchope, General Wauchope's second cousin.[35]

Major G.E. Benson was the main guide that night. He was later a column commander during the guerrilla phase of the war specialising in night attacks and mortally wounded at the battle of Bakenlaagte on 30 October 1901. (McGregor Museum, with permission)

Ewart leaves one of the most detailed accounts, yet to emerge since the battle, of that dreadful night advance:

> It was inky dark and raining steadily. The outlook was most unpropitious. We had no idea what lay before us, beyond what we had observed on the previous evening and that the ground between us and Magersfontein was broken, intersected by hollows, strewn with rocks and boulders, and here and there slightly covered with patches of thorn and mimosa scrub. What possessed Methuen to let us start under such conditions I cannot conceive. Deployment of any kind was out of the question. We could only get along in the closest formation and it was extremely difficult to keep touch with each other.
>
> At 12.30 am we started on our disastrous adventure, led by Major Benson DAAG and Captain Cumming Bruce (Black Watch Regiment). Before we advanced, Wauchope told me that he would move with the Guides in front and

32 Meyer, *Kommando-Jare*, pp.63-64. That I. Meyer referred to rain water running through the trench as a liquid stream from two to three feet deep, reinforces the author's point that this was an existing rainwater runoff gulley that was improvised into a trench.

33 MMK: 7654/37A: General Sir J.S. Ewart, Unpublished Autobiography, p.451.

34 Amery, *The Times history*, p.398.

35 Amery, *The Times history*, p.398.

> he wished me and his ADC, Rennie, to keep in rear of the brigade so as to try to keep up. This was not an easy task. Things grew worse and worse from the moment we started. The rain descended in torrents. Drenched to the skin we stumbled along over the broken ground. Darker and darker and more difficult did matters become and at one time our uncertain path was only from time to time illuminated by the constant flashes of lightning. Our compasses were quite useless, being choked with rain, and the pitiless rain ran down our backs and chilled us to the bone.[36]

Hore-Ruthven recalled that:

> One had to grab hold of the man in front so as not to lose touch and even then touch would have been lost if the left guides had not been provided with ropes which ran from front to rear. The pace, of course, had to be a crawl–just moving on and halting and moving on again. The only relief to the darkness was the frequent flashes of lightning and occasionally the beam of the searchlight at Kimberley.[37]

On the Boer side, Lane wrote that at:

> About one o'clock this morning burghers were ordered out of laager, some going in batches, others in twos and fours and single, no one seems to be in command, the order is to push out, to your individual commando at 'positions'. Everything is quiet as if nothing was about to happen. It is mostly sand veld and that deadens any noise.[38]

On 11 December 1899, at around 2:00 a.m. Cronjé ordered that the Boer outposts be abandoned, yet his order did not reach The Skandinaviskå-kåren.[39] At the same time Ewart received a message from Benson at the head of the column that he wished to see him. He found Benson with Wauchope, Benson saying that his compass was full of water and that he could no longer make out where they were. For some time already, Ewart thought they were bearing away to the left (West) and had almost got their backs to Magersfontein Hill. Benson had the same opinion and with difficulty they changed the direction of the column until they faced what they thought was the correct direction. While arranging this, Wauchope and Ewart lost Benson in the intense darkness, so Wauchope asked Ewart to replace Benson and try to guide the column. Forty-five metres on, they stumbled into Benson who said that he had completely lost the column in the dark. By 3:00 a.m. the rain had pretty much stopped. Between 3:30 a.m. and 4:00 a.m. they drew near to Magersfontein Hill, occasionally discernible by the brilliant flashes of lightning. They were approximately 730 metres from the

36 MMK: 7654/37A: General Sir J.S. Ewart, Unpublished Autobiography, p.452.

37 MMK: 7654/41a: Colonel C.M. Hore-Ruthven, A personal account of the battle of Magersfontein, 1933.

38 Lane, *The War Diary*, p.40.

39 Bojerud, 'Scandinavian volunteers', p.171.

hill,[40] although it was hard to tell the distance to the objective. Ewart felt 'that was high time we halted and deployed'.[41] He made his way forward to express this and on reaching the head of the column view, it halted, just as he reached the General.

The Boer sentries placed some distance in front of the trench below Magersfontein Hill heard the troops advancing towards them through the dark. As they fell back into the trench they warned the drenched burghers to prepare for action. Burgher E.P. Steinhobel recalled: 'Throughout the night the Korhaane birds flew up with their distinctive cry, kaka-rakka-kaka and because a Korhaane never in the night, and especially in the rain, leaves its nest, we knew that something had disturbed them. We observed these natural signs, including small Steenbuck that fled off the veld and through our positions'.[42]

The column had halted; as further progress was barred by what appeared in the darkness to be an impenetrable thicket of mimosa thorn, which grew along a wire farm fence with a gap of about 3.5 metres in it, presumably a farm paddock gate.[43] 'Well we halted about 3.20 and must have been visible to anybody on the koppies. Halted in brigade mass of quarter column'.[44] Ewart said, 'it was high time that we deployed'. Wauchope replied, 'Yes, but it will take some time to get through this, if necessary I shall pass the Black Watch through in single file and then go on with them alone. You must try and get the other three battalions through as best you can and then follow me.'[45]

Ewart went back and repeated this order to Hughes-Hallet of the 2nd Seaforth Highlanders and they then edged the three battalions towards the right where they found the ground more open and freer of bushes. After a detour of some 90 metres to the right, Ewart guided the battalion's half left and regained contact with the 2nd Black Watch, who were gradually reforming after crossing through the thorns.

Wauchope said to Ewart, 'Now I am going to deploy the Black Watch. Tell the Seaforths to prolong to my left and direct the Argyll and Sutherland to come up to my right. The Highland Light Infantry are to remain as a central reserve and come no further'.[46] 'These were the last words he ever spoke to me, possibly they were the last he ever uttered in this world'.[47]

Wauchope had altered the order of the regiments by sending the 1st Argyll and Sutherland Highlanders to the right instead of the left. His reason was clear to Ewart, as Wauchope had remarked that apparently, they were too much to the left (West) of the hill. Wauchope's aim was to flank the hill to its

---

40 MMK: 7654/37A: General Sir J.S. Ewart, Unpublished Autobiography, p.452.

41 MMK: 7654/37A: General Sir J.S. Ewart, Unpublished Autobiography, p.452.

42 F. Conradie, *Met Cronjé Aan Die Wesfront (1899–1900)*, p.79. The Karoo Korhaan (*Eupodotis vigorsii*), also known as Karoo Bustard, is a species of bird in the bustard family, Otididae, from Southern Africa. The Steenbuck or Steenbok (*Raphicerus campestris*) is a common small antelope of southern and eastern Africa.

43 MMK: 7654/22: C.E. Stewart: an account of what occurred on 10 & 11 December 1899.

44 MMK: 7654/30: C.E. Stewart, Unpublished Diary.

45 MMK: 7654/37A: General Sir J.S. Ewart, Unpublished Autobiography, p.453.

46 MMK: 7654/37A: General Sir J.S. Ewart, Unpublished Autobiography, p.453.

47 MMK: 7654/37A: General Sir J.S. Ewart, Unpublished Autobiography, p.453.

eastern edge and outflank it. Ewart conveyed the order to deploy promptly to Hughes-Hallet, Goff and, to Kelham that he was not now to advance any further.[48] Kelham replied, 'I suppose I had better deploy and then lie down'.[49] Ewart agreed.

Burgher Meyer stared towards the oncoming formation.

> And then we saw them, here right before us, a huge compact mass of humanity. The Scottish, the famous Black Watch, they all had recognisable kilts. They had just come through a thick patch of thorn bushes and were milling around as if to reassemble into one or another formation. My heart bouncing in my throat. My overexcited pulse. The enemy was right in front of us and apparently totally unaware of our presence.[50]

The Boers were well prepared. They used lanterns in various parts of their Central Defensive Cluster to signal as to when to open fire. Some distance away to the left of the 2nd Black Watch a small light became visible on the hill.[51] Suddenly from the hillside another bright light flashed twice followed by a couple of rifle shots.[52] Another signal lamp flashed brightly, about 90 metres to the left of the Highland Light Infantry. Drummer F. Gordon recalled that it was a bright red light.[53] It was 3:53 a.m.[54] Kelham, 'uttered an exclamation but the words were hardly out of my mouth before a sheet of flame blazed a few hundred yards to our front and a hail of bullets swept through us'.[55] 'Immediately on the level in front of us, a concealed trench opened a terrific fire. The front of the hill was lit up by the flashes of rifles as though someone had pressed a button and turned on a million electric lights'.[56]

This fire was opened by the Kroonstad and Hoopstad Commandos, and some of the Potchefstroom burghers, 400 metres ahead of the 2nd Black Watch. 'All hell broke loose'.[57] Cronjé recalled his experience of this moment.

> There, beneath the trees, there" – and he pointed with his finger towards a position below us, to the left or east of the slopes of the Magersfontein Hills – "I and my seven adjutants came across the Scotsmen early in the morning. It was totally

48 Lieutenant Colonel G. Goff was killed in action. His body was recovered from the battlefield before the British withdrawal on 132 December 1899, and buried in Cemetery 1, in marked grave Number 11 at Doorns A, Modder River. Author's collection: Modder River, Graves of those fallen during Anglo Boer War 1899–1900–1–2, Colonel D.E. Lines of Communication, September 1902.

49 MMK: 7654/37A: General Sir J.S. Ewart, Unpublished Autobiography, p.453.

50 Meyer, *Kommando-Jare*, p.64.

51 MMK: 7654/4: Lieutenant C. West, Account of the Battle of Magersfontein.

52 R.P. Dunn-Pattison, *The History of the 91st Argyllshire Highlanders* (Edinburgh and London: William Blackwood and Sons, 1910), p.272.

53 E.M. Spiers, *Letters from Kimberley*, p.85.

54 MMK: 7654/291: H.G. Chandos Pole Gell, 2nd Battalion Coldstream Guards, Unpublished Diary, p.15.

55 MMK: 7654/7B: Brigadier General H.R. Kelham, The First Battalion H.L.I. in South Africa 1899–1901, Unpublished Manuscript, p.42.

56 Dunn-Pattison, *The History of the 91st*, p.272.

57 Meyer, *Kommando-Jare*, p.64.

> unexpected. One of my men thought that it was ostriches – you know of course how strange these guys are clothed – but I knew that they were Scotsmen and I cried out: 'Schiet, kerels! Schiet hulle!' Immediately my bodyguard jumped from their horses and started to shoot at them. Soon the [Boer] rifles were rattling from all sides: thus the battle of Magersfontein began."[58]

Caught up in the chaos, Kelham:

> Just had time to shout at my loudest: "H.L.I. lie down". This was instantly done and looking back I saw all the companies prone and in good order, but it was useless, the whole column was broken up. The next instant a disorganized mob swept over us, there was no stopping them, I was knocked down, twice, lost my helmet, and was badly kicked on the head then swept away by the crowd, towards our right. I kept on shouting "H.L.I. halt, lie down" and the order was repeated by one or more sergeants with the result that in a few minutes I had a good many men in hand, but the bullets still phitted; like angry wasps and many men were shot.[59]

Another survivor recalled: 'The intensity of the fire seemed tremendous. I can distinctly remember standing absolutely thunderstruck at what seemed like a shower of bullets whistling past on all sides. It gave me the impression I could almost feel and see them, and that I had only to stretch out my hands to catch them'.[60] 'There was a considerable panic for the moment and I was knocked down by a number of men rushing back my helmet being kicked away or shot off my head.[61]

Wauchope was standing with some of his Staff in front of the brigade waiting for the completion of deployment, when this heavy fire commenced.[62] He observed the gap in the Boer firing line, for the rifle flashes were less in this area compared to those ahead and across Scrub Ridge to his right. He shouted above the noise and ordered Coode of the 2nd Black Watch to advance his men towards the gap. This order was passed along and the 2nd Black Watch, together with some of the 2nd Seaforth Highlanders, rushed towards the gap and the Boer earthwork line, fixing bayonets as they ran. Some of them got into the Boers defending this extremity of the line before the gap started towards Scrub Ridge. Private J. Ingram of the 2nd Black Watch being one.

> There were about 100 of us. We got round by the right and into the back of the trenches. We rushed into the trenches and gave them the bayonet, when our own troops in front started firing and we were catching it all. So the officer made us retire.[63]

---

58 Conversation between General A.P. Cronjé and N. Hofmeyr, mid-January 1900. See: N. Hofmeyr, *Zes Maanden bij de Commando's* (Gravenhage: W.P. van Stockum & Zoon, 1903), p.259.

59 MMK: 7654/7B: Brigadier General H.R. Kelham, The First Battalion HLI in South Africa 1899–1901, Unpublished manuscript, p.42.

60 Dunn-Pattison, *The History of the 91st*, p.272.

61 MMK: 7654/37A: General Sir J.S. Ewart, Unpublished Autobiography, p.453.

62 MMK: 7654/37A: General Sir J.S. Ewart, Unpublished Autobiography, p.454.

63 E.M. Spiers, *Letters from Kimberley*, p.87-88.

The charge of the Black Watch at Magersfontein. From A.C.R. Carter, *The Work of War Artists in South Africa*, p.6 (London: H. Virtue and Co Ltd, 1900)

> I saw A Company dropping and prolonged to their right doubling up. I got my bayonets on as we went thinking we were meant to rush it and B troop came on like bricks. Meanwhile ½ C company who were of course just behind me, tried to reinforce too, so I managed to edge off to my right and keep my lot extended. I had only my left ½ company with me as the right half in the half-light edged off too much and the other ½ C company got mixed up with them.[64]
>
> We got along 100 yards or so when we got into the dreadful flanking as well as frontal fire, and lost heavily. I could see now that the enemy were in trenches about 200 to 250 yards off. We managed to get 40 yards nearer, losing heavily all the time, and there we lay down (what was left of the lot with me) and began firing. I was about 15 or 20 yards in front, and had just got back to get in line when I got a bullet through my thigh, a quarter of an hour later it was quite light, and then we began to get it properly. The men on each side of me were hit straight away, and in a few minutes very few were left unhit. It was quite impossible for any ambulance or doctor to advance, so all our wounded lay within 200 yards or so of the Boer trenches all day.[65]

It was about this time that Major General A.G. Wauchope was shot dead, as was Lieutenant Colonels Coode and Goff, in the first few minutes of the fighting.

> I never saw him again after I left his side to convey his orders. To the best of my belief, he walked on when the firing began, in the direction of the Boer trenches and was one of the first to fall, as his body was found slightly in advance of the spot

64 MMK: 7654/30: C.E. Stewart of the 2nd Black Watch, Unpublished Diary.

65 Author's collection: Lieutenant F. Tait, Unpublished Diary, copy of a portion of the diary.

> where the brigade was caught. He had been stuck by a bullet over the left eye and killed instantaneously.[66]

Confusion prevailed. Some men lay down, others charged forwards, and others fell back or continued extending rightwards. Much of this confusion was due to there being no alternative plan if caught in closed formation, at close range, by the commandos. 'An extreme emergency without any plan leads to chaos'.[67] Officers and NCOs made strenuous efforts to preserve formations but the noise of the intense Boer rifle fire and shouting of confused men further worsened the situation. A withdrawal did occur, yet not by the majority of the force. 'We were very much disorganised'.[68]

> Then it was that I witnessed one of the bravest deeds I ever saw, for suddenly there broke forth the strains of "The Campbell's are Coming", and there was Jimmy McKay, the Corporal Piper of the 91st, standing up fearlessly playing the regimental tune, facing the storm of bullets in a valiant attempt to stop the retirement becoming a rout. The players of the various regiments broke out playing almost immediately after, and there can be no doubt that this altered the aspect of the fight considerably.[69]

After initially lying down, A and B Company charged the trenches but were brought to ground at varying distances, not closer than 100 metres from the Boer position from where they returned fire. For these men, their ordeal had just begun. In closing with the Boer trench, they would remain trapped under fire throughout the day.

> I got them to crawl up a bit (without the least difficulty) and there we lay and blazed away about 300 yards from the trench. The boers shot very badly and only after about 10 minutes did I hear many men hit. I looked to see what was comming [sic] on behind and lo and behold nobody. Well to cut a long story short,

Lieutenant Colonel J. Coode. (McGregor Museum, with permission)

Lieutenant Colonel G. Goff. (McGregor Museum, with permission)

66 MMK: 7654/37A General Sir J.S. Ewart, Unpublished Autobiography, p.454.

67 MMK: 7654/41a: Colonel C.M. Hore-Ruthven, A personal account of the battle of Magersfontein, 1933.

68 Author's collection: Midge Carter, 'Lieutenant Colonel B Lang, Interview: "The Boer War"', Durban (9 March 1970).

69 D Sutherland, *The Argyll and Sutherland Highlanders* (London: Leo Cooper Ltd, 1969).

"The Campbell's are Coming" (From A.C.R. Carter, *The Work of War Artists in South Africa*, p.6 (London: H. Virtue and Co Ltd, 1900))

we lay there from 3.30 am until 7pm. About 4.30am I think the guns began on them which drew them off a bit into their casemates where we could hear them talking and shouting and occasionally swearing, but the moment the guns stopped firing out they were again. There were two or three black boys among them. About 10 am I could only find 3 sound men within 30 yards of me on each side. We all hugged mother earth pretty close after we had finished our rounds.[70]

Lance Corporal E.T. Brown, 2nd Black Watch, remembered this dreadful experience.

I shall never, never, forget the disaster of my noble regiment and the remainder of the Highland brigade. It is a sad tale indeed; all that mortal man would do we did. We tried, we failed it seems but a dream. I myself got wounded at the beginning of the dreadful affair. I got hit with a Mauser bullet in the left thigh while carrying a wounded comrade. My second in the back and travelled out from the lower part of my stomach which was very painful. I can assure you I thought my day of rest had come. My third was in the thigh and my fourth in the elbow. I was in great pain all day–lay on the field for 29 hours. All that fatal day we wounded men lay close to the Boer lines under a blazing sun with shots of friends as well as foes passing over our heads. Many gallant deeds were done by our comrades. Men were shot through the body, lay without water, enduring all the agony of thirst, the pain of their wounds, and the heat of the day. Many a last farewell was whispered by pain drawn lips between the ringings of guns and firing of rifles. The battle raged all day long.[71]

Before these soldiers ran out of ammunition, it was not a one sided exchange. 'In fact all the time I lay there, I only saw one Boer, and he was a tremendous swell in a yellow jacket. He was sauntering along quite coolly, and we loosed off at him, and presently he disappeared, but I don't know if he was hit or not'.[72]

As daylight broke, Ewart endeavoured to collect and rally leaderless men who were falling back uncertain as to what to do. He advanced them up to the left flank where there were a number of 2nd Black Watch and 2nd Seaforth Highlanders, all under a severe fire. Gradually they advanced over a glacis-like slope up to about 450 metres from the main Boer trench, the existence of which, at the foot of Magersfontein hill, could clearly be seen.

70 MMK: 7654/30: C.E. Stewart of the 2nd Black Watch, Unpublished Diary.

71 MMK 7654/7: Ernest T. Brown of the 2nd Black Watch.

72 MMK: 7654/39a: T.M. Berkley, A pencilled sketch of Magersfontein giving Boer and British positions.

Never shall I forget the bravery of Corporal Shaul of the HLI, a stretcher bearer, who seemed to bear a charmed life. He was here there and everywhere dressing men's wounds as best he could. As he came by the man who was wounded on my left and encouraged him, I asked the Corporals name and said that, if I ever got out of the business alive, I would see that he was not forgotten. Maxwell and I subsequently recommend Shaul for the V.C. which he received.* (McGregor Museum, with permission)

* MMK: 7654/37A: General Sir J.S. Ewart, Unpublished Autobiography, p.455.

> Beyond this point we could not make any progress, despite the gallantry of Lindsay, who bravely stood up and with his wire cutters, cut a way through a wire fence for his machine gun. When at about 400 to 500 yards [450 to 550 metres] from the enemy's line we lay for a long time, returning the Boer fire as best we could; it seemed an eternity of mental strain and stress. Poor Rutherford Clark was killed, and a man next of the Black Watch, laying next to me to me on the right, had his head smashed. On my left, a man of the A&S Highlanders was shot through the thigh. The whistling of the bullets was incessant and it seemed certain death to stand up or raise one's head for any length of time. It seemed to me that there was no possible hope of our getting across the glacis up to the Boer trenches and that all we could hope for, if we hung on, was to see the enemy outflanked and manoeuvred from his position by the arrival of reinforcements on our right.[73]

Ewart and other officers observed Corporal J. Shaul of the 1st Highland Light Infantry perform several specific acts of bravery. Shaul oversaw the stretcher bearers; yet at one period of the battle he was seen encouraging men to advance across the open. He was most conspicuous during the day in dressing men's wounds, and in one case he came, under a heavy fire, to a man who was lying wounded in the back, and, with the utmost coolness and deliberation, sat down beside the wounded man and proceeded to dress his wound. Having done this, he got up and went quietly to another part of the field.[74]

To their right (East), a brief yet ruthless struggle occurred. The Skandinaviskå-kåren had a direct line of fire, into the Highland Brigade's right flank. They opened fire, as the initial rightwards attack to outflank the Boer main trench through the gap occurred, during the initial confusion

73 MMK: 7654/37A: General Sir J.S. Ewart, Unpublished Autobiography, p.455.

74 Corporal J. Shaul joined the Highland Light Infantry at the age of 15 and, after being first posted to Crete, arrived in South Africa in 1899. Corporal J. Shaul played in the regimental band and along with other bandsmen served as stretcher-bearers when in combat. He was awarded the Victoria Cross at Magersfontein and served with his regiment throughout the war. He remained in South Africa and, during the First World War, served with South African Forces in the East African Campaign.

caused by the opening fusillade. This enfilading fire 'appeared to me to be a serious menace to the whole Brigade. The fire from this direction was not so heavy as that from the front, but it was evident that if this enemy was not tackled and pushed back he might eventually envelope'.[75]

> As none of our troops appeared to be facing or deploying in that direction, and as I knew it was the flank to which my Company had been ordered to deploy, and as my Company, being in the rear, would have been the extreme right of our line, I proceeded to conduct an attack with the party we had collected on the enemy who were enfilading us. I had of course no orders and there seemed to be no one to give any. It therefore appeared to be an occasion when one must act at once on one's own initiative.[76]

Hore-Ruthven with approximately 100 1st Argyll and Sutherland Highlanders, 2nd Black Watch and 2nd Seaforth Highlanders, also led by Lieutenants B. Lang and W.B. King, advanced in the weak light towards the rifle flashes ahead.

> I heard some rifle shooting in the bushes. I said "My God there is something doing there". I got hold of the piper and got him to play the regimental march and that collected fellows together. When you are fired at from a certain direction you naturally go towards that. We deployed and went into the bushes.[77]

The Highlanders were discernible in the weak light as dark blobs moving across the veld. One group crossed a wire farm fence reaching the dead ground at the southern base of the ridge. Others swung around to their left and advancing East towards the ridge, crossed an open pan, which due to the rain, was knee deep with water. Another, led by Lieutenants Lang and King attacked the far left or northern edge of the ridge, the right flank of the Skandinaviskå-*kå*ren., thus enveloping them.[78] King advanced with a detachment to where Baron Fagerskjold lay with some others and summoned them loudly to surrender. In reply, Fagerskjold drew his revolver and shot King through his heart. With a cry: '"Oh my God"! he seized his breast and fell dead'.[79]

The Skandinaviskå-kåren who, when standing to fire or move around their position, were illuminated by the sun rising behind them. From the dead ground, for the Highlanders, it was a quick dash up the slope with bayonets fixed.[80]

---

75 MMK: 7654/41a: Colonel C.M. Hore-Ruthven, A personal account of the battle of Magersfontein, 1933.

76 MMK: 7654/41a: Colonel C.M. Hore-Ruthven, A personal account of the battle of Magersfontein, 1933.

77 Author's collection: Midge Carter, 'Lieutenant Colonel B Lang, Interview: "The Boer War"', Durban (9 March 1970).

78 Their axis of advance was through the area where the twin Waldemaar Crosses stand and then up the slopes. Author's collection: Midge Carter, 'Lieutenant Colonel B Lang, Interview: "The Boer War"', Durban (9 March 1970).

79 MMK: 7654/265: William Baerentzen. Personal experiences in the Boer War, pp.28–33. There was only one officer killed in action on this ridge that day and that was Lieutenant W.B. King.

80 On 11 December 2018 and 11 December 2019, the author tested line of sight and visual conditions in this exact area at 4:25 a.m. until daylight.

Officers of the 1st Argyll and Sutherland Highlanders prior to sailing to South Africa. Lieutenant Bertram John Lang stands to the far right of the photograph. Seated centre is Lord Roberts and next to him, to the right, in the bowler hat is Colonel O.C. Hannay, the then Officer Commanding, later killed in action at Paardeberg whilst leading the Mounted Infantry on 18 February 1900. (McGregor Museum, with permission)

The Highlanders fired as they went:

> From the standing or kneeling position and from the hip and often at close range, the enemy retiring before in like manner. One Boer I particularly remember; he waited behind a bush after his comrades had retired and opened fire on us at about 20 yards range just as we are approaching; this made our men very angry and they riddled him.[81]
>
> These fellows were lying behind the bushes you see, singly all over the place. I don't think they were in a cohesive command in any way. They were more or less single warriors. The result was when you saw a man over there, scratching or wriggling about. "There he goes"! And everybody has a pot at him. And I am sorry he was killed. In the meantime, he would have a pot at us. I think we must have wiped them out. Our blood was up then. We didn't make any bones about it. We took no prisoners.[82]

A desperate fight ensued with the Skandinaviskå-kåren, firing from, and dodging behind the anthills and bushes. Caught in their position, the majority were unable to fall back on Scrub Ridge, and overwhelmed.

> Captain Flygare received first a bullet through the legs and thereafter a second bullet hit his bandolier of which five cartridges exploded and ripped up his right side fully. He lived until the next morning.

Burgher W. Baerentzen, fighting with the Skandinaviskå-kåren, was severely wounded and narrowly escaped receiving the fatal coup de grace shot.

81 MMK: 7654/41a: Colonel C.M. Hore-Ruthven, A personal account of the battle of Magersfontein, 1933.
82 Author's collection: Midge Carter, 'Lieutenant Colonel B Lang, Interview: "The Boer War"', Durban (9 March 1970).

> We attempted immediately to seek cover partly behind the many ant hills of about one to one and a half yard high, of which there are many in this region, each one sufficient to cover partly two men, partly where we could cover in the high grass, steadily loading and firing. There were enough to shoot at, for instead of laying down as well hidden as possible, as we did, the British remained standing all the time and offered excellent targets to shoot at. I could literally see them fall when I shot.
>
> I got my rifle bullets. Both came from the left side, first a bullet through my right arm which went in mid into the under lower arm and out through the elbow. I felt a heavy blow on my arm and an electric shock and the rife [sic] was struck from me. But I was not so severely wounded that I could not take the rifle up again and continue to shoot. But soon thereafter I received my second bullet which went into the left side one fourth inch under the heart, right through the underbody and out on the right side through the liver, crushing underway [sic] some ribs.
>
> I lay and gasped for breath, fidgeted under the heavy pain and suffered from a burning thirst, indeed I could not keep silent. Particularly because I did not lose consciousness for one moment. But I was not the only one in this spot that suffered. Around me all our men lay either dead or wounded, winding themselves in heavy pains.
>
> The first Scot who approached where I lay was of the regiment Black Watch. He came first to Lindstrom who lay wounded and helpless, and with the exclamation: "Better finish off the bastards at once!" he drove his bayonet through the unlucky Swede. Thereafter he lifted his rifle and took carefully [sic] aim at me at a distance of about four yards. He must have been about to fire when an officer seized his arm and said:" Don't kill the wounded." Then he lowered his rifle and went quietly further.[83]

This killing of wounded was not an isolated event. Private G. Walker of the 1st Argyll and Sutherland Highlanders wrote home that:

> I and a lot more of our fellows, H.L.I., Seaforth's, Black Watch went to the right to try and stop the cross fire that was coming from the right. We found the enemy's picket here in small trenches, they were mostly Scandinavians. We completely wiped them off the map. One of them said, "Give me chance mate, I am a Glasgow man". One of the Seaforth's promptly ran him through, accompanied with the remark, "Then take that [expletive] you traitor".[84]

The Skandinaviskå-kåren suffered the highest proportional losses of all the commandos at Magersfontein. Twenty-four men were killed in action or died of wounds, six managed to reach the Boer lines while the remainder, all wounded, fell into British hands.[85]

During this time the first breach in the Boer defences took place, behind the Boers' front line. When the initial firing started from the main Boer trench beneath the Magersfontein Hill, F Company 2nd Black Watch, sprinted off to

83 MMK: 7654/265: William Baerentzen. Personal experiences in the Boer War, pp.28–33.
84 E.M. Spiers, *Letters from Kimberley*, pp.88-90.
85 Benneyworth, 'SCANDINAVIA'S MAGERSFONTEIN DEAD', p.142.

their right and became mixed up with D and G Companies.[86] They went through two wire farm fences to the immediate East of the main Boer trench and its earthwork extension, arriving completely behind Magersfontein Hill in its rear, facing its northern slopes.[87] This was Wauchope's original aim. These officers and senior NCOs carried out his orders, despite the confusion, shock and panic in the opening Boer fusillade. Much now hung in the balance.

Lieutenant Cox served in the Sudan Campaign, saw action at Omdurman, and was killed in action while scaling Magersfontein Hill. (McGregor Museum, with permission)

About 100 2nd Black Watch under Captain W. MacFarlane, Adjutant of the 2nd Black Watch and another group of the 2nd Seaforth Highlanders, under Lieutenant E.S. Cox, clambered up the northern slopes.[88] It was 5:00 a.m. and the British artillery started shelling the hills. Cox's group were all killed or wounded by this shell fire.[89]

Forced back by rifle fire from about 400 burghers[90] on top of the hills, and from Boer fire from their right flank and rear, the survivors retired North to seek cover in the scrub and bushes. A third group, of between 100 to 200 soldiers, led by Lieutenant R.S. Wilson of the 2nd Seaforth Highlanders and assisted by Sergeants F. Sackett and Frazer of the 2nd Black Watch, with some 2nd Seaforth Highlanders, got up along the North West slopes of the hill, overlooking the bend in the road. They struck a Boer tented camp and tethered horses, situated behind the neck.[91] In the weak light, they mistook the tethered horses for Boers and shot them before starting up the northern slopes of Magersfontein Hill itself. Approximately 407 horses were killed in this area.[92] As too were Agterryers with those horses, caught up in the crossfire. Soon these Highlanders were engaged by the Boer riflemen along the summit, who had just had their horses killed, and from an attack in their rear.[93]

86 MMK: 7654//39a: T.M. Berkley, A pencilled sketch of Magersfontein giving Boer and British positions, and MMK: 7654/31: Sergeant Sackett, G Company 2nd Black Watch, Unpublished Diary.
87 MMK: 7654//39a: T.M. Berkley, A pencilled sketch of Magersfontein giving Boer and British positions.
88 Maurice, *History of the War*, p.319.
89 Lieutenant E. Cox being killed in action. See: TNA: WO108/83: South Africa Field Force Casualty List 1899–1902. Lieutenant E. Cox being killed in action. See: TNA: WO108/83: South Africa Field Force Casualty List 1899–1902. Lieutenant E. Cox was later disinterred and reburied in Cemetery 1, in marked grave Number 13 at Doorns A, Modder River. Author's collection: Modder River, Graves of those fallen during Anglo Boer War 1899–1900–1–2, Colonel D.E. Lines of Communication, September 1902.
90 MMK: 7654/12c: Sergeant W. du Plessis. Written account in English.
91 MMK: 7654/31: Sergeant F. Sackett, G Company, 2nd Black Watch, Unpublished Diary.
92 MMK: 7654/12a: Sergeant Willie du Plessis, p.7.
93 MMK: 7654//39a: T.M. Berkley, A pencilled sketch of Magersfontein giving Boer and British positions.

Above and below are two scenes of the Boer horses killed in action. Note that they are stripped of their equipment and also the varying stages of decay. (Western Cape Western Cape Archives and Records Service, with permission)

The exact spot on 23 November 2021. Note the Highland Brigade Memorial roughly centre of picture on the slope. (Author's collection)

(McGregor Museum, with permission)

The exact spot on 9 November 2021. (Author's collection)

Kommandant A.P.J. Diederichs and his Ladybrand Commando, having just returned from the attack on Enslin Siding, were watering their horses at Magersfontein farmhouse when the action commenced.[94] A contingent of the Ficksburg Commando were with them. Kommandant Diederichs, Veldkornet H.J. De Wet and Kommandant F.J. du Plooy immediately got the approximately 400 strong[95] commandos into action, splitting their force in two, thus creating two Boer mobile reserves that played a key role in deciding the outcome of the battle. Their attack being supported by one 75 mm Krupp which was with their commandos.[96]

The first group headed towards the neck (and valley) in order to gain its crest, repulse any threat and block this threatened area of the Central Defensive Cluster. The second group, namely the Ficksburg Commando, as ordered by General I Ferreira, galloped towards the Western edge of Scrub Ridge; to plug any further penetration through this sector and threat to the Eastern Defensive Cluster.[97]

Diederichs' burghers took cover in a donga, behind the horses killed earlier by Wilson's group, and opened fire on the backs of those Highlanders scaling the hill. The 75 mm Krupp opened fire with shrapnel from a position near the dirt road at them and, combined with British shells exploding just ahead along the summit, forced the survivors to scramble down.[98] Some 2nd Black Watch and 2nd Seaforth Highlanders formed an East to West firing line adjacent to the northern side of the dirt road, while others took cover amongst the scrub North of and about 600 to 700 metres from the base of the hills and this road. At 7:00 a.m. the Howitzer shells started exploding in the veld behind the hills, facing the northern slopes, right amongst the Boer mobile reserve moving around this area and about 20 metres from a group of Highlanders in the scrub. These Highlanders then re-joined the firing line along the dirt road.[99]

The survivors continued firing at the Boers, resupplying themselves with rifle ammunition from their dead and wounded comrades. 'Gradually nearly everyone in the line seemed to be either dead or badly wounded. We had plenty of ammunition passed on to us from our left but eventually there were such big gaps of dead and wounded it could no longer be passed along'.[100] At 10:00 a.m. with ammunition running low, they retired, falling back on the 2nd Seaforth Highlanders firing line.[101] All but 40 of Wilson's group were

94 MMK: 7654/12a: Sergeant Willie du Plessis. No page number on typed document. The farmhouse is located at: Latitude 28°57'19.84"S and Longitude: 24°43'49.98"E.

95 MMK: 7654/12a: Sergeant Willie du Plessis, pp.7–11.

96 MMK: 7654/12a: Sergeant Willie du Plessis, p.8.

97 WMBR: 04426/00001 Recollections by Burgher (later General) J.J. van Niekerk.

98 MMK: 7654/12a: Sergeant Willie du Plessis, p.8. It is worth noting that this artillery fire support to this Boer attack escapes all Official Histories written about the battle, yet it happened. No one has ever commented that it was not just British shells exploding on the summit and slopes, and it has always been assumed to have been British only shellfire that inadvertently thwarted this attack. This Boer gun played a key role in doing so having a clear line of sight to its targets.

99 J. Van Rensburg, *My Persoonlike Ondervinding Magersfontein Slag*, 24 November 1949.

100 MMK: 7654//39a: T.M. Berkley, A pencilled sketch of Magersfontein giving Boer and British positions.

101 MMK: 7654//39a: T.M. Berkley, A pencilled sketch of Magersfontein giving Boer and British positions.

The fighting area in the neck and along the Northern slopes of the Magersfontein hills. The horses killed in this area by Wilson's group are visible, as is the donga in which Diederichs' burghers took cover and opened fire from. It is possible that these horses belonged to this Boer commando and were killed by return British rifle fire. These were the Boers firing from a donga (gulley) at the foot of the hills, visible in this photograph. Of interest is that this donga was, post battle, strengthened with sandbags, and is another example of the Boer forces adapting water courses into an entrenched position, as they did with their main trench. No comment on this donga playing a role in the Boer defences after the battle has ever been made before, as too with the author's view of the main trench being an improvised water run-off sloot. (National Archives of South Africa, with permission)

killed, wounded, or forced to surrender. The dawn attack had finally failed. Diederichs and De Wet were killed during this decisive counterattack, that turned the outcome in the Boer forces favour.

The Ficksburg Commando at this stage arrived in the rear of Scrub Ridge and, after cutting a wire farm fence, started running up the rear slopes and into position.[102] Those approaching the outer Western side of Scrub Ridge ran into some Highlanders, from the groups that had earlier attempted to scale the rear slopes of Magersfontein Hill, and from the fighting behind it. Burgher J.J. van Niekerk leapt from his horse and opened fire. His brother shouted, 'Wait man, they are surrendering'. 'Oh yes,' van Niekerk replied. 'It looks like a surrender. I have heard a lot about this before, but never yet seen it'. 'All around you could just see how the enemy waved their little white handkerchiefs'.[103] After securing their prisoners, these Ficksburger's then moved into position. later playing a key role in the final stages of the battle.

Back at the main Boer trench at around 8:00 a.m. the Highland Brigade were pinned down at varying distances of 90 metres to 550 metres from the Boer positions.[104] The slightest movement drew Boer fire. What prevented their casualties from being higher was supporting artillery fire. Earlier,

102 WMBR: 04426/00001: Recollections by Burgher (later General) J.J. van Niekerk.
103 WMBR: 04426/00001: Recollections by Burgher (later General) J.J. van Niekerk.
104 Maurice, *History of the War*, p.320.

General Babington, Officer Commanding the cavalry and mounted infantry, ordered G Battery Royal Horse Artillery and the 12th Lancers, to occupy the ridge on which the Skandinaviskå-kåren were wiped out.[105] The ridge offered a clear view of the Central and Eastern Defensive Clusters, later becoming known as Horse Artillery Hill.

Shortly before 4:00 a.m. Babington ordered the mounted troops to advance in an easterly direction to turn the Boer left flank on Scrub Ridge. He also ordered two squadrons of the 12th Lancers and Major P.W.A.A. Milton's Mounted Infantry to dismount and reinforce the Highland Brigades' right flank.[106] The 9th Lancers were to force Moss Drift but only got to within 750 metres of the crossing, being stopped by rifle fire.[107] As for the 12th Lancers' The ground' as Sergeant Woodhead recalled,

> Was not suited for cavalry, nor the position of the enemy's strongholds either, so we galloped to a place of safety for our horses, and dismounted, and with carbines did the duty of the foot soldier. We advanced in splendid formation on the right flank, where we thought the Guards were, but only to find that they had been driven back. We advanced and retired several times on our stomachs, and lay there banging away until four in the afternoon, amidst groans which made you cry almost.[108]

This sector of the Boer Eastern Defensive Cluster held firm, ably supported by shellfire from the single 75 mm Krupp near Brown's Drift and two 37 mm Pom-Poms, positioned on Scrub Ridge.

At 6:00 a.m. G Battery opened fire from Horse Artillery Hill. While the wire fence was being cut in order to run the guns up the reverse slope, Major R. Bannatine-Allason, the Battery commander, reconnoitred the summit. He came under rifle fire and decided instead to position the guns on the southern reverse slope.[109] Although artillery drill then in practice specified that guns were not to be operated from reverse slope positions, G Battery continued firing from these positions.

Gunner E. Jackson of G Battery recalled that, 'We were in action for over 15 hours and fired over 1,000 shells. We had one officer and four men wounded, and had nine horses killed, besides a lot wounded. One of my horses was shot through the leg. How we escaped so easily God only knows'.[110]

Their fire added to the Howitzer and 4.7-inch naval gun fire onto the main Boer trench and also at targets along Scrub Ridge.

> Our guns started shelling the kopje shortly after daylight most of the shells went right over the Boers trench and burst on the kopje where at the time there were no Boers. A good many of our shrapnel shells burst behind where we were lying and

105 This ridge is commonly known as Horse Artillery Hill.
106 TNA: WO132/16: Major General J.M. Babington, Despatch on the Magersfontein Action, 13 December 1899.
107 Maurice, *History of the War*, p.322.
108 Spiers, *Letters from Kimberley*, p.92.
109 Maurice, *History of the War*, p.322.
110 Spiers, *Letters from Kimberley*, p.91.

Boer Pom-Pom in action on Scrub Ridge. In centre is Kommandant T. de Beer of the Schweizer-Reineke Commando, holding in his right hand, a Krag-Jorgensen rifle.* Note the Boer riflemen all armed with Mauser rifles, as evidenced by the charger clips in their bandoliers. One exception being the Artillerist who held a .303 Lee Enfield rifle with fixed bayonet. He was a member of the Transvaal Staatsartillerie, and probably a reservist with a previously captured weapon. The Pom-Pom loader crouched, poised to reload, with an ammunition belt loaded with 23 high explosive rounds. (McGregor Museum, with permission)

* The Krag–Jørgensen is a bolt action rifle designed by the Norwegians Ole Herman Johannes Krag and Erik Jørgensen in the late 19th century. Adopted as a standard arm by Norway, Denmark, and the United States, about 300 were delivered to Boer forces of the South African Republic, making it an extremely rare weapon used in the conflict, and favoured by Boer officers.

One of a few known action photographs taken at Magersfontein, it depicts airburst and percussion shells detonating along the trench line. (McGregor Museum, with permission)

> several of our men were hit by them. The lyddite shells from the naval gun were mostly short of the trench and falling in the soft sand did not burst.[111]

The 75th Battery Royal Field Artillery soon arrived, unlimbered on the summit of Horse Artillery Hill and opened fire. The two batteries then divided their targets. G Battery Royal Horse Artillery firing on targets from the centre of Scrub Ridge and running East along it to Moss Drift; and 75th Battery Royal Field Artillery firing on the Central Defensive Cluster and northern end of Scrub Ridge. They drew return fire from a Boer Pom-Pom positioned on Scrub Ridge. G Battery Royal Horse Artillery returned fire, knocked out the Pom-Pom, and continued shelling Scrub Ridge. By keeping down the Boer fire, these two Batteries saved the Highland Brigade and Guards Brigade from suffering far heavier losses.

However, they suffered losses under this intense Boer fire. A gunner of the 75th Battery R.F.A wrote of this.

> Well, we trotted 1,000 yards and it came 'Halt, action front', and then we caught it…Our leading driver got shot through the stomach, and one of his horses was shot, and when going down dead the two horses fell on top of them, and the wheel horses went on top of the lot. Well, the wheel driver got up, and unhooked his horses…and while he was doing that he had a bullet through the helmet…I was serving ammunition to the gun, and I got a bullet deep in the leg.[112]

From 11:00 a.m. to 1:20 p.m. Colonel Hall ordered the guns to keep up a slow rate of fire for two reasons. There was little or no movement on either side, so infantry fire had virtually ceased, and 'a large amount of ammunition had been used'.[113] That day G Battery Royal Horse Artillery fired 1,153 shells and 75th Battery Royal Field Artillery 820 shells at the Boer positions, which included supporting the later Guards Brigade attack.[114] The 18th Battery Royal Field Artillery fired 940 rounds, the 62nd Battery Royal Field Artillery about 1,000 rounds and the 4.7-inch naval gun 73 rounds.[115] The amount of ammunition expended by G Battery Royal Horse Artillery was the highest by a single battery in one day during the war.

The 62nd Battery Royal Field Artillery, took up position West of Horse Artillery Hill, 1,830 metres from Magersfontein Hill. At 4:20 a.m. they opened fire on the hill, adding to the woes of the Highlanders scaling its northern slopes.[116] Soon they realised their error and reduced their range

---

111 MMK: Military History Collection: Lieutenant M Bullock, B Company 2nd Black Watch.

112 Spiers, *Letters from Kimberley* p.91. The Gunner shot through the stomach, the author has identified as 20752 Gunner C. Lacey, as he is the only member of this Battery listed as wounded that day. TNA: WO108/83: South Africa Field Force Casualty List 1899–1902.

113 TNA: WO132/16: Lieutenant Colonel F.H. Hall, Despatch on the Magersfontein Action, 13 December 1899.

114 TNA: WO132/16: Major General J.M. Babington, Despatch on the Magersfontein Action, 13 December 1899.

115 Maurice, *History of the War*, p.327.

116 TNA: WO132/16: Lieutenant Colonel F.H. Hall, Despatch on the Magersfontein Action, 13 December 1899.

The 75th Battery Royal Field Artillery firing positions on Horse Artillery Hill, marked with a commemorative gun, erected in 1999 for the centenary of the battle. The author identified the exact site where to place this marker, based on T Friction firing tubes, used to fire the guns, found by the author on the ground. (Author's photograph)

Dispatching Howitzer ammunition to the firing line from Modder River. In the background stands the Crown and Royal Hotel. (McGregor Museum, with permission)

The same scene on 18 March 2010. (Author's photograph)

to 1,555 metres onto the main Boer trench.[117] At 6:00 a.m. Hall ordered the 18th Battery Royal Field Artillery to endeavour to enfilade the trenches. They took up position adjacent to the 62nd Battery Royal Field Artillery, 1,252 metres from the Boer trench, opening fire at 7:00 a.m.[118] Together these two batteries fired 1,940 shells that day.

The Royal Engineers balloon observers coordinated this bombardment and, spotting Boer reinforcements advancing towards Scrub Ridge, directed fire onto them. This included the Howitzer battery who shelled the reverse slopes of Scrub Ridge.[119] This is the first recorded instance of aerial fire control over artillery during warfare. Sergeant Edwards, Royal Engineers, inside the balloon observed that, 'The Boer loss was terrific, we could see from the balloon the effect of the lyddite shells, and gave the batteries the result, and where they were bursting'.[120]

Methuen and his Staff on Headquarters Hill realised that their initial attack had failed. Their immediate two options; use the artillery to deny Boer mobility, contain them in their positions, suppress their fire and interdict any attempts to reinforce their positions, which they did. Simultaneous to the artillery fire, then use the available forces of the 9th Brigade to press home their demonstration against the Western Defensive Cluster, thus containing Boer forces in that sector. Or bolder still, attack the hills immediately East of the main Boer trench and enfilade it; and or, with the available remaining infantry, namely the Guards Brigade and the 1st Battalion Gordon Highlanders, deliver a concerted attack against the Eastern Defensive Cluster

117 Maurice, *History of the War*, p.321.

118 TNA: WO132/16: Lieutenant Colonel F.H. Hall, Despatch on the Magersfontein Action, 13 December 1899.

119 Amery, *Times history of the war*, p.410.

120 E.M. Spiers, *Letters from Kimberley* pp.93-94.

Commanded by Captain H.B. Jones and Lieutenant A.W.H. Grubbs of the Royal Engineers, the 1st Balloon Section arrived at Modder River camp on 9 December 1899. The balloon section played a key role in the battle, as were it not for accurate artillery fire, the Boer forces would have routed the Highland Brigade. (McGregor Museum, with permission)*

*In 1899 the standard British military observation balloon was manufactured by joining seven overlapping layers of caecum (the blind intestine of an ox) into a near spherical envelope. This substance, also known as "Goldbeaters skin," was impenetrable to gas, flexible, strong, and lightweight. The observation balloon was inflated with hydrogen, had a capacity of 10,000 cubic feet and operated to a maximum altitude of 1,000 foot. When on campaign, the balloon section manufactured hydrogen by applying sulphuric acid upon Zinc. Another method of hydrogen manufacture was electrolysis of water but this process was performed in England and the hydrogen shipped out to South Africa. Hydrogen was stored inside pressurised steel cylinders and transported in specially adapted wagons, known as tube wagons. Between 3 and 4 tube wagons accompanied each balloon section and contained a system of pipes and valves connected to the hydrogen cylinders to facilitate the rapid filling of the balloon. The balloon was anchored with a retaining cable to a wagon and raised and lowered with a winch. Two observers occupied the balloon and relayed messages to the ground crew using either a telephone or a message bag attached to the retaining cable. See G. Benneyworth, Magersfontein Battlefield Museum display, 1999.

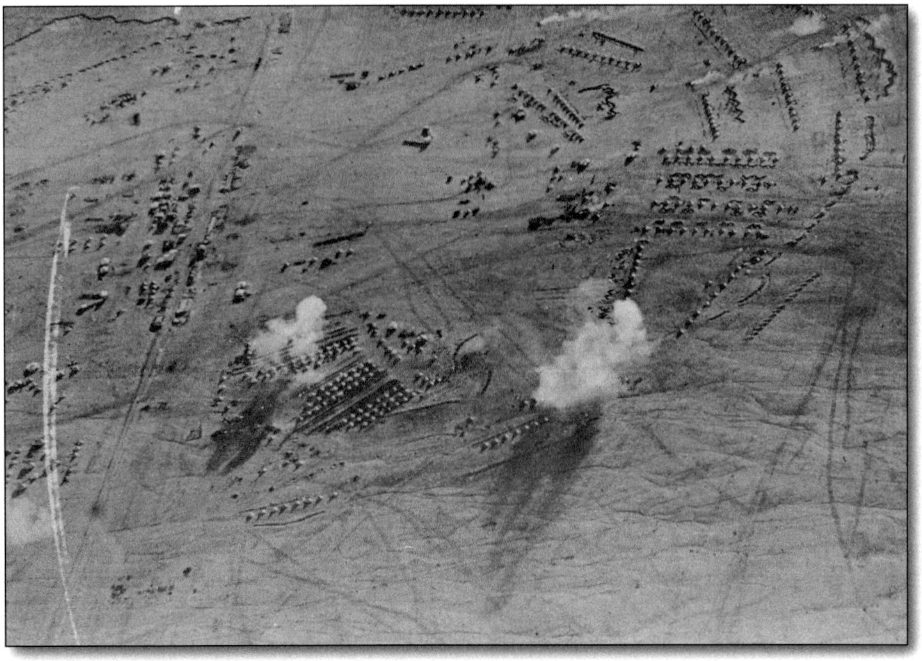

This is the only identified image taken from an observation balloon during the war, from a height of 300 metres (1,000 feet) of a British infantry camp. Accurate observation enabled accurate artillery fire during the battle. (Local History Museums' Collection, Durban, with permission)

and break through. Then roll up the Eastern Defensive Cluster thus collapsing the Boer Central Defensive Cluster at Magersfontein through manoeuvre.

Would it have worked? Yes. It had every possibility of succeeding. British artillery superiority could prevent the main trench from being reinforced and that of Scrub Ridge and the Eastern Defensive Cluster. British numbers were greater, and the Boer forces could not be in every place at the same time. The Eastern Defensive Cluster was initially weakly defended and therefore breakthrough highly possible, which all officers with military acumen were advocating, even before and immediately after the Modder River battle.

Did it work? No. For it was haphazardly and partially attempted. The Guards Brigade who held the only possibility of unlocking the deadlock were deployed in a lacklustre manner. Yet Methuen was not entirely responsible for this failure. He ordered Colvile's Brigade to attack and occupy Scrub Ridge, with the clear intention that this attack must break the Boer defences anchored on the Eastern Defensive Cluster and roll up the Boer left flank. These orders are critical to understanding the subsequent failure.

From Colvile's perspective, he later claimed on 12 December 1899, that Methuen ordered him to avoid becoming seriously engaged with the Boer forces on Scrub Ridge, and to use his discretion in supporting the Highland Brigade. According to Colvile, at 8:00 a.m. he received, from the Chief Staff Officer Douglas, a message that the Highland Brigade:

> Was holding their own but required support on their right. I accordingly ordered Major Hon. A. Henniker Major Commanding 2nd Battalion Coldstream Guards to afford this as far as possible, which he did by bringing up his supports on his left, and as I did not consider this reinforcement sufficient I prolonged his line to the left by bringing up 2 Coys of the Grenadiers. The 1st Coldstream being fully occupied with the enemy on the right I did not feel justified in withdrawing any of that battalion, but shortly afterwards. Codrington succeeded in collecting about 200 details and being thus strengthened detached two of his companies in support of the Highlanders.[121]

What actually happened? Before the advance of the Guards Brigade from the general area of Headquarters Hill against Scrub Ridge, Crabbe briefed Codrington as to the plan. He presumably received his orders from a Staff Officer, which in turn originated from Methuen, for at that stage, according to Codrington, Colvile could not be found. His orders were:

> That the Scots Guards had been made into Divisional Troops, both Coldstream Battalions were to advance in Easterly direction, and occupy a ridge which appeared to cut the skyline (but there was no really marked feature), that I was to guard my right flank carefully; that the Grenadiers were to be in support, and that they would guard their own right flank. The first Battalion Coldstream was to be the directing Battalion.

121 TNA: WO132/16: Major General H.E. Colvile, Magersfontein Despatch, 12 December 1899.

> A few minutes afterwards Colvile came up and I told him what had passed; he laughed and said he had been close at hand all the time. He repeated the above orders except that the Second Battalion Coldstream was to be the directing battalion instead of the First Battalion as mentioned by Crabbe. He said it was not known if the ridge was occupied; or not, but that if it was occupied the enemy were to be turned out.[122]

These orders were clear, that Scrub Ridge was to be attacked and captured. During the Guards Brigade's advance and extension of their firing lines, the Boers opened fire on the Highland Brigade, opening the battle. Shortly afterwards Ruggles-Brise sent Codrington and Henniker Major a written order that they were 'to be careful not to become seriously engaged, if I could help it, and that I was to report when I had occupied the ridge'.[123] This order would have come from Colvile, yet the question stands, did he originate this order or did Methuen? Who changed their mind and turned what could be a decisive strike into an ineffectual manoeuvre? Methuen or Colvile? It was Colvile, as the evidence shows.

Codrington relayed this order about not becoming seriously engaged to as many Captains as he could, approximately four or five of them. Others did not receive it and followed their original orders, pressing home their attack. During their advance the 2nd Battalion Coldstream Guardsmen came upon a Highlander who informed them that, 'The Highland Brigade has been cut to pieces'.[124] Ewart was brought to Henniker Major and:

> Begged him most earnestly to go to the support of the Highlanders. Their attack, he said, had failed. They were 'hanging on' as best they could, but their position was well-nigh desperate and, unless immediate help were forthcoming, they must be destroyed to the last man. In view of the orders which he had received, Col. Henniker could not possibly send them any material assistance. All that he felt justified in doing was to allow Lieut. Studd to take half his company (No 2) to their support. Lieut. Studd lost no time in acting upon this permission.[125]

The battalions then:

> Advanced through scrub and bushes for I think 300 or 400 yards [270 to 370 metres] and came under fire, the enemy being quite invisible, and there being nothing beyond the mere sound of their rifles to enable one to guess where their position was. We took cover and fired at a line of bushes that seemed a likely place for the enemy to occupy about 600 yards off. There appeared to be a nullah with a wire fence on the further side it [was] about 50 yards in front of what I considered to be the enemy's position. The three Companies (No1, 2 and 3) remained in

122 MMK: 7654/264: Lieutenant Colonel A. Codrington, Unpublished Diary, 1905, p.28.
123 MMK: 7654/264: Lieutenant Colonel A. Codrington, Unpublished Diary, 1905, p.28.
124 MMK: 7654/291: H.G. Chandos Pole Gell, 2nd Battalion Coldstream Guards, Unpublished Diary, p.16.
125 Hall, *The Coldstream Guards*, p.73.

Methuen with his staff on Headquarters Hill observing the battle. (McGregor Museum, with permission)

their position the whole day and fire was kept up with occasional lulls, and in some instances their fire was very accurate.[126]

The right flank of the 1st Coldstream Guards ended about 2,300 metres from the Modder River, the gap being filled by the 9th Lancers and Mounted Infantry. During the morning Codrington received a message from the observation balloon at Headquarters Hill that there were approximately 300 Boers in front of his 1st Coldstream Guards, with another 400 in rear of them in support.[127] The two battalions 1st Coldstream Guards sent to support the Highlanders' right flank reached Horse Artillery Hill and established the required link. The 3rd Grenadier Guards deployed facing the Boer positions running halfway East to Voetpads Drift on the Modder River. The 1st Scots Guards, who accidentally disengaged from the Brigade when advancing during the dark, were held in reserve as an escort to the Royal Field Artillery, until later sent by Methuen to plug the gap created by the Highland Brigade collapse during the afternoon.

When Methuen realised that Colvile's attack was deteriorating into a holding action and not the decisive strike so urgently required, he again ordered him to initiate a concerted attack, break through the Boer positions and roll up their flank.[128] This attack would succeed as the positions were still weakly held, yet urgency was essential. The balloon observers were reporting Boer reinforcements moving into position behind Scrub Ridge. If the Eastern Defensive Cluster could be breached and the Boer flank rolled up before additional reinforcements strengthened the Boer line, then the initial Highland Brigade attack would not have been in vain. Such a manoeuvre would collapse the Central Defensive Cluster.

Yet Colvile refused to press home his Brigade's attack and countermanded Methuen's orders, relayed to him by Benson. Douglas was clear on this matter:

> My recollection of the matter is this–You did send Colvile a message to push on if possible, by Benson but he would not do so. Benson and I often talked of it

126 MMK: 7654/264: Lieutenant Colonel A. Codrington, Unpublished Diary, 1905, p.29.

127 The balloon was sent aloft at 5:55 a.m.

128 MMK: 7654/205: C.W. Douglas, Letter to Lord Methuen, 26 August, Headquarters, 2 Division, Aldershot.

afterwards. Codrington I know twice that day sent back a message asking Colvile to be allowed to push on, but he was told in reply he was not to do so. Lock would be able to tell you this. The statement is untrue, incorrect and without foundation.[129] I should have thought it was Colvile's place to send to you [Methuen] to say he was going to push on, and to have pushed on without asking, when he was found, he was sitting down looking at the enemy whom he felt he could have pushed back. If a "General" is going to wait for orders to "push on" when he can he should, even in a battle.[130]

An officer, known only as Lock, recalled that:

As far as I can remember you did send a message to General Colvile. In fact, I go further than Colonel Douglas and think you sent two, one by Benson and one by Bell Smythe – I distinctly remember Benson talking about it afterwards, especially on one occasion when I went for a walk with him.

Again I remember riding over the ground with Colonel Douglas after Cronjé's departure and his saying that the Coldstream ought to have been pushed forward as a wedge –

I am very sorry I cannot give you anything more certain, but the impression I have always had was that you ordered Gen. Colville to press forward if possible, and to this day I have wondered why he did not do so.

Reading the last part of your letter again you say "the Brigade could not get forward as the Boers were well concealed covering a broad front." This is true during the latter part of the day after the Boers had brought up reinforcements on the bushy ridge, but in the morning, when Codrington asked to be allowed to advance it was perfectly possible, at least I believe this to be the opinion of the Brigade.[131]

Despite the situation of the Highland Brigade, Colvile threw away the single remaining opportunity to win the battle. Any chance of collapsing the Eastern Defensive Cluster and turning the Boer left flank was lost for good. From the burghers' perspective, laying behind their defensive works beneath the trees and the bushes, looking down towards the grass plain they could see the attacking Guardsmen. Burgher A.C. Schulenburg observed that:

In front of us the soldiers advanced in long rows firing, we too opened fire and fired continuously so that the barrels of the rifles sometimes became too hot and our people had to stop for a while. The khakis [the British] lay flat on the ground and crept closer through the grass. Next to me beneath the small tree lay Piet van Vuuren and we were covered with fallen leaves from the trees because the khakis fired too high and shot the leaves from the trees. The enemy came closer; luckily we could clearly see them in the grass as they crept forwards because they had

129 A statement by Major General H.E. Colvile that he received no such instructions.
130 MMK: 7654/205: C.W. Douglas, Letter to Lord Methuen, 26 August, Headquarters, 2 Division, Aldershot.
131 MMK 7654/207: Letter from Lock to Lord Methuen, dated Guards Club, concerning Colvile's role in the battle of Magersfontein, 7 September 1903.

A Boer sanger on Scrub Ridge facing the direction of the attacking Guardsmen. In the middle distance, towards the horizon, the Guards Brigade burial site and memorial can be seen. (Author's photograph)

> food tins on their backs and these shone in the sun. It was a cloudless warm day. Approximately ten paces to our right lay the two Benade brothers. One of them had some binoculars; he raised them to observe and was shot dead.[132]
>
> Further right from us were Ward Three, under Command of Veldkornet Hennie Coetzee. Next to the aforementioned was his farm foreman, Dick Dauth who lay firing. Suddenly he got a bullet in the head and Coetzee saw this and lifted him up slightly to check the wound and also to help him and with that, he too got a bullet through the head.[133]

The balloon observers reported on Boer reinforcements moving towards the Eastern Defensive Cluster across the veld between Scrub Ridge and Magersfontein Farm. Hence the urgency for a concerted effort to capture Scrub Ridge. Yet, to compound and reinforce his numerous errors, at 7:00 a.m. Methuen ordered the half battalion, 1st Gordon Highlanders, to give direct support to the Highland Brigade. For Ewart this:

> Seemed be a most foolish instruction [by Methuen], as every available man, instead of being thrown against this part of the enemy's position in this senseless

132 Burgher Benade is not commemorated on the Magersfontein Battlefield Museum Roll of Honour and represents a newly identified casualty, as of 2021.

133 Veldkornet K.J.C. Coetzee and Burgher Dick Dauth, both of the Lichtenberg Commando, were killed in action and are commemorated on the Roll of Honour at the Magersfontein Battlefield Museum. Veldkornet K.J.C. Coetzee's son was killed in action during the Modder River battle. See: Lane, *The War Diary*, p.42.

The 2nd Gordon Highlanders attacking in extended order towards Magersfontein Hill. Note the shell explosions above the Boer main trench. (McGregor Museum, with permission)

> manner, should have been pushed to the right, along the line of the Modder River, so as to make a bid for victory by turning the enemy's left flank.[134]

They came into action before 11:00 a.m. When within 2,000 metres from this Boer position, Lieutenant Colonel G.T.F. Downman extended and, in successive waves of skirmishers, passed through the Highland Brigade. They advanced at the double over the open battlefield straight towards the trenches. Companies were running 50 or so metres, then flinging themselves flat, yet every time they rose a tremendous fire was opened. In one trench the Boers were armed with Martini Henry rifles; for each time they rushed forwards, a long line of white smoke marked the well-concealed trench.[135] 'It was beautifully done and in perfect order, but as the position was approached, the rushes became shorter and weaker, finally when about in line with and on the left of the remnant of the Highland Brigade, the attack fizzled out'.[136] The closest they got to the Boer trench was 290 paces.[137]

Lieutenant H.E.M. Douglas, Royal Army Medical Corps, despite being under very severe rifle fire, advanced in the open to attend to Captain and Adjutant W.E. Gordon; also attending to Major S.L. Robinson and other wounded men.

Methuen had committed his entire force, either on the battlefield or to defending his camp at Modder River Station, while his only other infantry brigade was engaged in a failed diversion along the Western Defensive Cluster. He had no further reserves. The British cavalry were checked at Moss Drift and the Mounted Infantry were deployed into the firing line facing the Boer defences that stretched down towards Moss Drift. The 2nd

134 MMK: 7654/37A: General Sir J.S. Ewart, Unpublished Autobiography, pp.456–457.

135 MMK: 7654/7B: Brigadier General H.R. Kelham, The First Battalion H.L.I. in South Africa 1899–1901, Unpublished Manuscript, p.50.

136 MMK: 7654/7B: Brigadier General H.R. Kelham, The First Battalion H.L.I. in South Africa 1899–1901, Unpublished Manuscript, p.50.

137 Maurice, *History of the War*, p.327.

Lieutenant H.E.M. Douglas; V.C. 'I had made up a concentrated solution of Morphia, which I gave hypodermically to all the seriously wounded cases; I told them that I would come back to pick them up as soon as the firing stopped. The morphia appeared to ameliorate their misfortunes considerably'. However, struck in the face by a British shrapnel bullet, he was severely wounded.* (McGregor Museum, with permission)

* MMK: 7654/134: Lieutenant Colonel C.H. Burtchaell, 1912, 'Journal of the Royal Army Medical Corps', United Services Medical Society, Volume XVIII, p.553. Magersfontein Battlefield Museum Display: Lt Douglas joined the Royal Army Medical Corps (RAMC) in 1899 and first saw action at Magersfontein where he was severely wounded while performing various acts of gallantry. Douglas was awarded the VC and, for further service later in the war, he received the Distinguished Service Order (DSO). Between 1903–1904 Douglas participated in the Somalia Campaign and during the First World War he saw service in Serbia. Appointed a Commander of the Bath, Douglas remained with the RAMC and rose to the rank of Major General. He retired in 1933 as Deputy Director of Medical Services in India.

King's Own Yorkshire Light Infantry had entrenched at Voetpads Drift, as ordered. They observed a commando moving towards Moss Drift which would threaten the far right British flank. At 9:00 a.m. five companies were pushed forward towards Moss Drift and successfully frustrated this endeavour, despite coming under heavy fire.[138] During this engagement at least one soldier was hit by Boer fire, while in the act of pulling back his rifle bolt to reload his empty rifle magazine. In the tumult of combat it was abandoned on site.[139] The Battalion suffered 10 wounded during the battle.[140]

Cronjé and his officers were not going to risk a British breakthrough in their Eastern Defensive Cluster. They redirected forces from the Western Defensive Cluster (Langberg) against which, the 9th Brigade's demonstration was clearly that, not an attack in force. Much like Kommandant Diederichs' earlier attack and whose forces functioned as a mobile reserve, the Potchefstroom Commando, Ladybrand Commando and elements of the Ficksburg and Kroonstad Commandos were dispatched to assist the other commandos on Scrub Ridge. However, this was not a mere reinforcement of the Eastern Defensive Cluster.

It was the Boer force's moment to seize victory, by delivering a decisive strike.

Under the overall command of General Ferreira, the burghers dismounted behind Scrub Ridge, leaving their horses with their Agterryers and, at 1:30 p.m. moved into their attack, the lead force being the Ficksburg Commando.[141] Their point of effort was the weak link between the Highlanders' right flank and the Guards Brigade's left flank. They advanced under terrific and

138 Maurice, *History of the War*, p.325.

139 The author has seen this rifle and been taken to the exact site by a Kimberley resident who found it.

140 TNA: WO108/83: South Africa Field Force Casualty List 1899–1902.

141 Amery, *The Times history*, p.411.

Burgher A.C. Schulenburg (far left) as a prisoner of war in Bermuda later during the war. (War Museum of the Boer Republics, with permission)

accurate shellfire, directed by the balloon observers, and rifle fire from the Highlanders and Guardsmen. This shellfire was so intense that a number of burghers refused to advance through it, yet Ferreira, dressed in his brown 'morning coat'[142]:

> Behaved with distinguished bravery. During the severest fire–he galloped up across the flats, dismounted and ran forward a few hundred yards, all in the open, followed by the Ladybranders and Kroonstaders, and took up his position on the bare flats at the central point of the main British attack. A stranger, who has fought in three wars, who witnessed this incident, told me that the Ladybranders walked into the very gates of Hades with the nerve and coolness of old soldiers.[143]

Schulenburg was one, seeing his close friends killed around him. Burgher Eddie Hamman, a personal family friend from Lichtenburg, being hit in the left side of his skull. Half-conscious, he repeatedly screamed and mumbled incomprehensibly, yet could not be helped, due to the continual British fire. Hamman died later that night. The burghers were tormented by hunger and thirst, exacerbated by the heat and anxiety, that at any moment they might be shot in the head.[144]

Burgher J. van Rensburg, also part of this counter attack, virtually ran into the Highlanders.

142 WMBR: 03213/00001: Recollections by J.S. Kruger.

143 M. Cleaver, *A Young South African: A Memoir of Ferrar Reginald Mostyn Cleaver Advocate and Veldcornet* (Johannesburg: WE Hortor & Co. Ltd, 1913), p.42.

144 MMK: Military History Collection: A.C. Schulenburg, My Experiences in The Boer War, 1960. Burgher E. Hamman of the Lichtenberg Commando is commemorated on the Roll of Honour at the Magersfontein Battlefield Museum.

> Eventually we managed to get ourselves in front of the forward fighting line, where I saw groups of people spread out in a line lying and shooting. We landed up with 10 or 15 burghers, all of them Ficksburgers and Ladybranders. I was about 10 or 15 paces in front of the other bunch that followed me and when I passed the people lying there one of them said to me to watch out as I was going in among the English. I went about 10 paces forward and saw a Scots soldier for the first time, about 30 paces from me. He jumped from behind a vaalbos and ran to another. I yelled back at my mates to look at the ostrich. Suddenly I saw that the English troops among the bushes were all Scots. I fell flat and started shooting from 30 to 50 paces. One of the people lying there called me back, saying I was lying in their way. After a heavy fight we managed to drive them back about 200 paces. Then again they charged closer to about 30 to 50 paces. After a heavy fight we forced them back and this time for good.[145]

Burgher J.J. van Niekerk also participated in this attack. He recalled that some of them pushed so far forwards that at one point they were ordered to pull back a bit, as with van Rensburg, the concern being shot by their own side, firing from behind them.

> I was shooting from the kneeling position at the enemy. We couldn't lay flat because then the enemy wouldn't be visible.[146] My brother again joined me as Kommandant with an order to hold this position.[147] Uncle Jan and the two Veld Kornets were already wounded. Uncle Jan's leg was shot off above the knee. Veld Kornet Gert Fourie's knee shot off and Veld Kornet Jan Groenewald's arm was off.[148]

However, his luck could not last, with all the bullets cracking past and shrapnel shells exploding.

> I was wounded through my right shoulder. It was a terrible shock. I tried falling back with my friend Paul Botha who was also wounded. Not far from me was Roelof van Schalkwyk and he asked me what it was. "I think a shell fragment has smashed my shoulder" was my reply. He crept closer to examine and told me it was a Dum Dum.[149] It had entered from the front and exited from the back, because in front was a small hole and in rear a huge exit wound. My shoulder behind was ripped apart. Paul Botha fainted and fell across my chest. I shouted for my mates to pull this man off me. Thys Snyman was prepared to do so and came immediately. He pulled my wounded friend off and laid him next [to] me. He had just finished working on me and just as he was about to return when a bullet hit him through his neck and he fell with a part of his body on me. I pushed him off with my healthy hand. Botha writhed away next to me and later died.[150]

---

145 MMK: Military History Collection: Burgher J van Rensburg, My Persoonlike Ondervinding Magersfontein Slag, 24 November 1949.

146 Due to the length of the grass.

147 A battlefield appointment to replace casualties.

148 WMBR: 04426/00001: Recollections by Burgher (later General) J.J. van Niekerk.

149 An explosive bullet.

150 P.H. Botha of the Ficksburg Commando is commemorated on the Roll of Honour at the Magersfontein Battlefield Museum. Also on the Roll of Honour are two Burghers of the

Not for a lack of courage, yet there was talk of falling back. Despite being seriously wounded, van Niekerk shouted to his comrades, 'No chaps you must not abandon the position, let us die here like men!'[151]

Laying among dead and wounded burghers, from his position on Scrub Ridge, van Rensburg could clearly see the 12 guns of G Battery Royal Horse Artillery and the 62nd Battery Royal Field Artillery, on Horse Artillery Hill, firing at them. The airburst shrapnel shells, shattering the sky around his head. He saw, in the distance, Methuen and his Staff on Headquarters Hill, directly next to the tethering point for the observation balloon.[152] Agterryer S. Maine, serving with the Schweizer-Reineke Commando, was so taken by the sight of the balloon aloft, that it left an indelible impression on him for the rest of his life. His next born son, born after the war, he named Balloon, a tribute befitting a veteran of the battle.[153]

The Fauresmith Commando, led by Kommandant P.T. van der Merwe, 'A very proud man with a large beard', received a message from Ferreira,[154] delivered by Burgher J.S. Kruger, who galloped over on his white horse, under shellfire, all the while aware of the balloon in the nearby sky, ominously observing him. Kommandant van der Merwe replied that he 'would not allow his men to be shot to pieces'.[155] Yet approximately 200 burghers volunteered, following Kruger back, under intense fire, to reinforce the Ladybrand Commando.[156] Ferreira then ordered his men to push forward and, together with a group, including Kruger, they advanced, despite the shellfire, exploding about them. This determined attack was going to be the final deciding factor. With this attacking party ran van Niekerk. He recalled that, 'Here and there a Scot leapt up with his kit and turned to flee. These we simply shot flat.'[157]

Hughes-Hallett, now commanding the Highland Brigade after Wauchope's death, realised the threat that this attack posed to his right flank.

> About 1 p.m. I found that a large party of the enemy were getting round my right flank and a very heavy fire was poured in on us here at the same time also from the left. I then saw it was necessary to bring round to my right to intercept this movement and I ordered the men near me to get round to the right which we did under a very heavy fire.[158]

Ladybrand Commando, Burghers M.I. Snyman and M.J. Snyman, one of whom could be the T. Snyman, shot while rendering aid, assuming a spelling error in the original sources from which the author compiled the Roll of Honour. Also possible is that is that the two Snyman's are in fact the same person, and whose first name was Marthinus, and therefore called Thinus, hence the casualty is Thinus Snyman.

151 WMBR: 04426/00001: Recollections by Burgher (later General) J.J. van Niekerk.

152 MMK: Military History Collection: Burgher J. van Rensburg, My Persoonlike Ondervinding Magersfontein Slag, 24 November 1949.

153 C. van Onselen, *The Seed is Mine: The Life of Kas Maine, a South African Sharecropper 1894–1985* (Johannesburg: Johnathan Ball Publishers SA, 1996), p.24.

154 WMBR: 03213/00001: Recollections by J.S. Kruger.

155 Kommandant P. van der Merwe led the commando at this stage, taking over from Kommandant B. Greyling after the Modder River battle.

156 WMBR: 03213/00001: Recollections by J.S. Kruger.

157 WMBR: 04426/00001: Recollections by Burgher (later General) J.J. van Niekerk.

158 TNA: WO132/16: Lieutenant Colonel JW Hughes-Hallet, Despatch on the Magersfontein Action, 13 December 1899.

Lieutenant Colonel Downman leapt up shouting, 'Who sounded the retire'.* He ordered the 1st Gordon Highlanders to align with the 2nd Seaforth Highlanders, running along the line, waving his arm to direct this realignment, yet fell shot, mortally wounded. (With permission, McGregor Museum)

* Dooner, *The Last Post*, p.101.

Hughes-Hallett consequently ordered the right flank of the 2nd Seaforth Highlanders to swing back and form a defensive line with the 1st Coldstream Guards to meet this threat. To the Highlanders in this area of the battlefield, many presumed it heralded a general withdrawal.

To those watching, his actions were misinterpreted, and hundreds of Highlanders stood up and started to withdraw. The right flank first gave way and by 1:30 p.m. it became a general rout, albeit covered by artillery fire.[159]

Those troops neither wounded nor pinned down within the immediate vicinity of the Boer trench stood up and started walking back towards Horse Artillery Hill. For the burghers this presented an ideal target, opening fire into the backs of the retiring soldiery. Despite the covering British shellfire, the burghers 'were firing as hard as they could fill their magazines at the retreating columns'.[160]

For the British troops on the far right flank facing Scrub Ridge they watched in horror as they, 'Saw men of the Highland Brigade away to our left, in front of the main hill, commence to retire and I remember feeling appalled and exasperated at the folly of it. It was certainly a great mistake; it was so obviously dangerous to retire across very open ground in front of the main position'.[161]

It was during this retirement that the greater part of the casualties occurred.[162] During the retirement, Captain E.B. Towse attempted to carry the dying Downman on his back; but finding this not possible, supported him until joined by Colour Sergeant D. Nelson[163] and Lance Corporal W.C.H. Hodgsen, who then helped to carry him away. Hodgsen recalled this moment:

159 Maurice, *History of the War*, p.327.

160 Lane, The War Diary, p.41.

161 MMK: 7654/41a: Colonel C.M. Hore-Ruthven, A personal account of the battle of Magersfontein, 1933.

162 TNA: WO132/16: Lieutenant Colonel J.W. Hughes-Hallet, Despatch on the Magersfontein Action, 13 December 1899.

163 Colonel G.T.F. Downman was buried in Cemetery 1, in marked grave Number 10 at Doorns A, Modder River. Author's collection: Modder River, Graves of those fallen during Anglo Boer War 1899–1900–1–2, Colonel DE. Lines of Communication, September 1902. Colour Sergeant D. Nelson and Lance Corporal W.C.H. Hodgsen received the Distinguished Conduct Medal (DCM) for these acts of bravery. See: South African War Honours and Awards (London: Arms and Armour Press, 1902), p.97.

Captain E.B. Towse; V.C. Photograph taken after his return from South Africa.* (McGregor Museum, with permission)

* Magersfontein Battlefield Museum Display: Captain EB Towse later received the Victoria Cross for this and other heroic acts. Captain EB Towse joined the army in 1883 and after various postings in Egypt, Malta and Ceylon (Sri Lanka), saw combat service in India. Posted to South Africa in 1899, Towse was blinded in action and although invalided out of the army, he overcame this disability and taught himself Braille. In 1901 Towse joined the National Institute of the Blind and during the First World War, he went to France as an unpaid Staff Captain. Towse worked tirelessly, assisting blinded soldiers at the various base hospitals, and wrote letters to their parents, wives or friends on their behalf. In 1927 Towse became a Knight of Grace of the Order of St John of Jerusalem but was forced by ill health to resign his chairmanship of the institute in 1944.

> The 'Retire' was signalled and as long as I live I shall never forget that retirement. We hadn't retired a dozen yards before we lost our brave colonel, Colonel Downman, who fell with a bullet through his right breast. I was near him at the time, and together with a colour sergeant, carried him out of danger. I grieve to say that he died almost two hours afterwards.[164]

Private H. Anderson, 1st Coldstream Guards who was lying to the Highland Brigade right flank saw:

> The Highland Brigade running towards us as if the devil was after them. Some had no rifles, others no hats. They were complexly demoralised. It was just like a fire at a theatre. Highlanders were dropping off by the score, all shot in the back. The Highlanders ran past us, and no wonder, as nearly half the Highland Brigade lay on the field, dead and wounded.[165]

Many Highlanders ran past the artillery positions to an area midway between Horse Artillery Hill and Headquarters Hill. By 3:30 p.m. Colonels Hughes-Hallet and Kelham[166] managed to rally and regroup some of the men near Horse Artillery Hill, while Ewart arranged for water carts to be brought up to them. They reformed in rear of the 18th and 62nd Battery's Royal Field Artillery[167]. The Boer 75 mm Krupp, positioned on top of Magersfontein Hill, had remained silent all day, when:

> Suddenly the enemy's artillery, which had been kept out of sight, or had not come into action earlier, suddenly opened up a rapid shrapnel fire. To my horror I saw the exhausted brigade begin to dissolve again under this fresh trial, many of the men retiring straight to the rear. At one time some of the guns were absolutely

164 E.M. Spiers, *Letters from Kimberley* p.94.

165 E.M. Spiers, *Letters from Kimberley* p.95.

166 Lieutenant Colonel H.R. Kelham had been wounded earlier in the battle.

167 Maurice, History of the War, p.327.

> abandoned and I feared we were in for a debacle. Happily, however, the officers were able to rally enough men to regain the line of the guns.[168]

This 75 mm Krupp also shelled the 62nd Battery Royal Field Artillery positions,[169] and possibly too the Krupp near Magersfontein farm which had shelled the attack on the North slopes of the hill earlier in the day, and the Krupp near the drift, and the 37 mm Pom Poms on Scrub Ridge. This shellfire finished off the battle. Many exhausted, shocked and demoralised troops fell back towards their initial bivouac area near Headquarters Hill. Thereafter, firing petered out and by 4:00 p.m. the battle spluttered into semi-silence.

During their final retirement Lieutenant C.M. Hore-Ruthven:

> Came across 2nd Lieutenant R.A. Bullock who was severely wounded, and assisted him. We fortunately met a Cavalry Officer mounted. We peremptorily demanded his horse to carry Bullock. He readily agreed and assisted us personally. We did not know who he was but discovered later he was General Babington, Commanding the Cavalry Brigade, and felt a little nervous about having demanded the horse of so exalted an Officer, and also about some rather disparaging remarks we let fall about the Higher Command.[170]

The 1st Scots Guards closed the gap created by the collapse of the Highland Brigade, advancing to within 1,370 metres from the main Boer positions.[171] The Guards Brigade were ordered to hold their positions, while the cavalry and artillery withdrew a short distance as night fell. Food and drink, the first for some in over 24 hours, were brought to the lines and the British soldiers spent the night on the veld.

Despite the carnage of the day, the intensity and ferocity of close combat, scenes of humanity prevailed. After a discussion between a Boer Kommandant and Major C.E. Stewart, walking British wounded in front of the main trench below the hill were permitted to rejoin their forces, after leaving behind all weapons and ammunition. Stewart and 15 men, including Lieutenant Tait, got up at approximately 7:00 p.m. and stumbled back to the British positions.[172]

Stewart recalled:

> Well about 6pm the Boers I suppose saw we were comparatively harmless and two of them came down with water bottles. I yelled to them to go away but couldn't stop them so they just gave the wounded water and took stock of us. They then got an interpreter who said they wouldn't fire on the wounded if they lay still. I said I wasn't wounded but they said it didn't matter. At about 6.30 pm they again shouted from their trench and asked someone to come up, so I shouted back I'd

168 MMK: 7654/37A: General Sir J.S. Ewart, Unpublished Autobiography, p.459.

169 As evidenced by 75 mm Krupp segment shrapnel in this area, identified by the author in 1999.

170 MMK: 7654/41a: Colonel C.M. Hore-Ruthven, A personal account of the battle of Magersfontein, 1933.

171 Maurice, *History of the War*, p.328.

172 MMK: 7654/22: C.E. Stewart: an account of what occurred on 10 & 11 December 1899.

> go if I could come back to my men. Well I went up and they seemed quite a decent lot that I saw though I hear of some pretty low things done by them. Then their commandant wanted to take me prisoner but I declined the honour and said I had only come under his promise that I might go back. He then said he'd go and see his general to find out about the ambulances, so I said "right" and then he came back and said he wouldn't open fire if I took all the men that could walk away without arms or ammunition. I told him he had got all our ammunition earlier but the men should leave their rifles only about six could have carried them anyway. He also said he wouldn't fire on the ambulances if I ordered them up. There were about 15 men who could walk so I got hold of Bullock's arm and lugged him along a bit then went to look for an ambulance.[173]

On Scrub Ridge, van Rensburg lay with four dead and three wounded burghers in his immediate vicinity. He spotted an ambulance collecting wounded, sprinted towards it, and sought help to collect these casualties. Between 4:00 p.m. and 5:00 p.m. they arrived at Magersfontein farmhouse, the Boer field hospital. If the day was not traumatic enough, there he observed a grim sight. The bodies of 30 burghers being buried in one mass grave. They were laid out in rows, head to toe, and then covered in.

At the farmhouse, to his surprise, were about 200 burghers who never took part in the battle. They sat, making a noise, boiling water and braaing meat.[174] Exhausted, yet furious, van Rensburg shouted at their apparent officer, 'Who are you to stand here and make a noise, I have brought out wounded and am going back again–come with me then you will see what it looks like there'.[175] The officer replied that he was Judge Hertzog and his role was to collect those who fled the battlefront and force them back. Hertzog never forgot this experience and many years later, related to van Rensburg when they met, that he often thought about this manly boy, whose hardness he admired.[176]

Once it was completely dark the Boer commissariat brought water onto Scrub Ridge. For Schulenburg, 'never before had water tasted so delicious'.[177] A little while later they brought pots and tins filled with stywe pap, and this 'tasted so nice, better than a feast' in a prestigious hotel dining room during peacetime.[178] All throughout the battle he thought of his brother in the Kimberley siege lines, knowing that he could hear the Magersfontein battle raging. Alone in the dark, he thought of him again, and felt his brother's angst and worry for him.[179]

---

173 MMK: 7654/30: Diary C.E. Stewart of the 2nd Black Watch.

174 To braai is to barbeque meat on an open fire.

175 MMK: Burgher J. van Rensburg, My Persoonlike Ondervinding Magersfontein Slag, 24 November 1949.

176 MMK: Burgher J. van Rensburg, My Persoonlike Ondervinding Magersfontein Slag, 24 November 1949.

177 MMK: Military History Collection: A.C. Schulenburg, My Experiences in The Boer War, 1960.

178 MMK: Military History Collection: A.C. Schulenburg, My Experiences in The Boer War, 1960. Stywe pap is a thick porridge made from maize meal, a relatively coarse flour produced from mealies/corn in southern Africa.

179 MMK: Military History Collection: A.C. Schulenburg, My Experiences in The Boer War, 1960.

On Headquarters Hill the British troops spent a miserable night. Ewart did not sleep a wink, being 'too wretched and exhausted to close my eyes'.[180] Chandos Pole Gell, was emotionally shattered, like those around him. These experiences reflect something of the traumatic impact of combat, battle shock, exposure to extreme violence, brutal death and crippling injury.

Chandos Pole Gell was:

> Offered a whisky and soda and some stew which I could not face, then he gave me bread and jam. I ate the jam but the bread was too much for me so I put it in my jacket. The night which was the worst I ever spent, very cold and to add to the delights of sleeping in wet clothes with no coat or blanket, we had a stampede of horses over us followed by our mules.[181]

Burgher van Rensburg returned to Scrub Ridge to the East of the 37 mm Pom-Pom position, occupied by the Fauresmith Commando. There he found Burgher Roos laying under a buffalo thorn bush with both his knees shot off. There was nothing van Rensburg could do. Roos bled to death in front of him.[182] Despite all this, and the traumatic day, he went out that night towards the British positions around Horse Artillery Hill on sentry duty. Van Rensburg never slept, unable to, given the shock and adrenaline of mortal combat. He, and Burgher Page, walked out into the pitch dark close to British positions on Horse Artillery Hill, to listen out for any threatening activity.[183]

Ambulances from both sides scoured the battlefield, searching for wounded, and, after dark, by the light of lanterns. A haunting sight. The wounded crying out for water, their wives, mothers and sisters.[184] Lane recorded the numbing effect that the exposure to battle wrought on ordinary men.

> I suppose it is seeing so many dead and dying all round you, but no one seems to take it as a matter of fact. I daresay when the war is over I will then realise it more. I see poor devils with bullet wounds, that in ordinarily times I would think a man could not live. I see men walking about joking and laughing with their clothes all bloodstained some with as many as three bullet wounds. One man I saw on horseback, coming in, when his clothes were taken off I saw the bullet had entered at the left breast and out of the left shoulder, and yet he lives.[185]

At 9:00 p.m. Methuen confidentially told the Division's Principle Medical Officer that, 'the whole force would probably have to fall back'. Consequently, arrangements were made to evacuate the wounded to Modder River. At

180 MMK: 7654/37A: General Sir J.S. Ewart, Unpublished Autobiography, p.460.
181 MMK: 7654/291: H.G. Chandos Pole Gell, 2nd Battalion Coldstream Guards, Unpublished Diary, p.8.
182 Burgher J.H. Roos of the Fauresmith Commando is commemorated on the Roll of Honour at the Magersfontein Battlefield Museum.
183 MMK: Burgher J. van Rensburg, My Persoonlike Ondervinding Magersfontein Slag, 24 November 1949. pp.11–12.
184 MMK: 7654/12a: Sergeant Willie du Plessis, p.12.
185 Lane, *The War Diary*, p.31.

10:00 p.m. the first convoy of ambulance wagons started and by midnight the remaining wagons left.[186] Their rumbling wheels, audible to the Boer artillerists on Magersfontein hill.[187]

After dark, at great personal risk, Methuen's intelligence officer, Major Reade and a colonial scout named Harding, crossed the battlefield to investigate the trenches, yet found them occupied.[188] A 1st Scots Guards patrol were also heavily fired on from the trenches.[189]

12 December 1899

Any hopes that, as at Modder River, the Boers would abandon their positions during the night, were dashed by daylight. Why should they have? After all, they had fired into the backs of the retreating Highland Brigade and held all three of their defensive clusters, in particular the Central and Eastern Defensive Clusters, albeit with losses.

At sunrise on 12 December 1899, the burghers on Scrub Ridge exchanged fire with the Guards Brigade. Methuen made a personal reconnaissance which confirmed reports from the night before that the Boers remained strongly in position. At 6:00 a.m. a Boer messenger under a flag of truce approached the 1st Scots Guards outposts to report that there was a large number of dead near the point of the hill and requested medical assistance to be sent to the wounded laying near their trenches. Captain J.E. Carter went ahead and met with a Kommandant at the South Eastern point of the hill. He said he would not permit a burial party to approach his lines but would allow wagons with African drivers to remove the dead. Six wagons removed 38 wounded, including Lieutenant Arthur Grenville Wauchope, some of them only 100 metres from the trench and well behind the hill.

> They had lain for nearly 26 hours, exposed to the sun and a bitterly cold night, their position in the direct line of British fire. 'Many were very badly wounded, the majority suffering from fractured legs, amongst which were a number of severely fractured thighs. Captain Beach put up one of these with a rifle splint, but the Boer commandant objected to any rifles being taken away even as splint. The trenches were fully manned with Boers while the work of loading the ambulance wagons was going on. General Wauchope's body was found and sent into Modder in a wagon after the wounded had been removed.[190]

---

186 MMK: 7654/134: Lieutenant Colonel C.H. Burtchaell, 1912, 'Journal of the Royal Army Medical Corps', United Services Medical Society, Volume XVIII, p.567.

187 MMK: 7654/12a: Sergeant Willie du Plessis. No page number on typed document. It is an important point to note, that this vehicular movement was heard on top of the Magersfontein Hill that night, supporting the point that the night advance by the Highland Brigade was heard by the Boer forces, despite the thunderstorm.

188 Either Trooper H.H. Harding or Trooper G.H. Harding of the unit Colonial Scouts. See: TNA: WO127: Discharge books.

189 Maurice, *History of the War*, p.330.

190 MMK: 7654/134: Lieutenant Colonel C.H. Burtchaell, 1912, 'Journal of the Royal Army Medical Corps', United Services Medical Society, Volume XVIII, p.568.

On 12 December 1899, at 7:00 a.m. the 2nd Seaforth Highlanders returned to Modder River camp and the 1st Argyll and Sutherland Highlanders moved to Voetpads Drift to protect the right flank of the Division. At around 9:00 a.m. both sides agreed to a temporary armistice, so that the wounded could be collected.

Captain Carter was later made a prisoner of war, while assisting two wounded Highlanders in the vicinity of Scrub Ridge. His Boer escort became interested in his saddlery and concluded that an unloaded revolver inside a saddle wallet was in breach of the Geneva Convention. Carter was taken to a Boer Kommandant some distance away who was clearly annoyed by his detention. However, he had seen far too much of their positions and was sent to Jacobsdal that afternoon and locked up in jail. Five days later he was returned, blindfolded, to the British lines.[191]

On Scrub Ridge two wounded British soldiers approached van Rensburg, one of whose jaw was shot off. They struggled to help him drink some water as he couldn't swallow.[192] Van Rensburg then walked forward about 200 paces to where, the day before, a British shell had exploded among some British troops, killing five of them. He was surprised that in this small area where he had fought, according to him, there were approximately a hundred dead British troops. He then rode over to the main Boer trench where he was shown Wauchope's body, lying about 15 paces from the trench.[193]

However, no one informed the naval gunners that a ceasefire was in effect and, seeing movement around the main Boer trench, they opened fire with their 4.7-inch naval gun. The Boer artillery replied, shelling G Battery Royal Horse Artillery, yet the Battery did not return fire. Chaplain J. Robertson of the Highland Brigade galloped over to the naval gun to inform them of their error, while a medical officer went over to the Boers to explain the error. This brief shelling petered out.[194]

That morning the first batch of 41 prisoners of war from the 2nd Seaforth Highlanders and 1st Argyll and Sutherland Highlanders arrived in the Boer main laager. 'Poor fellows, they look bad on it. They are halted about fifty yards from me, are allowed to rest with a guard of about 20 men round them in a circle'.[195] Lane got one of them to help him get them coffee and biscuits and make them as comfortable as possible. There was no enmity of any sort. One of them was badly wounded in the arm and a Boer nurse assisted to dress his wound. 'In conversation they seemed awfully wild with their officers, and blamed them right and left'.[196] That afternoon another 22 prisoners were

191 MMK: 7654/134: Lieutenant Colonel C.H. Burtchaell, 1912, 'Journal of the Royal Army Medical Corps', United Services Medical Society, Volume XVIII, pp.568–569.

192 MMK: Burgher J. van Rensburg, My Persoonlike Ondervinding Magersfontein Slag, 24 November 1949, p.13.

193 MMK: Burgher J. van Rensburg, My Persoonlike Ondervinding Magersfontein Slag, 24 November 1949, p.14.

194 Maurice, *History of the War*, p.330.

195 Lane, *The War Diary*, p.44.

196 Lane, *The War Diary*, p.44.

Highlanders, as prisoners of war being marched into a Boer laager after the Battle of Magersfontein. (McGregor Museum, with permission)

brought in, including Captain Carter.[197] From the laager they were then sent to Jacobsdal, from thence to Bloemfontein and finally to Pretoria.

A little time later, in the British force, it became known that Methuen did not mean to renew the battle, disappointing many senior officers who hoped that he would. Colvile strongly urged him to do so, asking that he make another attempt with the Guards Brigade supported by the Highland Brigade Yet, 'Methuen was a beaten man who would take no further risks'.[198] He seemed much upset the day before, remarking to Ewart that, 'I shall have to stand the shock of what has happened'.[199] He later cited the defeat of the Highland Brigade, scarcity of artillery ammunition, and a lack of water, as his main reasons.

At 12:00 noon, Methuen's forces began a retrograde movement to Modder River:

> A defeated and dispirited force. We had an unpleasant time, as the enemy shelled us nearly all the way back to the Modder, our progress being necessarily slow as the field hospitals took a lot of moving and all the wounded had to be carried on stretchers. Before we retired, George Rennie went out with a stretcher and flag of truce and recovered Wauchope's body, which we brought into Modder with us.[200]

The artillery returned fire, including the naval gun, which fired 50 rounds in return. By 4:00 p.m. the forces were back in camp around Modder River Station.[201] This brought to a close a three day action, opening with the bombardment on 10 December 1899, and ending with a withdrawal under shell fire.

> As soon as they [Grenadier Guards], began to move, the enemy's guns turned most of their attention to them, and at times Crabbe's lines could hardly be see

197 Lane, *The War Diary*, p.44
198 MMK: 7654/37A: General Sir J.S. Ewart, Unpublished Autobiography, p.461.
199 MMK: 7654/37A: General Sir J.S. Ewart, Unpublished Autobiography, p.458.
200 MMK: 7654/37A: General Sir J.S. Ewart, Unpublished Autobiography, p.461.
201 Maurice, *History of the War*, p.330.

For the stretcher bearers, drawn from the Highland Brigade, this was exhausting work. Six men were assigned to each stretcher, four carrying and two in relief.* Photograph taken during the withdrawal from Magersfontein on 12 December 1899. (McGregor Museum, with permission)

* MMK: 7654/134: Lieutenant Colonel C.H. Burtchaell, 1912, 'Journal of the Royal Army Medical Corps', United Services Medical Society, Volume XVIII, p.569.

> through the dust; but when we did see them they were strolling quietly along in slow time, utterly unconcerned, alternate files halting and facing the enemy, while the others retired to a fresh position, in which they halted till the advanced files had passed through them.[202]

That last day, only one British soldier was killed in action; Lance Corporal W. Cooksey, 3rd Grenadier Guards.[203] While watching the retiring British force, the, 'Agterryers picked up the discarded Tommies' helmets off the veld, throwing them upwards into the air, in an act of jubilation'.[204]

The Boers suffered some 250 casualties, of whom at least 105 were killed in action or died of wounds.[205] Lane recorded in his diary on 12 December 1899 that, 'I hear our loss is put down at over three hundred'.[206] The likelihood is strong that Boer losses were even higher, when considering Agterryers in the fighting area, and for whom records were never kept. According to van Rensburg, he was amazed that the Boer death toll was not higher; 'the wonderful and most incomprehensible thing about the entire battle is that on our side 147 were shot dead'.[207] As with Lane's account, this is relevant, in that both Burghers state higher casualty figures than contemporary publications; and they would know for they heard this information at the time, particularly Lane, who was in the main Boer laager. De la Rey, later wrote that when he thought of Magersfontein, he thought of the Joubert brothers[208], all three of whom were killed in action that day, and the shock and distress that this impacted on the Lichtenberg community.[209] Many senior Boer

202 Colvile, *The Work of the Ninth Division*, p.4.
203 TNA: WO.108/83: South African Field Force Casualty List, 1899–1902, p.11.
204 WMBR: 03213/00001: Recollections by J.S. Kruger.
205 Roll of Honour, Magersfontein Battlefield Museum. Compiled by the author in 1999 using the following sources: MMK: 104/87: Staatscourant ZA Republiek, Woensdag, 17 Januarie 1900. MMK: 7654/93a: National Monuments Council Casualty List, 30 June 1999.
206 Lane, *The War Diary*, p.45.
207 MMK: Military History Collection: Burgher J. van Rensburg, My Persoonlike Ondervinding Magersfontein Slag, 24 November 1949, p.15.
208 Magersfontein Roll of Honour: C. Joubert, G.L. Joubert and P.J. Joubert of the Lichtenburg Commando.
209 MMK: 7654/24: General J. de la Rey, Unpublished Manuscript, p.18.

officers, Kommandants and Veld Kornets, were killed in action or suffered horrific and disabling injuries, as did their burghers. Of note is Veldkornet J.C.K. Coetzee, who is attributed to having fired the first shot in the war at Kraaipan. For small communities from where the commandos originated, bonded through marriage and friendship, the aftershocks reverberated, remaining for generations afterwards, and in some cases still do.

British losses were considered high, even when viewed against losses in World War One.[210] Approximately 876 casualties in Methuen's force, of whom at least 241 were killed in action or died of wounds,[211] 675 wounded and 63 missing in action or taken prisoner.[212] However, dependent on which account is consulted, casualty figures vary.

The Times History of the War in South Africa records, '46 officers and 706 men killed and wounded, and of these casualties again by far the greater part fell on the two leading battalions, of whom the Seaforth's lost 11 officers and 200 men, and the Black Watch 17 officers and 338 men, the latter figures giving a percentage of 60 percent, among the officers and 37 percent among the men'.[213] 'The Black Watch lost 38.5 percent of their strength'.[214] The Royal Army Medical Corps recorded casualties as being 169 killed, 692 wounded and 34 died of wounds; total fatalities being 203. As a percentage of the troops engaged, this was 7.5. percent.[215] In the Highland Brigade senior leadership losses included killed in action or died of wounds hours later, Wauchope, Coode, Goff and Downman, and many other officers and NCOs killed or wounded, including Major Milton, who lies buried in an unmarked grave on the battlefield, locked within the heart of the South African veld. Kelham and Codrington were both wounded, along with many others who led and remained with their troops throughout the action, attesting to their courage.

The feeling in the Highland Brigade was:

> Of chagrin and disappointment at the fiasco of the morning was, as well as can be imagined, very acute. One felt that with a little better management or better luck the affair might have been a success, and that a magnificent Brigade had been shattered and almost destroyed through sheer bad generalship. All ranks felt stunned, angry and rather bewildered.[216]

As if the defeat was not enough for the Highland Brigade, with their dead not even finally buried:

---

210 MMK: 7654/41a: Colonel C.M. Hore-Ruthven, A personal account of the battle of Magersfontein, 1933.

211 Magersfontein Battlefield Museum, Roll of Honour.

212 Maurice, *History of the War*, p.209.

213 Amery, *Times history of the war*, p.416.

214 MMK: 7654/41a: Colonel C.M. Hore-Ruthven, A personal account of the battle of Magersfontein, 1933.

215 MMK: 7654/134: Lieutenant Colonel C.H. Burtchaell, 1912, 'Journal of the Royal Army Medical Corps', United Services Medical Society, Volume XVIII, p.668.

216 MMK: 7654/41a: Colonel C.M. Hore-Ruthven, A personal account of the battle of Magersfontein, 1933.

Wounded arriving and receiving treatment in Modder River camp after the Battle of Magersfontein. African wagon drivers look on, while to the right, a British soldier urinates in front of a tent. Secondary infection from germs and bacteria claimed many lives during the war. (McGregor Museum, with permission)

A wounded Highlander bandaged up to the left. Note the white forearm band with the letter M on the central medical orderly and the bicep white band on the other orderly to the right. (McGregor Museum, with permission)

> Lord Methuen made another very grave error. A few days after the fight he summoned either all the Officers of the Brigade, or the whole Brigade, – I forget which – and made them a speech in which he said more or less in so many words, that the Brigade had not done its best and he hoped we would do better next time. The effect was to make us feel extremely resentful, almost mutinous, and if anything could be calculated to complete the destruction of morale this was felt to be about it.[217]

'The Brigade, and especially the Black Watch, had been very hard hit and were feeling sore and depressed. To administer further stripes was a monstrous and ungenerous thing to do; what was needed was balm to heal the wounds. Methuen's name was anathema to the Battalion (Black Watch) for the remainder of the war'.[218]

Ewart recorded that:

> The remainder of the Highland Brigade at this time were exasperated beyond measure with Lord Methuen, who was trying to make us scapegoats for the disaster which he had brought upon our heads, and there was a very bitter feeling against him. While I was absent with the Boers burying our dead, his Lordship, I learnt, had made a most injudicious speech to the brigade declaring that they had only themselves to thank for their failure. As I was not present, I don't know exactly how he put it, but the effect was deplorable in the brigade.[219]

This dressing down of the Highland Brigade remains a controversial point in the history of Magersfontein. Other sources recalled it differently. Writing to Methuen on 22 March 1900, Hughes-Hallet said:

> I myself have seen some of the reports in the papers to which you refer to, and must confess that I was mad and exhausted at the time. I cannot from memory quote your exact words to the Highland Brigade, on the 13th December last, but I myself most certainly never for a minute thought that you meant to say anything unkind or of an uncomplimentary nature to us that day, from what you said in conclusion to me personally is you thanked me by the hand, having said, "I thank you Hughes-Hallet for what you did last Monday and console with you on the loss of your officers and men."[220]

Queen Victoria communicated her views on the matter through one of her Aides to Methuen:

217 MMK: 7654/41a: Colonel C.M. Hore-Ruthven, A personal account of the battle of Magersfontein, 1933.

218 MMK: 7654/41a: Colonel C.M. Hore-Ruthven, A personal account of the battle of Magersfontein, 1933.

219 MMK: 7654/37A: General Sir J.S. Ewart, Unpublished Autobiography, p.466.

220 MMK 7654/203: Lieutenant Colonel J. Hughes-Hallet letter to Lord P.S. Methuen, 22 March 1900.

> My dear General
> The Queen has read the enclosed and I am sure that Her Majesty is relieved to know that the story generally circulated that Methuen had severely reproached the remains of the Highland brigade after their disaster at Magersfontein is absolutely without foundation.
>
> But in any case Methuen may rest assured that the Queen is the last person in the world to disparage let alone condemn those who are fighting for her, be they Generals or drummer boys.
>
> All Her feelings are for the suffering and what she does always hope is that the leaders will achieve their ends with the least possible loss of life – fully recognising that gains are not secured without losses![221]

On balance, however, one has to consider the views of Ewart and Hore-Ruthven who were there and wrote about it later when, unlike Hughes-Hallet in 1900, who had his career to consider if speaking out about his senior command.[222] In particular, Ewart who, as Brigade Major, had access to all the leading personalities involved in the action, then and afterwards, and insights into their viewpoints and actions; including that of Wauchope. These two officers were clear on the matter; that Methuen saw the disaster as 'ill luck'[223] and, faced with a defeat of his own making, scapegoated his troops, in particular the Highland Brigade.

Analysis: Victory and defeat on the South African veld

The Magersfontein Battle followed a British defeat and Boer victory at Stormberg in the eastern Cape Colony on 10 December 1899. Another resounding Boer victory followed on 15 December 1899 at Colenso when Buller attempted to break through the Boer defences on the Tugela River and relieve Ladysmith. These three defeats in one week became known as Black Week for the British Empire.

The British defeat at Magersfontein is essentially a case of two symbiotic parts; the failure of the night attack, followed by the failure of the day attack.[224] From the outset Methuen allowed the failure of one part of his force to then accept a failure by his entire force, thus paralysing his judgement. In throwing away the Gordon Highlanders, as opposed to attacking Scrub Ridge, he repeated his tactics at Modder River, revealing a lack of sound judgement.

---

221 MMK 7654 / 209: Letter from an Aide to Queen Victoria, Windsor Castle to Lord P.S. Methuen, 6 March 1900.

222 Lieutenant Colonel J. Hughes-Hallet view was used in 1999 by a historian to exonerate Lord Methuen, who stated that he was too magnanimous to blame the deceased, Major General A. Wauchope, for the failure of the battle; and cited Hughes-Hallet. This historian made no reference to the unpublished autobiographies by Lieutenant Colonel J.S. Ewart and Lieutenant C.M. Hore-Ruthven. See: S.M. Miller, LORD METHUEN AND THE BRITISH ARMY Failure and Redemption in South Africa (London: Portland, Frank Cass, 1999), p.141.

223 MMK: 7654/37A: General Sir J.S. Ewart, Unpublished Autobiography, p.466.

224 Amery, *Times history of the war*, p.417.

Defeat is attributed to various factors, the fundamental of these being poor leadership and generalship by Methuen. There is no getting around this point, as many apologists attempted to do, both during the war, and since. At the Battle of Modder River, Methuen narrowly averted defeat, the only decisive military acumen being shown by Pole-Carew. Methuen's conduct at Modder River demonstrated that he was unfit for further Divisional command, for in the overall battle he lost command and control. It was his subordinates, such as Wauchope and Ewart, who saw the obvious options available, when confronted by an impending action at Magersfontein. Yet he bludgeoned on, incapable of adjusting his thinking and actions to changing and challenging environments.

It is important to note the skills set and experience not only of Methuen, yet also of his subordinates. Yet the selection of Methuen as a divisional commander was based on seniority and not experience. Unlike his three Major Generals, he had served his entire career as a Staff Officer and, as a divisional commander had no experience of command, even at Brigade level, set off to relieve Kimberley with a scraped together Division that had never trained together, let alone fought together. Good luck played a role in his victory at Belmont and Graspan, yet his inability manifestly revealed itself at the battle of Modder River.

Wauchope's career saw him rise through various regimental commands, backed up with extensive combat experience. Yet, until Magersfontein, he had no experience of the Boers, other than the scrap at Enslin. Colvile also rose through regimental command, saw active service prior to South Africa and thus had more experience than Methuen. Prior to South Africa, Pole-Carew served mainly as a staff officer, yet had experience commanding a battalion. Prior to Magersfontein he commanded a brigade at Modder River, where his military acumen was exemplary.

A want of reconnaissance was not an excuse. He had the option of delaying by one day, given that the Kimberley garrison was nowhere near capitulating. On 4 December 1899, Kekewich signalled that Kimberley had 40 days' provisions and plenty of water.[225] A day's delay therefore would have enabled the observation balloon to reconnoitre the Boer Central and Eastern Defensive Clusters. The observers would have clearly seen the main Boer trench and all the other defensive works laid out beneath them. This coup de grâce would have avoided defeat and opened viable alternatives, ones already suggested, such as an outflanking manoeuvre to the East. 'This should have been ascertained and one cannot help thinking it could have been. This seems to be error No.1'.[226] A reconnaissance in force, such as that, which Wauchope attempted on 10 December 1899, would have clarified the matter, through forcing the Boers to reveal themselves. The lack of reconnaissance left one with 'a feeling of being aboard a ship in shallow water and in a fog, from which no surroundings were being taken'.[227] Also to blame

225 Amery, *Times history of the war*, p.390.

226 MMK: 7654/41a: Colonel CM Hore-Ruthven, A personal account of the battle of Magersfontein, 1933.

227 Maydon, *French's Cavalry Campaign*, pp.61–62.

for a lack of reconnaissance was Colvile, who held temporary command from 2 December 1899, while Methuen recovered from his wound, until handing back command on 6 December 1899. No serious reconnaissance was undertaken in the direction of Magersfontein or Langberg, when the main Boer effort was spent creating their Central Defensive Cluster, literally beneath the noses of the British force. For this Colvile was solely responsible.

The total absence of secrecy was a complete blunder. 'The point of our attack was well advertised by our over-night bombardment.'[228] The Boers were forewarned and the column made a racket during its advance, scaring up ground nesting birds, cackling into the sky. The bombardment left the Boers in no doubt that their Central Defensive Cluster was to be, as like Belmont, attacked at dawn.

The want of timely support to the Highland Brigade after its early reverse played a key role, as 'the supporting troops were too far away altogether'.[229] The Guards Brigade had the opportunity of attacking the Eastern Defensive Cluster and rolling up the Boer East flank, with the evidence showing that this had every chance of success. Had the entire Brigade, together with the whole of the 1st Battalion Gordon Highlanders been ordered into a concerted and determined attack against Scrub Ridge, supported with artillery, the battle would have turned into victory for the British. Instead, half of the 1st Battalion Gordon Highlanders were frittered away into a pointless attack, for which Methuen bears responsibility. The Guards Brigade potential was squandered into an ineffective holding action, for which, the blame rests with Colvile. Between these two Generals, victory for the British, was lost.

Ewart summed it up succinctly.

> I am, however, quite certain that the battle could have been won. The whole of the 9th Brigade and the Grenadiers and Scots Guards never drew trigger all day and practically no effort was made to extricate the Highlanders from the unfortunate position in which they were placed. Lord Methuen seemed to have quite lost his nerve in the face of the sudden crisis and to have accepted defeat from the moment he heard of our reverse.[230]

Hore-Ruthven was clear on this, despite writing of it, 34 years later.

> My own experience, and the ease with which my party reached the low ridge, would suggest that a properly organized attack in any strength might have captured the low ridge in daylight. The Guards Brigade and Cavalry Brigade failed to do so, it is true, but they were sent in piecemeal on an enormous front with little or no artillery support. The contour of the ridge was favourable and one could get within a few hundred yards of the Boer trenches without serious loss and a concerted attack in strength against one part of the line – say the north end of the ridge where I was – might have succeeded, and also witness the fact that many

228 MMK: 7654/37A: General Sir J.S. Ewart, Unpublished Autobiography, p.460.
229 MMK: 7654/37A: General Sir J.S. Ewart, Unpublished Autobiography, p.460.
230 MMK: 7654/37A: General Sir J.S. Ewart, Unpublished Autobiography, p.460.

> of the leading Companies of the Black Watch did get through the Boer lines and climb some distance up the main hill.
>
> If the low ridge had been captured for a length of a few hundred yards the remainder would have easily been taken. There was no depth in the Boer position here – just one line – and the Boer never stayed once his flank was threatened.[231]

Methuen never planned for any alternative option, should something actually go wrong during the initial assault. His only thought, once his forces were checked, was to hold on in front of the trenches until nightfall, in the hope that Boers, as at Modder River, would abandon their positions.[232]

Hore-Ruthven saw this point clearly.

> The assault on the key position having failed, could Lord Methuen have done anything more? I think however, he should have had a plan in his head to carry out in case the palpably risky night march did not succeed. I believe the best plan really would have been to take the low ridge first (Scrub Ridge) as one day's operation and then make a flank attack on Magersfontein Hill from the east as a second operation and I am not sure even if the second operation would have been necessary – I believe the Boers would have quitted.[233]

Finally, one question remains. Had Wauchope deployed his Brigade sooner, could the disaster have been averted? The answer is not. The unfavourable nature of the weather caused significant delays and, 'The rough and intersected character of the ground which made deployment impossible until it was too late'.[234] He also knew that once he ordered the deployment, control would initially be lost. He thus attempted to get as close to the Boers, and the correct position as possible, before initiating deployment. At most, he could be accused of being overly cautious, yet he knew the complexities and difficulties of an attack at dawn, in particular after a night march such as the one the Brigade experienced. Had he deployed earlier, his attack would have failed. Shot dead, at the head of his Brigade, Wauchope fell, facing the Boers.

For the Boers at Magersfontein, when seeing the British force retire to Modder River, there was much jubilation.

> If the British had held their ground, it would have had a very depressing effect. Now the burghers are told and harangued they have a glorious victory, have killed five thousand of the enemy, they are the 'chosen people,' 'God is with them,' etc, etc. The war fever is stronger in this quarter than it has been since the commencement of hostilities.[235]

---

231 MMK: 7654/41a: Colonel C.M. Hore-Ruthven, A personal account of the battle of Magersfontein, 1933.

232 Amery, *Times history of the war*, p.410.

233 MMK: 7654/41a: Colonel C.M. Hore-Ruthven, A personal account of the battle of Magersfontein, 1933.

234 MMK: 7654/37A: General Sir J.S. Ewart, Unpublished Autobiography, p.460.

235 Lane, *The War Diary*, p.45.

The Boer forces prepared their three defensive clusters extremely effectively. Constructing their entrenchments and other defence works at night ensured camouflage and secrecy. Deception being an art of war, which they perfected in their preparations. Leaving nothing to chance, their three defensive clusters covered the likely attack options available to Methuen.

The Boer Generals intuitively read their enemy commander correctly, having learnt from the three prior battles, that Methuen lacked the military acumen for a war of manoeuvre. That, as before, in particular at Modder River, he would blunder forwards using the bludgeon tactics of frontal attacks. In order to concentrate his strength, he could not attack all three defensive clusters. He had to pick at least one for an initial frontal attack. That then left the Boer officers with an option of using their mobility to reinforce a threatened sector by switching forces from a non-threatened sector. These mobile reserves enabled them to plug weak points, threatened sectors and the gap between their Central and Eastern Defensive Clusters, during the actual action. Through conserving their artillery throughout the day, they saved their guns from destruction from the combined weight of the British artillery; firing only at the critical moment, to force the final outcome.

Although not present during the Magersfontein action, de la Rey combined and applied the lessons of Belmont, Graspan and Modder River, adjusting his tactics to his enemy and the terrain. Ground level defences were pivotal to the Boer victory at Magersfontein. For this he deserves the credit. Cronjé was in command during the action and, his actions and that of his forces, led to victory. However, as with Modder River, he would squander this victory through subsequent inertia and a failure of military acumen.

Furthermore, the Boer officers seized the initiative when opportunities presented themselves for independent action. Officers such as Ferreira, Diederichs, H.J. De Wet and du Plooy played key roles at decisive moments, along with many other unknown officers. Yet, fundamentally it must be remembered that the burghers fought with great determination, tenacity and courage against superior numbers of soldiers and artillery. Despite all, they prevailed, winning victory at Magersfontein, on the South African veld.

9

Magersfontein. Burying the dead

Burial parties initially set to work on 12 December 1899, and continued doing so for some years after the battle. There were a number of reasons for this. Many of the British dead were initially hastily buried and required reburial immediately after the war. The Boers, who held the ground until mid-February 1900, had more time to do a proper job.

On 13 December 1899, Ewart, by order of Methuen, rode out under a flag of truce to bury the British dead. 'They would not, naturally, allow us to approach close to their trenches, yet they supplied us with working parties, searched the ground for us in quest of bodies or any remaining wounded, and eventually listened to Doctor Robinson's services by the grave sides'[1].

It was a grim task, remembered by an unidentified Sapper of the Royal Engineers:

> The first grave we dug was about thirty feet long and three feet deep, and would you believe it? – we put fifty-three Scotsmen into it. Thirty-four of the Black Watch alone. It was something horrible, and every man of us was crying all the time we worked; and when after we placed them all in, the burial service was going on before we covered them over, three or four fainted, whilst the others cried so loudly that you could hardly hear the minister.[2]

This burial site is marked on the battlefield by a memorial, recording that Captain A.F. Lambton[3] (1st Highland Light Infantry), Captain J. Rutherford Clarke, Lieutenant W. Russell Cowie (2nd Seaforth Highlanders) and 15 men of the Highland Brigade were buried there, thus totalling 18 burials.[4] That

1 MMK: 7654/37A: General Sir J.S. Ewart, Unpublished Autobiography, pp.462–463.

2 E.M. Spiers, *Letters from Kimberley*, p.97.

3 Yet there is also evidence that Captain A.F. Lambton's body was later disinterred and reburied in Cemetery 1, in marked grave Number 1 at Doorns A, Modder River. Author's collection: Modder River, Graves of those fallen during Anglo Boer War 1899–1900–1–2, Colonel D.E. Lines of Communication, September 1902.

4 These graves were exhumed in 1962 and reburied in the West End Garden of Remembrance, Kimberley, however the original site still stands on the battlefield, marked with one monument.

'Altogether we buried 31 bodies in the course of the day including that of Captain Rutherford Clarke and Lambton of the 71st. Lambton's body was lying on the site of the first disaster to the brigade. We also identified and took particulars of 43 other bodies.'* (Author's photograph)

* MMK: 7654/37A: General Sir J.S. Ewart, Unpublished Autobiography, pp.462–463.

leaves 13 other bodies buried elsewhere on the terrain that day, presumably soldiers killed closest to the main Boer trench, as two graves were established in the area close to the trench.[5]

These 43 bodies would be buried the next day. This grave, as with all the burials by Ewart, are valuable in ascertaining, where possible, exactly where individuals and battalions were during the action. That he refers to Lambton's body lying on the site when the action first opened, it can be accepted that this burial site is in the immediate vicinity where the Highland Brigade were when fire was opened. The Black Watch had gone further ahead with Wauchope and thus were between this memorial and the Black Watch Memorial, a white marble obelisk, approximately in the centre of the Highland Brigade position, when fire opened, and 350 metres ahead.[6] The line of mimosa thorns and wire fence which delayed the dawn deployment is located 120 metres behind the burial site and monument.

Located at Latitude: 28°58'39.08"S. Longitude: 24°41'55.32"E.

5 Western Cape Archives and Records Service (KAB): GH 35: Vol 2, Reference 197. Evidence of the disturbed ground where these graves were can be seen on the battle site.

6 The night advance started in mass of quarter column with a front of about 38 metres and a length of 155 metres. However by the time they were in this vicinity the front companies of the Black Watch were ahead of the column and in the act of extending.

This burial site still stands on the battlefield,* marked by two memorials, recording that Lieutenant Colonel J. Coode, Captain W. McFarlane and Lieutenant N.G. Edwards (2nd Black Watch), Lieutenant W.B. King (1st Argyll & Sutherland Highlanders), Major G. Ray (1st Northumberland Fusiliers), and 35 NCOs and men were buried there.** This totals 40 burials, a post war error, as Ewart stated that he buried 43 bodies in this grave, and would know, for he counted the corpses. (Author's photograph)

* Located at Latitude: 28°59'0.88"S. Longitude: 24°42'11.95"E.

** These graves were exhumed in 1962 and reburied in the West End Garden of Remembrance, Kimberley, however the original site still stands on the battlefield, marked with two monuments.

Ewart returned to Magersfontein the next day to continue with this grim work, joined by Chaplain J. Robertson (Highland Brigade), Doctor Godshaw [Unknown] and Corporal A. Bettington (Cape Medical Staff Corps)[7]. These four men would not have dug the graves themselves, so black labourers did the deed. They finished, as best as possible, their horrific task as recalled by Ewart:

> We completed our sad task of identifying and burying the dead. We were all very sick, for the task of handling, in the great heat, the swollen, distorted, and rapidly

7 *The London Gazette*, 16 March 1901. Corporal A. Bettington of the Cape Mounted Rifles, attached to the Cape Medical Staff Corps, and together with Private Johnson, Argyll and Sutherland Highlanders, were instrumental in removing a wounded Highlander to safety while under heavy fire. Corporal A. Bettington was awarded the Distinguished Conduct Medal for this act of bravery. *The London Gazette*, 27 September 1901.

> decomposing bodies of our dead comrades was trying beyond all words. On the right of our position, we buried 43 bodies in one long trench, Lieutenant and Adjutant MacFarlane's remains being at the Northern end of the grave.[8]

Of interest is that Colonel Coode was killed in the opening stages of the action, so why he was buried here, and not closer to where he died, or removed to Modder River remains unknown, as too, with McFarlane and Edwards. King perished in the immediate vicinity, in combat with the Skandinaviskå-kåren. Ray served with the Mounted Infantry, also killed in the vicinity of this gravesite, while trying to rally some 'broken highlanders'.[9] The unnamed other ranks all perished in this area of Horse Artillery Hill and Scrub Ridge.[10]

While undertaking this grim task, the British burial party interacted with Boer burial parties working nearby, clearing the ridge of bodies from the Skandinaviskå-kåren and preparing their burial sites, of which there were three.[11] 'We buried the eighteen men in three graves where they had fallen and said a prayer there'.[12]

Ewart mentioned that some of the burghers listened to Chaplain Robertson's services by the grave sides. The Guards Brigade buried their own dead much further afield, out of sight given the distance, hence Ewart never commented on this.[13] However, they would have retrieved bodies of Coldstream Guardsmen in this vicinity, though closer towards Scrub Ridge.

During the battle, the Boer commandos started burying their dead at the site of their field hospital at Magersfontein Farm.[14] These casualties would have been evacuated from the Eastern Defensive Cluster (Scrub Ridge) as the field hospital was in direct line of sight, and despite the intense shellfire, accessible, unlike the main Boer trench and Magersfontein Hills. Casualties from Diederichs, De Wet and du Plooy's attack, were also evacuated. Subsequent post battle disinterment saw reinternments at this site, continuing until the 1960s when the battlefield was apparently cleared of all burgher graves. On 6 April 1931, the Boer Memorial was unveiled and later incorporated into the Burgher Monument, unveiled on 10 October 1969.[15]

---

8 MMK: 7654/37A: General Sir J.S. Ewart, Unpublished Autobiography, p.463.

9 Amery, *Times history of the war*, p.416.

10 Of interest is that a Lieutenant J.B. King was listed as being buried in Cemetery 1, in marked grave Number 11 at Doorns A, Modder River. Author's collection: Modder River, Graves of those fallen during Anglo Boer War 1899–1900–1–2, Colonel. DE Lines of Communication, September 1902. There was only one other officer with the same surname killed during the South African War and that was Captain J.B. King of Kitchener's Fighting Scouts on 8 March 1901. See: M.G. Dooner, *The Last Post*, p.204. Therefore, the possibility exists that Lt J.B. King's body was recovered off the battlefield before the British withdrawal on 12 December 1899, and that the memorials at Magersfontein Battlefield are incorrect. Although on balance it is unlikely that he was buried at Modder River, Cemetery I.

11 Bojerud, 'Scandinavian volunteers', p.171.

12 F Hale, 'The Scandinavian Corps in the Second Anglo-Boer War' *Historia, 40*, (2000), 220–236.

13 No information about these burials surfaced during the author's research, yet hopefully it will at some stage, if it exists. Presumably the Guards Brigade Major H.G. Ruggles-Brise, supervised this, immediately after the battle.

14 Latitude 28°57'19.61"S and Longitude 24°43'50.23"E.

15 Located at: Latitude 28°57'13.22"S and Longitude 24°44'3.53"E.

3rd Grenadier Guards officer's mess. Photograph taken after the Magersfontein battle in Modder River. Left side of the table standing: Captain F.EW. Hervey-Bathurst and A.H. Travers, both wounded in the Modder River battle. Seated Unknown; Major H.G. Ruggles-Brise; Major M.R. Compton-Roberts; G.C. Tygon; and G.W. Duberly.
Right side of table standing: Lord O'Hagen (died 1900); Captain G.F. Trotter; the Honourable E.H. Lygon (killed in action 1900); E.G. Spencer Churchill; and T.F. Falkner. Seated: Captain L.R. Fisher-Rowe; the Honourable B. Gordon Lennox; the Honourable Lieutenant A.V.F.V. Russell; Captain A. St Leger Glyn; and Lieutenant Colonel E.M.S. Crabbe. (With permission, McGregor Museum)

It is possible that isolated Boer graves may yet remain on the terrain. Additionally that of Agterryers, for whom there is no single identified grave, despite them being on the terrain from 5 December 1899, until Cronjé abandoned the position during February 1900, after Kimberley was relieved.[16]

The question of where the Skandinaviskå-kåren were buried needs clarification, as three memorials stand on the battlefield today commemorating this Corps.

A 1974 publication refers to the crosses being the Scandinavian burial site and a 1980 publication has them buried beneath these crosses.[17] This article states:

16 Over the last 30 years the author has seen numerous grave mounds in various areas of the battlefield.

17 Duxbury, *Magersfontein 11 December 1899*, pp.18–19.

On 25 April 1908, General Louis Botha unveiled the Scandinavian Memorial, which made of rough-hewn Swedish granite, stands on an outlying ridge North West of the main Magersfontein hills, in an area holding no connection to where the Skandinaviskå-kåren fought, died and were buried.* (McGregor Museum, with permission)

* Located at: Latitude 28°57′42.90″S and Longitude 24°41′4.99″E.

On 16 December 1927, General J.C. Smuts unveiled the twin Waldemaar crosses, approximately 230 metres North-North-West from the summit.* These crosses are widely believed to mark the Skandinaviskå-kåren graves.** These are two of the three memorials to the Skandinaviskå-kåren. (Author's photograph)

* Located at: Latitude 28°59′3.32″S and Longitude 28°59′4.39″S. Latitude 28°59′4.39″Sa and Longitude: 24°42′31.95″E.

** For the author this seemed, from the 1980s, an anomaly. Why would these be the only Boer forces graves on the battle site, given the exhumations and reburials until the 1960s? Hence a deeper look into the matter ensued.

> Twin Waldemaar crosses of reddish granite stand in the veld atop stone mounds, about 1.5 kilometres south east of the main Magersfontein Koppie. These mark the graves of the Scandinavians killed during the battle, and the approximate area where they fell. While other Boer and British dead have been exhumed for reinternment elsewhere, the Scandinavians still rest in their original graves on the battlefield.[18]

However, this is incorrect.[19]

In 1903, Major A.R. Cameron, (Military Secretary of the Cape Colony), inspected the graves at and around Modder River Station and Magersfontein. In June 1903, he submitted his report to Sir W.H. Hutchinson, Governor of the Cape Colony. [20] This report offers much insight into the burials and reburials of British dead after the battle and Cameron numbered these burial sites against a sketch he made:[21]

- Grave 1: Grave of 10 highlanders covered with limestone and surrounded by a wire fence.
- Grave 2: Grave of 15 highlanders similar to Grave 1.
- Grave 3: A fenced grave containing a number of unidentified bodies and then being burrowed into by animals.
- Grave 4: A memorial stone to Captain A.F. Lambton, Captain J. Rutherford Clarke, Lieutenant W. Russell Cowie and fifteen men of the Highland Brigade. The grave was surrounded by an iron spiked railing, lightly cemented over, with weeds growing through the cement. Cameron's report and notes on his sketch state this grave was not to be moved. This burial site is currently marked with a granite memorial erected by the SA War Graves Board in 1963. Yet there is also evidence that Captain A.F. Lambton's body was later disinterred and reburied in Cemetery 1, Grave Number 1 at Doorns A, Modder River. [22]
- Grave 5: Grave number five includes the graves of Colonel Coode, Captain and Adjutant MacFarlane and Lieutenant Edwards of the 2nd Black Watch, Lieutenant King of the 1st Argyll & Sutherland Highlanders, Major Ray of the Northumberland Fusiliers, and 35 NCO's and men. The grave was surrounded by a good stone wall, well cemented over and an admirable piece of work. Cameron recommended that this burial site should not be moved. Although the South African War Graves Board later exhumed and reburied the remains in Kimberley, the wall and its original memorial remain, thus forming a fixed reference on the terrain. As for King originally buried there, he died fighting the Scandinavians. Therefore, this burial site is directly related to the action with the Skandinaviskå-kåren.

18 F. Barbour, Magersfontein Monuments (Kimberley: Kimberley Litho, 1980), p.9.

19 As established by the author in: Benneyworth, 'SCANDINAVIA'S MAGERSFONTEIN DEAD', pp.142–147.

20 KAB: GH 35: Vols 2 and 3, Reference 197 and Reference 172.

21 KAB: GH 35: Vols 2 and 3, Reference 197 and Reference 172.

22 Author's collection: Modder River, Graves of those fallen during Anglo Boer War 1899–1900–1–2, Colonel D.E. Lines of Communication, September 1902.

- Grave 6: A wire fenced burial site stated to contain Scandinavians and disturbed by burrowing animals. No trace of this grave exists on the battlefield today.
- Grave 7: An unfenced burial site containing unknown bodies and disturbed by burrowing animals. Graves in bad repair.
- Grave 8: A simple unfenced grave.
- Grave 9: An unfenced burial site containing unknown bodies and disturbed by burrowing animals. Graves in bad repair.
- Grave 10: Was unfenced with two burgher graves, one of whom had the name Roos cut into a stone. This was Burgher J.H. Roos of the Fauresmith Commando whose knees were shot off and who bled to death under a thorn bush, as witnessed by Burgher J. van Rensburg.[23]
- Grave 11: A number of unknown bodies covered by a pile of stones and badly fenced.
- Grave 12: Was unfenced, a mere heap of stones with the name Naudé cut into a stone. Burghers B. Naudé and S. Naudé of the Hoopstad Commando are commemorated at the Magersfontein Battlefield Museum and the Burgher Monument.

Except for Graves 4 and 5 and the Guards Brigade memorial, Cameron recommended that all burial sites, as listed in his report, were to be concentrated into one:

> Big grave immediately beneath the Black Watch memorial which stands where the action commenced. So far as remains could be identified, the British would be placed at one end of the grave and the Boers on the other and they could be divided from one another by a fence should it be considered necessary. The remains will be coffined and buried deep, which will obviate the necessity of cementing over the grave. It should be surrounded by a strong, iron spiked railing.[24]

He further stated that a benefit in reducing the number of graves at Magersfontein to three was that less ground would need to be expropriated to create lengthy right of ways to access them across privately owned ground. The only right of way required would be from the 'high road to grave No 5, about 500 yards in all'.[25] He got his measurement short, as grave number five is 1,500 yards from the road. Perhaps he meant to include the figure 1 before the 500, either way grave five has never been moved, other than the human remains in the 1960s. Assuming his recommendations were carried out, then all the human remains in all the burial sites referred to were relocated to the Black Watch Memorial, in particular graves seven, eight and nine, which were in the immediate area where the Waldemaar Crosses stand.

---

23 MMK: Burgher J. van Rensburg, My Persoonlike Ondervinding Magersfontein Slag, 24 November 1949. There is only one Burgher Roos listed as killed or died of wounds on the Magersfontein Battlefield Museum Roll of Honour.

24 KAB: GH 35, Vol. 3, Reference 172.

25 KAB, GH 35, Vol. 2, Reference 197.

On 22 June 1905, Mr Westerman, contracted to move the graves, reported to Cameron that his work was finished and furnished a report. He relocated 62 bodies of Highlanders, one unknown, and possibly four Boers. The following are some of the particulars of the various graves that he moved:

- From Grave 1 he removed the remains of eight Highlanders.
- From Grave 2 he removed the remains of 15 Highlanders, some having identifying regimental numbers on the uniforms, all of the 2nd Black Watch, namely:
  - 4221. Lance Corporal John McDonald.[26]
  - 4664. Private John Ogg, listed as Missing in Action in the casualty roll.[27]
  - 4484. Private Robert Henderson.[28]
  - 5886 and 4176.
- Grave 3: eight bodies were recovered, all Highlanders based on bits of their uniforms.
- Grave 6: nine bodies were recovered, all Highlanders based on bits of their uniforms.

Westerman found graves that Cameron did not refer to in his report, and without a sketch by Westerman these are difficult to position on the terrain. Of these, were eight graves containing either one or two burials, all stated to be Highlanders. Some were marked with a wooden cross indicating R.H. (Royal Highlanders). A body in one of these single graves was a Highlander with the regimental number, 7894. The distances of these graves from Magersfontein Hill varied between 730 metres East to 2,300 metres East and near a small pan. Many of these bodies must have been located by the Boers after the British burial parties left and were buried by them, for Ewart does not mention them. Three graves near this pan may have been created after the Boers abandoned their positions and these bodies were found.

As for the removal of the Skandinaviskå-kåren graves and their reinternment at the consolidated burial site at the Black Watch memorial, additional archival evidence corroborates that this happened. On 20 April 1906, the Danish Consul wrote to Sir W.H. Hutchinson on the matter of the Scandinavian Memorial. The Consul's letter leaves no doubt as to what happened to the original burial site of the Skandinaviskå-kåren graves. The Consul reported that the friends and relatives to the fallen Scandinavians had raised funds in Denmark, Norway and Sweden.

> For the purpose of erecting a monument to their memory on the spot where these men fell to which the owner of the farm Magersfontein a Scotchman, Mr

26 Identified by the author 19 April 2021, using: TNA: WO.108/83: South African Field Force Casualty List, 1899–1902, p.53.

27 Identified by the author 19 April 2021, using: TNA: WO.108/83: South African Field Force Casualty List, 1899–1902, p.59.

28 Identified by the author 19 April 2021, using: TNA: WO.108/83: South African Field Force Casualty List, 1899–1902, p.53.

> Bissett, had given verbal permission. The necessary money was subscribed and a monument was sent out to East London, where it is now lying and storage being paid for same; as since that time that the verbal permission was given the bodies of the fallen have been removed to some ground fenced in by the Government for that purpose and the farmer refuses to let the monument be erected anywhere else. As the money was subscribed under the stipulation that the monument be erected on the spot where the fighting took place and the men actually fell, as is an old custom in the North, the Committee of the Memorial Fund have approached me to try to secure for them permission to remove the corpses of the fallen back to their original grave and erect the memorial there.[29]

The fact that the landowner verbally agreed to the monument being erected where the Scandinavians were initially buried and subsequently refused after the monument arrived in East London offers another clue. A 2016 publication states that, 'When the monument was erected it was not, as originally planned, placed on the site of the Scandinavians' graves because the owner of the land opposed this suggestion'.[30]

The hypothesis is that the farmer [Mr Bissett] initially agreed as the graves were located where, Cameron found them. He subsequently changed his mind once these graves (numbered seven, eight and nine) were exhumed and reinterred in the immediate vicinity of the Black Watch monument. Perhaps he objected to the two memorials erected virtually next to each other. That the Danish Consul states that he was approached to re-exhume the human remains and return them to their original burial site is clear on the fact that the Scandinavians were reburied as per, Cameron's recommendation, at the Black Watch memorial.

The Danish Consul arranged for Mr G. Christensen, a survivor of the Skandinaviskå-kåren to inspect the battlefield. Not only was Christensen a veteran of the battle, he assisted in burying the fallen Scandinavians immediately after the battle. The Consul reported on what Christensen reported to him, namely that,

> The bodies of the fallen Scandinavians at Magersfontein have been exhumed, and all traces of their graves have been done away with. The stones that covered their graves have been carted a distance away and strewn in a heap near a big English grave, that bears a Cross and inscription of a Lieut. Col, a Capt, an Adj. Major. Two Lieuts, and 35 Non Com. Officers and Men, who fell in action before the Boer trenches on the 11 December 1899. [This is the contemporary British Grave Site Memorial Two and the Grave Number Five in Cameron's report.] The Scandinavians fought and fell about 60 to 70 yards North East of this grave, and at that time there were no trenches. After the fight when the Scandinavians were put to rest, the above mentioned English grave was there, so Mr Christensen is quite certain about the spot, the Committee now request that the corpses of the fallen be left alone, as there is no means of identification. And they only apply for

---

29 KAB: GH 35/197: Vol. 3, Reference 172.

30 C. Gerdov, 'A Scandinavian "Magna Charta"? The Scandinavian Corps and the politics of memory in South Africa (1899–1927)', *Historia* 612 (November 2016), pp.54–78.

One of the dumping sites of the original burial site rocks and grave mound spoil. (Author's photograph)

> permission to erect the Memorial on the spot where the Scandinavians fought and fell that is 60 to 70 yards North East of the above mentioned English grave on Magersfontein.[31]

On 24 April 1906, Cameron wrote to the Army Quarter Master General in Cape Town about these graves.

> When the bodies were exhumed from the different graves on Magersfontein Battlefield, it was impossible to tell which graves contained Scandinavians and even after exhumation identification was in many cases impossible. The Scandinavians are now buried in the big grave at the foot of the Blackwatch Memorial, placed where the action commenced. The Governor is of opinion that the best place for the Scandinavian memorial would be close to the railings of the grave and from the letter it would appear that Mr. Bissett would have no objection to its erection there. Should, however the Scandinavian community be anxious to erect the memorial where the Scandinavians were originally buried it may be possible to legally expropriate a plot of ground there to Government, though it would not be a burying place. Re-exhumation is of course out of the question.[32]

A final point about Christensen's site inspection is his reference to the stones that covered the original Scandinavian graves being carted a distance away and strewn near the British grave site. A 2016 examination of Magersfontein by the author located the stones referred to exactly where Christensen described them to be. Two areas of this surface scatter include dolerite rocks

31 KAB: GH 35/197: Vol 3, Reference 172.
32 KAB: GH 35/197: Vol 3, Reference 172.

and calcrete stones which originally formed the grave mounds. A small pile of stones comprising both dolerite and calcrete is located 40 metres from the British grave at: Latitude: 28°59'2.33"S and Longitude 24°42'11.31"E. The second larger collection of stones is 70 metres from the British grave site at Latitude 28°59'3.40"S and Longitude 24°42'10.96"E.[33]

In 2018, the author located the original burial site of the Skandinaviskå-kåren.[34] Surface evidence is disturbed soil, remains of barbed wire fencing and, most importantly a circular ration tin lid, probably a condensed milk tin. Right in the centre of the lid is a bullet hole, made by a .455 Webley revolver bullet, suggesting a close range shot by a British officer, which hit the recipient through a pouch or haversack, in which the tin was stored. The authors' impression of this is that it was a *coup de grace* shot at a wounded Scandinavian, trying to shield his face behind a pouch or haversack.

Who fired the shot? It may have been Lieutenants King or C.M. Hore-Ruthven, yet there was at least one officer carrying a .455 Webley that day.[35] Lieutenant Lang, whose father gave him this revolver before leaving for South Africa in 1899, and who stated years later, that, 'Our blood was up then. We didn't make any bones about it. We took no prisoners.[36]

Finally, it should be noted that, at the time of the erection of the twin Waldemaar Crosses, it was widely believed that they marked the site of the Skandinaviskå-kåren burial site. Correspondence between a Mr T. Ericson, interested in the maintenance of this burial site, and the Secretary of Lands, the Provincial Secretary and the Public Works Office to secure servitudes or right of ways from the British Grave number five to these twin Waldemaar Crosses refers to attempts to establish this right of way. On 1 July 1926, 'A number of Scandinavians fell and they are buried in two separate graves which are in a rather dilapidated condition.'[37] On 1 October 1927, the Secretary of Lands replied to Mr T. Ericson that:

> In order to do so he would have to make a detour around a pan which in the rainy weather is filled with water and in the dry season forms a valuable grazing ground for his stock. This new right of way would be about 900 yards [823 metres]. The graves in question are two isolated graves over which substantial monuments have been erected and they are well protected at the base with large stones.[38]

These twin crosses were therefore in position two and a half months before the unveiling ceremony by General Smuts on 16 December 1927. However, do they mark the actual grave site? The evidence uncovered and presented

33 Identified by the author on 16 March 2016.

34 As this site will be archaeologically surveyed in the near future, its location is undisclosed, at this stage, given the risk of battlefield looting.

35 The Webley Mk IV revolver rose to prominence during the South African War and, firing large .455 Webley cartridges, remains one of the most powerful top-break revolvers ever produced.

36 Author's collection: Midge Carter, 'Lieutenant Colonel B Lang, Interview: "The Boer War"', Durban (9 March 1970).

37 KAB: PAS, Vol 2/1078: Reference GX/MISC/7.

38 KAB: PAS, Vol 2/1078: Reference GX/MISC/7.

The funeral of Wauchope. Sixteen pipes played The Flowers of the Forest and Lochaber no More. From A.C.R. Carter, *The Work of War Artists in South Africa*, p.27. (London: H. Virtue and Co Ltd, 1900)

suggests not based on the inspection by Christensen and other archaeological evidence.[39]

On 12 December 1899, Wauchope was buried with full military honours in Cemetery 1, Modder River. Buried to his left in the same row were Lieutenant Ramsey, Lieutenant Colonel Downman, Lieutenant Cox, Captain Brodie, Lieutenant Colonel Goff, Captain Wingate and Lieutenant Campbell.

On 17 December 1899, Mr J.D. Logan, the owner of Matjiesfontein Village, located 236 kilometres North-East of Cape Town, arrived at Modder River camp. His Grandson Major J. Buist recounted that:

> When J.D. Logan heard of the death of Wauchope, he decided wisely, or unwisely, that it was inappropriate for this gallant, distinguished officer to be buried without due ceremony in so humble a resting place and obtained permission from Methuen, who was then chief of general staff, to exhume the body and to have it reinterred at Matjiesfontein. He also contacted Lady Wauchope in Scotland by telegraph, offering a vault at Matjiesfontein for the burial of her husband. Lady Wauchope, possibly confused by the similarity of the names Magersfontein and Matjiesfontein, is believed to have agreed to this at the time. Logan then travelled to Modder River by train himself, taking with him a handsome lead-lined coffin. He personally supervised the exhumation of Wauchope's body, which was placed

39 KAB: GH 35/197: Vol 3, Reference 172.

> in the coffin Logan had brought and put in Logan's compartment for the journey to Matjiesfontein.[40]

The site is marked with an impressive memorial on a hillside overlooking the cemetery, paid for by Logan.[41]

Nevertheless, one of Wauchope's closest comrades personally 'repelled this decision, for I feel sure that poor Andy would have preferred that his remains should continue to rest at Modder River alongside so many of his gallant comrades'.[42]

40 D. Allen, *Empire, War & Cricket in South Africa Logan of Matjiesfontein* (Cape Town: Zebra Press, 2015), pp.214–215.

41 Located at: Latitude 33°14'30.38"S and Longitude 20°28'42.13"E.

42 MMK: 7654/37A: General Sir J.S. Ewart, Unpublished Autobiography, p.464.

10

Monuments, Memorials, and Graves

After the war various monuments and grave memorials were erected at Magersfontein.

As for the human remains, all identifiable burial sites on the battlefield were exhumed over the subsequent six decades after the battle, and reinterred at two places. During 1961–1963 a misguided policy by the British Forces Committee resulted in the British graves at Magersfontein and on other battlefields in the Kimberley vicinity being exhumed and relocated to a newly established Garden of Remembrance in the West End Cemetery, Kimberley.[1]

The Boer graves fell under the care of the Burgergrafte Komitee and they relocated their graves to the Magersfontein Burgher Monument.

Records archived with the South African Heritage Resources Agency (SAHRA) identified one reason why the graves were moved. The members of the British Forces Committee decided to reinter the graves from the battlefields because in their view, 'the graves in their present position could not be properly cared for and maintained'.[2] This committee also decided that 'the remains from the historical battlefields, such as Magersfontein, Modder River, Belmont and Graspan, should be buried separately so that these graves can be readily identifiable in the new Garden of Remembrance'[3] It was agreed that markers be erected at all the sites where exhumations took place, recording the particulars of those soldiers originally buried there.

This never happened. Archaeologists were not present and the exhumations poorly coordinated, permanently damaging the military heritage record. Original hand engraved headstones deemed to have no historical value were smashed or buried in the original graves. Some graves were never exhumed, yet their memorials and grave markers removed. In certain cases, mass graves were partially removed, as exposed skeletal remains on some of the

1 Located at Latitude 28°44'4.89" S: Longitude: 24°44'10.24" E.
2 South African Heritage Resources Agency (SAHRA), Report by Lieutenant Colonel AJ Kenyon; MC and Mr AC Long, 1962.
3 South African Heritage Resources Agency (SAHRA), Report by Lieutenant Colonel A.J. Kenyon; M.C. and Mr A.C. Long, 1962.

The Highland Regiments Memorial, a granite Celtic cross, was unveiled by Lord Milner, on 11 December 1902, on the highest point of the Magersfontein hills.* Its inscription reads: Erected by Scots the world over in memory of the officers and men of the Highland Regiments who fell at Magersfontein 11th December 1899. Scotland is poorer in men but richer in heroes. (McGregor Museum, with permission)

* Located at: Latitude 28°58′6.03″S and Longitude: 24°41′4.99″E.

The Guards Brigade Memorial is a white marble cross erected at the approximate centre of that Brigade during the action, on the Brigades' burial site.* (Author's photograph)

* The memorial was paid for by Colonel E.M.S. Crabbe, with assistance from Lieutenant A.V.F.V. Russell. See: Russell, *Letters from South Africa*, pp.220–221.

Other solitary graves have been identified since the 1980s, for example that of Lance Corporal W. Cooksey, 3rd Grenadier Guards. In this instance, in early 1980, the farmer's son opened the grave without legal authority and removed artefacts. Consequently, the grave was archaeologically excavated by the McGregor Museum and the human remains identified through a regimental number embossed on a spoon and a regimental belt buckle. Interestingly, he had 81 Mark II .303 ball ammunition and 45 Mark IV soft nosed (dum-dum) rounds on him, when killed in action.[*] (McGregor Museum, with permission)

* MMK: Military History Collection: Report on W Cooksey, 1980.

sites still testify.[4] In 1985, tidying up was finally completed, 22 years after the process started. Mr A.C. Long, representing the British Forces Committee at that time, recorded that 'what there is to show for it is just a disgrace'.[5]

Mr R.E. Stevenson added:

> What they have done at Kimberley shocks me. All the graves at the famous battlefields in the vicinity have been rifled and the pathetic remains carted to Kimberley. Here there is an imitation of the gardens found in World Wars I and II areas; but conditions were entirely different there – the graves could not have been retained scattered all over the densely populated and heavily cultivated areas. In any event World War I gardens are hardly visited except on very special

---

4 As observed by the author at many of the original burial sites across South Africa, including the Guards Brigade memorial at Belmont farm.

5 SAHRA: WG/39: Volume 4, Letter from A.C. Long to Secretary British Forces Committee, 5 May 1974.

> occasion. I had relations buried at Magersfontein and Belmont. I would never have consented to their removal.[6]

Records reflect that certain British regiments requested that the British Forces Committee to stop their policy of exhumations, after hearing what was happening.[7] At the Kimberley Garden of Remembrance, the British forces' graves were not reinterred into separate areas as originally intended by the British Forces Committee in 1962. They were buried in one large pit which was grassed over. The individual headstones that survived the journey were aesthetically arranged on the lawn and are not indicative of the individual burial sites. In the centre of the garden, in grand military style, stands an imposing granite memorial, listing the names of the British dead, reinterred at this site.

---

6 SAHRA: WG/39: R.E. Stevenson, included in: Notes by G.E. Brink, 12 February 1967.

7 SAHRA: WG/39: Letter from the Highland Colonels, 1967.

11

Conclusion: the aftermath

The trilogy of British defeats, known as Black Week, led to a massive reorganisation of the South African Field Force. These military failures jolted the War Office and the empire's citizenry into a state of frenzied shock. Field Marshal Lord Roberts was immediately ordered to replace Buller and, upon arrival in South Africa on 10 January 1900, set to fulfilling the original objectives of the War Office plan. The lifting of the Kimberley Siege formed his secondary objective simultaneous to that of Ladysmith and the Relief of Mafeking his third. His second in command was Lord Kitchener.

Roberts set to tilting the strategic advantage away from the Republican forces. The key to this was creating room for manoeuvre on the military landscape. Cronjé rested on his laurels after his Magersfontein victory. He remained stubbornly convinced that the next attempt to relieve Kimberley would involve another attack against Magersfontein. His forces strengthened their defences yet became complacent. In the main Boer laager, inertia prevailed:

Lord Roberts in his study in Bloemfontein, shortly after capturing the city. From M Menpes, *War Impressions Being A Record In Colour* (London: Adam & Charles Black, 1901)

> It is quite impossible to imagine, or realise, that one is at the seat of war. The camps are dotted in groups of tents down the river for the space of ten miles. The laager is a rustic assemblage of wagons and tents, about twenty miles beyond the range of the enemy's biggest cannon, where we sit and smoke and play concertina all day long.[1]

For this they paid a bitter price.

On 15 February 1900, Roberts' Cavalry Division, commanded by Major General French, outflanked Magersfontein to the East and lifted the Siege of Kimberley. His infantry captured Jacobsdal, all movements previously advocated by Wauchope and others. This bold strike forced Cronjé to abandon his Magersfontein positions and attempt to withdraw to Bloemfontein.

However, Cronjé's forces were doggedly pursued by the 6th Infantry Division, kept barely at bay by the Boer rearguard. The Cavalry Division left Kimberley and after some more hard riding, closed the trap, arriving just ahead of Cronjé's forces at Paardeberg Drift. Roberts and Kitchener's forces surrounded the Boer force, heralding one of the largest conventional battles of the war, fought during 17–27 February 1900. The Boers capitulated on Majuba Day, sending a shock through the Republics. Cronjé, much like Methuen, displayed his lack of military acumen, indeed military incompetence, in a war of manoeuvre.

> One of the most interesting men I talked to was Major Albrecht. The Prussian artilleryman. He talked in a very open manner of General Cronje, whose conduct at Paardeberg he said was bad; in fact, the only excuse he could find for Cronje was that he must have lost his head. Many and many a time he and other officers went to General Cronje and begged him on their knees to retire from his position; but Cronje only scoffed at them, repulsing them in an almost brutal way, saying that they were talking nonsense. The English could not surround them, they would never travel so far from the railway, and he was not going to move for anyone. This obstinacy on the part of the Boer General seemed to impress everyone. I have often heard it said that, although General Cronje was a good defender of koppies, he was no good in the open.[2]

The British advance on Bloemfontein resumed and the Boer front crumbled, first at Poplar Grove on 7 March 1900. On 10 March 1900, despite determined resistance by De la Rey's forces at Driefontein, the commandos were forced from their positions at bayonet point. In Natal, Buller broke through the Boer lines at the Tugela Heights and lifted the Siege of Ladysmith on 28 February 1900. On 13 March 1900, Roberts's military steamroller captured the Orange Free State capital, thus ending the Western Campaign.[3]

---

1 Cleaver, *A Young South African*, pp.34–35.

2 M. Menpes, *War Impressions Being A Record in Colour* (London: Adam & Charles Black, 1901), pp.215–216.

3 Anglo Boer War Museum, 'Introduction to the war: Second British offensive', < https://www.wmbr.org. za/view.asp?pg=research&pgsub=intro1&pgsub1=5&head1=Introduction%20to%20the%20War>, accessed 22 Apr. 2020.

Two burghers with their makeshift shelter at Magersfontein. (McGregor Museum, with permission)

Magersfontein looking across the Central Defensive Cluster from its far Western end, where the Scandinavian Memorial stands. The white sandbags were added after the battle. (McGregor Museum, with permission)

This unique photograph depicts Cronjé surrendering to Lord Roberts. It is the only known photograph showing them shaking hands and conversing, during the act of surrender. To their right, a highlander marks time. (Author's collection)

Albrecht and Cronjé after surrender at Paardeberg. From M Menpes, *War Impressions Being A Record In Colour.* (London: Adam & Charles Black, 1901)

The final attack at bayonet point at Driefontein by an eyewitness artist. Note the soldier on the far right laying and firing and whose trousers were cut back to shorts. Most of the troops' clothing was in tatters when the army seized Bloemfontein. (Author's collection)

Whilst the Western Campaign achieved the British army's immediate objectives, in terms of pre-war strategic thinking, the effects of the Campaign lasted far beyond its operational arena, and determined military policy throughout the war. For the Boers, their pursuit of siege tactics proved ineffective and their use of conventional tactics against numerically superior forces, failed to stem the tide of invasion. This triggered a switch in strategy and tactics by Boer officers such as Generals C. R. de Wet and de la Rey, who experienced the Western Campaign first hand, and in de Wet's experience, the opening stages of the Natal campaign. These Generals later became renowned guerrilla fighters during the post conventional phase of the war, eluding capture and retaining some control over the military landscape, until hostilities ceased.

On 3 May 1900, Roberts' army struck north for the Transvaal, crossing the Vaal River two weeks later. Brushing aside the Boer conventional forces, the British troops seized Johannesburg on 31 May 1900, and occupied Pretoria on 5 June 1900.[4] Having captured the capital cities and Rand gold mines, Roberts initially believed that he could pacify the civilian population. Consequently, he issued proclamations promising British protection for those burghers and their families who desisted from further military action, handed in their weapons and signed an oath of neutrality. He became used to easy victories during his invasion of the Republics and was thus ill prepared for the subsequent guerrilla war which exploded along his rear logistic routes after the fall of Pretoria.

Yet his fundamental flaw was a failure to wrest control of the rural landscape from the Boer forces. Although the British invasion represented a steamroller flattening the opposition, his army flattened little apart from the roads, maize fields and river crossings. The commandos merely regrouped on his flanks, rear and front, attacking his troops from whichever position suited them.

The railway infrastructure, its bridges, track, trains, and telegraph lines all formed primary targets. Hit-and-run attacks against convoys and the capturing of isolated British garrisons further enabled their resupply of munitions and weapons. The commandos' support and supply bases were provided by civilians residing on farms and in small towns, unoccupied by British troops.[5] Consequently, the British army found itself chasing its proverbial tail in search of a conventional opponent, yet the Boers merely melted away into a landscape which proved capable of swallowing up British troops in ever-increasing numbers, with decreasing results to show for this.

The commandos also attacked garrisons guarding Vredefort Road, Honingspruit and Serfontein stations and sabotaged numerous railway bridges, culverts and telegraph lines located along the Vereeniging/

---

4 War Museum of the Boer Republics: "Introduction to the war The mobile war begins" (available at https://www.wmbr.org. za/view.asp?pg=research&pgsub=intro1&pgsub1=6&head1=Introduction%20to%20the%20War, as assessed on 22 April 2020).

5 J. Hattingh, 'The British blockhouse system', in F. Pretorius, E. (ed), Scorched Earth (Cape Town: Tafelberg, 2017), pp.218–220.

General de Wet ignited this new type of war on 7 June 1900. His commandos attacked and captured British supply dumps at Roodewal (Rooiwal) and Rhenoster River, inflicting many casualties on the infantry guarding these positions. This photograph depicts a heavily armed burgher leading a British soldier into captivity. The burgher is carrying the soldiers'.303 rifle and has opened the bolt to render it safe. Behind them a looting frenzy was underway. (Author's collection)

Kroonstad railway line.[6] This isolated Roberts from his southern army and the rear supply bases and cut his communications to Britain.

Faced with an escalating guerrilla war, he retaliated, striking at the Republican's Achilles' heel. In instituting a scorched earth policy, he targeted civilians deemed to be assisting the commandos. Targets were civilians residing close to points along the railway infrastructure that were attacked. Retaliation saw the destruction of their homesteads, most either dynamited or burnt. However, these measures failed to halt escalating Boer military activity.

Roberts was not the first British commander to follow such a path of action, for his tactics were identical to those first used in South Africa by Methuen in the Ramdam area of the Orange Free State Republic. During January 1900, on the pretext that several Boer farms positioned along his right flank formed supply bases for the commandos, Methuen ordered their destruction. Dynamited and burnt, this strike set the precedent for methodologies synonymous with the South African War.[7] From June 1900, farm burning became widespread British military practice, extending into

6 NA: Lord Roberts Papers, Various despatches detailing the numerous Boer attacks on the lines of communication, Volume 6.

7 These homesteads were in all likelihood used by the Boer forces as supply bases for at least one of them was owned by Kommandant D. Lubbe of the Jacobsdal Commando which was

Scorched earth. A Boer family watch their home burn, before being led into captivity inside a concentration camp. (War Museum of the Boer Republics, with permission)

all areas adjacent to the railway infrastructure. British column commanders in many instances interpreted their orders more widely than the narrow definition of civilian collaboration and destroyed Boer properties regardless of whether these were located near the scene of the Boer strikes or not.

In one respect, this indiscriminate arson has its roots in the Boers forces' earlier actions in the opening stages of the war. This involved the expulsion of civilians from the South African Republic at the outbreak of the war, causing destitution and bitterness; shelling civilians in Kimberley, Beaconsfield, Ladysmith and Mafeking as opposed to military targets; and, during the earlier occupation of British territories, mass scale looting and destruction of property.

Total War – 1900–1902. Seizing the Landscape

The war then immediately entered a more brutal phase, leaving its mark on South African society; scars which still exist today. Kitchener realised that to crush ongoing Boer resistance, it was fundamental to gain total control of the rural landscape, as this was crucial to winning the war.

Consequently, he immediately Roberts's retaliatory tactics by applying a systematic scorched earth policy throughout the annexed Boer Republics.

---

then deployed with General P.A. Cronjé's forces at Magersfontein. Kommandant D. Lubbe fought at Belmont and was severely wounded during the Graspan action

This was supported with a military strategy similar to that used by General V. Weyler during the Cuban War of 1868–1878 and again during the insurrection of 1895–1898 when General V. Weyler applied the Reconcentrado system.[8] The aim was to literally grind down the Boer commandos, and scour the landscape and destroy all life sustaining means. In Army Circular 29, Kitchener spelled out in no uncertain terms how he intended to claim ownership of the terrain.

In November 1900, Lord Kitchener succeeded Lord Roberts as Commander in Chief of the South African Field Force. (War Museum of the Boer Republics, with permission)

> Of the various methods suggested for the accomplishment of this object, one that has been strongly recommended, and has lately been successfully tried on a small scale, is the removal of all men, women and children and natives from the districts which the enemy persistently occupy. This course has been pointed out as the most effective method of limiting the endurance of the Guerrillas.[9]

Unlike Roberts' retaliatory strikes, Kitchener implemented a three-pronged approach to achieve this end, pursuing this with devastating efficiency. The first involved fencing the landscape to create military paddocks, achieved by the erection of some 8,000 fortifications (blockhouses) along the railway infrastructure and interlinking these with barbed wire entanglements. Once this logistics artery was secured, the blockhouse lines were then extended across the countryside, thus closing off a once porous operational terrain for the commandos. This military grid reduced the commando's mobility and operational space; the control of landscape being crucial to the outcome of military operations.

Then the civilian population experienced the full brunt of this strategy, known as Total War. Forcibly removed from their farms and towns to deny the commandos shelter, rationing and intelligence gathering networks, their homes, kraals and crops were burnt and livestock seized or destroyed. A number of towns suffered a similar fate, being either totally or partially destroyed.[10] This Total War strategy shattered the rural economy, resulting in a humanitarian crisis.

Captured civilians were interned in military managed camps known initially as refugee camps, and later as concentration camps. At the time, the

8 B. Nasson & A.M. Grundlingh (eds), *The War at Home* (Cape Town: Tafelberg, 2013), pp.11–12.

9 NA, Pretoria, Military Governor Pretoria (MGP), Vol. 258, Reference 21/12/1900: Army Circular 29, p.17.

10 Bluebook: Cd 324. Return on buildings burnt in each month, June 1900 to January 1901, including farm buildings, mills, cottages and hovels, London: HMSO, 1901).

Boer camps were known as Burgher Refugee camps, and in the case of black civilians, Native Refugee Camps.[11]

British policy dictated that black civilians were not rationed nor provided with adequate medical support and materials with which to build shelters, the aim being to reduce the financial cost of the war. This policy further coerced black civilians to provide labour in exchange for food, in line with colonial military policy of the time. Namely, doing the bare minimum for enemy civilians who were to be managed (or mismanaged) along the basis of 'let die'.[12] An estimated 27,927 Boer and 14,154 black civilians succumbed to infectious diseases, inadequate rationing, and medical neglect.[13] However, the figure for deaths within the black camps was higher; the author estimates this to exceed 30,000 people.[14]

A key objective for the alliance between the British political, military, and international capitalists was restoring economic activity through increasing gold, coal, and diamond mining output. On 4 May 1901, the first gold mine reopened in Johannesburg, the opening ceremony attended by Kitchener.[15] During May 1901, the military and Kimberley diamond mining industry finalised arrangements to increase diamond mining operations by coercing labour through the 'no work no food' policy. Internees refusing to work or cooperate were to starve.

Similar discussions occurred between the military and the owners of the Vereeniging coal mines.

By July 1901, the Transvaal camps were brought under the military control of the newly formed Native Refugee Department and by 1 August 1901, the Orange Free State camps followed.[16] This Department fell under direct British military command, with Kitchener as its ultimate head. It controlled all black civilian refugees, in order to underwrite the British war effort, reduce the financial cost of the war while redirecting labour to the British army and the mines. Women, children, and elderly men inside these camps worked as forced wartime agricultural labourers, growing vegetables for the military. Non-compliance led to the immediate suspension of rations.

---

11 J.S. Mohlamme, 'African refugee camps in the Boer Republics', in F. Pretorius, (ed), *Scorched Earth* (Cape Town: Tafelberg, 2017), p.112.

12 R. Chickering, 'Total war: The use and abuse of a concept', in M.F. Boemke, R. Chickering, S. Forster (eds), Anticipating Total War: The American and German experiences 1871–1914 (Washington/Cambridge, German Historical Institute, Cambridge University Press, 1994), pp.13–28.

13 P. Warwick, *Black People and the South African War 1899–1902* (Johannesburg: Ravan Press Pty Ltd, 1983), p.145.

14 G. Benneyworth, 'Traces of forced labour: A history of black civilians in British concentration camps during the South African War, 1899–1902' (PhD, UWC, 2017), p.23 <http://etd.uwc.ac.za/xmlui/ handle/11394/5466>, accessed 22 Apr. 2020; G. Benneyworth, 'Land, labour, war and displacement: A history of four black concentration camps in the South African War (1899–1902)', Historia, 64/2 (2019), 14–15, DOI 10.17159/2309-8392/2019/v64n2a1

15 H.W. Wilson, *After Pretoria: The Guerrilla War* (London: The Amalgamated Press Ltd, 1902), vol. 2, p.629.

16 G. Benneyworth, 'A case study of four South African War (1899-1902) Black concentration camps', New Contree, 84 (2020), 84.

Medical inspection inside a black forced labour camp, Orange River Colony, 1901. (National Museum of Military History, with permission)

These wartime forced labourers were to work or starve.[17] The Native Refugee Department also functioned as a labour reserve for the British army.[18]

December 1901 saw over 6,000 workers sent to the army as labour, while 13,000 camp internees were in military employ.[19] Men working on the mines or with the military had the cost of feeding their families deducted from their salaries. This employment was an obvious choice; rations received and cash wages enabled food purchases with which to save their lives and those of their families. The rationale being that the camps were to cost little or nothing at all, while functioning on the basis of 'let die'.[20]

The black concentration camps played an important role in fragmenting the operational terrain for the Boer commandos. Their placement along the railway line resulted in the line being less porous for the commandos. The establishment of these camps along the central line between Bloemfontein and Pretoria, the eastern line between Pretoria and Volksrust and the western line between Mafeking and Orange River Station interned some 115,700 people by May 1902. They also incorporated many thousands of hectares

17 Nasson & Grundligh, *The War at Home* (Cape Town: Tafelberg, 2013), p.176.

18 NA, Transvaal Administration Reports, Final Report, 1901, and NA, Superintendent Refugee Camps (SRC), Vol. 10, p.3422, 1 July 1901.

19 FSA, Chief Staff Officer (CSO), Vol. 86, Reference 358/02: Colonel De Lotbiniere to Major H.J. Goold-Adams, 1902.

20 NA, MGP, Vol. 245, 27 May 1901.

under agriculture, which effectively fragmented the operational terrain of the Boer Republics.

If one takes into account the camps and the presence of these internees on the military landscape, it is apparent that they augmented the blockhouse lines by making it increasingly difficult for the commandos to cross the railway lines and manoeuvre their forces. They had, in effect, unwittingly become the eyes and ears of the British army, forming an early warning system along the military's primary logistic artery, the railway line. Thus the camps served another purpose, one that escapes contemporary interpretations of this system, namely, that they acted as stopper groups for the British army.

Although the intensity of this phase of the war occurred primarily in the former Boer Republics,[21] the early battle terrain of the Western Campaign also shared this experience. Concentration camps for both Boer and black civilians opened at Orange River Station and Kimberley, with two black concentration camps near Kimberley and the western railway forming part of the western blockhouse anvil. These black camps were later broken up and the internees railed north to a black concentration camp near Dry Harts Siding, located 162 kilometres North of Kimberley. Between November 1901 and February 1902, Dry Harts camp experienced the highest death rate out of all the black concentration camps set up during the war and in those run by the Native Refugees Department.[22]

The final piece of the strategy was inserting British mobile columns into the countryside to hunt down and break apart the Boer fighting formations and to drive the commandos onto the blockhouse lines. These lines formed, for the British forces, both a static trap and anvil, upon which the brutal process of smashing apart the commando fighting formations could be finalised. These tactics, combined with the British military's arming and deploying sectors of the black population against the commandos, eventually forced Republican capitulation on 31 May 1902.

As a pall of smoke settled over the Republican landscape, it cast a shadow over subsequent interpretations of the war. The experience of Total War later shaped South African society, throughout the 20th century. A driving force, for the creation and establishment of an Afrikaner nationalist ideology, namely apartheid; arising as a Phoenix, from the ashes of a devastated landscape.

Indeed, the legacy of Total War still haunts South Africa today.

---

21 Some commando groups did 'invade' the Cape and Natal Colonies but the author is of the opinion that this was due to these forces running out of operational terrain and supplies, due to the impact of Kitchener's various strategies in the Orange Free State and Transvaal during this phase of the war.

22 For further information on these camps see the author's PhD, Traces of forced labour–a history of black civilians in British concentration camps during the South African War, 1899–1902, available at: http://etd.uwc.ac.za/xmlui/handle/11394/5466

Bibliography

Archives

Africana Library, Kimberley, South Africa

Africana, Kimberley Corporation Mayors Minute, Municipal Year ending 31 December 1899

Free State Archives, Bloemfontein, South Africa

Chief Staff Officer (CSO), Vol. 86, Reference 358/02: Colonel De Lotbiniere to Major H.J. Goold-Adams, 1902

McGregor Museum, Kimberley, South Africa

Military History Collection, 1st Division Diary: 13 November 1899

7654//39a: TM Berkley, A pencilled sketch of Magersfontein giving Boer and British positions

7654/7: Ernest T. Brown of the 2nd Black Watch

Sir R Buller, Correspondence to Lord PS Methuen, 9 November 1899

Military History Collection: Lieutenant M Bullock, B Company 2nd Black Watch

7654/134: Lieutenant Colonel CH Burtchaell, 1912, Journal of the Royal Army Medical Corps, United Services Medical Society, Volume XVIII

7654/264: Lieutenant Colonel A. Codrington, Unpublished Diary, 1905

7654/182c: Letter by Major General Sir Reginald Pole-Carew, Modder River, 2 December 1899

7654/183: Notes of conversation with Major General Sir Reginald Pole-Carew on 25th February 1903

7654/189: Letter by Major General Sir Reginald Pole-Carew to one of his officers, 16 January 1903

Report on W. Cooksey, 1980

7654/22: C.E. Stewart: an account of what occurred on 10 & 11 December 1899

7654/30: Extract of C.E. Stewart's Boer War diary – an account of the battle of Magersfontein and of Boer and British casualties

2589: Mr W.D. Fynn's Reminiscences, unpublished manuscript, 16 April 1951

7654/291: H.G. Chandos Pole Gell, 2nd Battalion Coldstream Guards, Unpublished Diary

7654/7B: Brigadier General H.R. Kelham, The First Battalion HLI I South Africa 1899–1901

Kimberley Meteorological Report, November 1899

Methuen, 'Diary Of War'

7654/194 b: 'Methuen', 26 November 1899

Military History Collection, Letter from Methuen to Buller, 2 December 1899, 25 December 1899

Military History Collection: P.S. Methuen, Diary of War, 1899, Unpublished Manuscript
7654/194 a: P.S. Methuen, 1899, Letter to Wife, Unpublished Manuscript
7654/194 a: PS Methuen, Letter to Wife, 18–24 November 1899
7654/194 b: PS Methuen, Letter to Wife, 26 November 1899
Report on W. Cooksey, 1980
7654/12a: Sergeant W. du Plessis
Burgher J. van Rensburg, My Persoonlike Ondervinding Magersfontein Slag, 24 November 1949
7654/24: General J. de la Rey, Unpublished Manuscript
7654/41a: Colonel C.M. Hore-Ruthven, A personal account of the battle of Magersfontein, 1933
7654/31: Sergeant Sackett, G Company 2nd Black Watch, Unpublished Diary
104/87: Staatscourant ZA Republiek, Woensdag, 17 Januarie 1900
Military History Collection: A.C. Schulenburg, *My Ondervindinge In Die Boere-Oorlog*, Unpublished Diary
7654/12c: Unnamed Witness Account. The battlefield at the foot of the ridge on Magersfontein
on the 11 December 1899.
7654/4: Lieutenant C. West, Account of the Battle of Magersfontein

Military Despatches

Babington, J.M., Major General, Despatch on the Magersfontein Action, 13 December 1899
Buller, Redvers, General Sir, 1899: Confidential Despatch to Under Secretary of State for War, Cape Town., National Archives of South Africa, Notes from Micro – Film No. A. 355 W.O. Box 32, 851, File 196.
Buller, Redvers, General Sir, 1904: *Evidence of General The Right Hon. Sir Redvers Buller Taken Before The Royal Commission on the War in South Africa*, London: Longmans Green and Co.
Colvile, H.E., Major General Sir, 1899: Despatch of the Belmont Action, 26 November 1899 as reproduced in *The True History of the War Part II* (London: Harrison & Sons, London, 1902)
Major General Colvile, Magersfontein Despatch, 12 December 1899
Crabbe, F.M.S., Colonel, 1903: Evidence and Statements as reproduced in Minutes of Evidence, Royal Commission on the War in South Africa (Unpublished Paper, London: Wyman and Sons Ltd.) vol. 2
Fetherstonhaugh, Major General, 1899: Despatch of the Belmont Action, 26 November 1899 as reproduced in *The True History of the War Part II* (London: Harrison & Sons, 1902)
Gough, 1899: Despatch of the Reconnaissance to Belmont, 11 November 1899, unpublished manuscript, PRO WO 32/7884, London
Methuen, P.S., Lord, 1899: Despatch of the Belmont Action, 26 November 1899 as reproduced in *The True History of the War Part II* (London: Harrison & Sons, 1902)
Methuen, P.S., Lord, Unpublished Despatch on the Magersfontein Action, 13 December 1899
Prothero, R., Captain, Despatch of the Belmont and Graspan Actions, 4 December 1899 as reproduced in *The True History of the War Part II* (London: Harrison & Sons, 1902)
Wauchope, A.G., Major General, Report called for in regard to the attack on Enslin, 7th December 1899

National Archives of South Africa, Pretoria

Notes from Micro Film No. A. 355 W.O. Box 32 / 851, File 196: Confidential – General Redvers Buller to Under Secretary of State for War, Cape Town, November 1899

Lord Roberts Papers, Various despatches detailing the numerous Boer attacks on the lines of communication, Volume 6
Pretoria, Military Governor Pretoria (MGP), Vol. 258, Reference 21/12/1900: Army Circular 29, p.17
Superintendent Refugee Camps (SRC), Vol 10.
Transvaal Administration Reports, Final Report, 1901

National Archives United Kingdom
WO132/16: Major General J.M. Babington, Despatch on the Magersfontein Action, 13 December 1899
WO 132/15: Major General H.E. Colvile, Despatch to CSO 1st Division, 30 November 1899
WO 32/7884: Lieutenant Colonel G.H. Gough, Despatch of Reconnaissance to Belmont, 11 November 1899
WO132/16: Lieutenant Colonel F.H. Hall, Despatch on the Magersfontein Action, 13 December 1899
WO132/16: Lieutenant Colonel J.W. Hughes-Hallet, Despatch on the Magersfontein Action, 13 December 1899
WO/32/7891: J. Jeppe, Captured Diary
WO132/15: Methuen-Buller, 2 December 1899.
WO 132/15: Methuen Despatch on the operations at Modder River
WO132/16: Lord P.S. Methuen Unpublished Despatch on the Magersfontein Action, 13 December 1899
War Office Library, London: Secret South Africa Despatches
WO.108/83: South African Field Force Casualty List, 1899–1902

South African Library, Cape Town
Microfilm 75/12: B.J. Bridges
OCLC Number:101723531: J.A. Glegg Collection
A 355 31 GRE: Staff Diary of the Guards Brigade, Brigade Orders, Belmont Farm, 22 November 1899
A 355 31GRE: Staff Diary of the Guards Brigade, 1st Division, South African Field Force, 1st Division Orders, 1899
AZF. 1991-15: Copy of Kommandant P.T. Van der Merwe War Telegram, 11 November 1899

Newspapers and periodicals

Black and White Budget, Volumes 1–3 (1900)
Illustrated London News
Morning Post
Penny Illustrated
Standard and Diggers News
The Cape Times
The London Gazette
The London Gazette, 27 September 1901

Private collections

Dr Garth Benneyworth Collection
Boer Shelling, Belmont, Heliograph message, 22 November 1899
General J.H. de la Rey, War Telegram, 25 November 1899.

General J.H. de la Rey, War Telegram, 26 November 1899
General J.H. de la Rey, War Telegram, 27 November 1899.
General Prinsloo, War Telegram, 23 November 1899
Imaged of the Boer farmhouse defending the Riet River crossing
Lieutenant Colonel B. Lang, Interview, London, 1970
Lieutenant F. Tait, Unpublished Diary, copy of a portion of the diary
Magersfontein Battlefield Museum, Roll of Honour, 1999
Modder River, Graves of those fallen during Anglo Boer War 1899–1900–1–2, Colonel. DE Lines of Communication, September 1902
Padre Eustace St Claire Hill: Unpublished Diary, 1899
Report by Lt Colonel A.J. Kenyon and Mr A.C. Long on South African War Graves situated along the railway line from Orange River Station to Magersfontein, 17 October 1962.
Sapper Charles Gwilliam, 17 Field Company Royal Engineers, Letter to his Mother from Station Hospital Wynberg, 4 December 1899
War with the Boers. Photocopy of Modder River battle map supplied the to the author by Major M. Everit of the South Wales Borderers Museum, Brecon, 2001

Dr Arnold van Dyk Collection, Bloemfontein
Telegrams and letters to J. van Tonder's father

Publications

"One of Them", *The 85th Kings Light Infantry* (London: Spottiswoode & Co., 1913)
Allen, D., *Empire, War & Cricket in South Africa Logan of Matjiesfontein* (Cape Town: Zebra Press, 2015)
Amery, L.S., *The Times History of the War in South Africa 1899–1902*, (1900–1909), vols 1–6
Anglesey, The Marquess of, *A History of the British Cavalry* (London: Secker & Warburg, 1986), vol. 4
Barthorp, M., *The Northamptonshire Regiment* (London: Leo Cooper Ltd, 1974)
Beet, A.J., and Harris, C.B., Kimberley under Siege, *Kimberley, Diamond Fields Advertiser*, 1950
Benneyworth, G., 'Scandinavia's Magersfontein Dead – Their Final Resting Place?', *South African Archaeological Bulletin* 72 (2017), pp.142–147
Bojerud, S., 'Scandinavian volunteers in the Anglo Boer War, 1899–1902', *Military History Journal* 14 (2009), pp.169–171
Breytenbach, J.H., *Die Geskiedenis van die Tweede Vryheidsoorlog, Vol. I* (Pretoria: Die Staatsdrukker, 1978)
Breytenbach, J.H., *Die Geskiedenis van die Tweede Vryheidsoorlog, Vol. II* (Pretoria: Die Staatsdrukker, 1978)
Buller, Redvers, As quoted in: Maurice, *History of the War in South Africa 1899–1902* (London: Hurst and Blackett Limited, 1906) vol. 1
Buller, Redvers, *Evidence of General The Right Hon. Sir Redvers Buller Taken Before The Royal Commission on the War in South Africa* (London: Longmans Green and Co., 1904)
Chickering, R., 'Total war: The use and abuse of a concept', in M.F. Boemke, R. Chickering & S. Forster (eds), Anticipating total war: The American and German experiences 1871–1914. (Washington/Cambridge: German Historical Institute, Cambridge University Press, 1994)
Cleaver, M., *A Young South African A Memoir of Ferrar Reginald Mostyn Cleaver Advocate and Veldcornet* (Johannesburg: WE Hortor & Co. Ltd, 1913)
Colvile, H.E., *The Work of the Ninth Division* (London: Edward Arnold, 1901)

Colvin, F.F., *Diary of the 9th Lancers* (Kensington: C. Roy, 1904)
Conradie, F., *Met Cronjé Aan Die Wesfront (1899–1900)* (Cape Town: Nasionale Pers Beperk, 1943)
Cooper, L., *The King's Own Yorkshire Light Infantry* (London: Leo Cooper Ltd, 1970)
Crabbe, F.M.S., *Minutes of Evidence, Royal Commission on the War in South Africa* (London: Wyman and Sons Ltd, 1903), vol. 2
Creswicke, L., *South Africa and the Transvaal War* (Edinburgh: TC & EC Jack, 1900), vol. 2
Dooner, M.G., *The Last Post* (Suffolk: JB Haywood & Son, 1980)
Dunn-Pattison, R.P., *The History of the 91st Argyllshire Highlanders* (Edinburgh and London: William Blackwood and Sons, 1910)
Duxbury, Geo R., *David and Goliath: The First War of Independence, 1880–1881* (Johannesburg: SA National Museum of Military History, 1981)
Fetherstonhaugh, R.S.R., Despatch of Belmont Action, 26 November 1899 as reproduced in *The True History of the War* (London: Harrison & Son, London, 1902)
Gerdov, C., 'A Scandinavian "Magna Charta"? The Scandinavian Corps and the politics of memory in South Africa (1899–1927)', *Historia,* 612 (November 2016), pp.54–78
Guest, WM., *With Lord Methuen and the 1st Division* (Klerksdorp: Printer and Publisher, 1902)
Gurney, R., *History of The Northamptonshire Regiment 1742–1934* (Aldershot: Gale & Ploden Ltd, 1935)
Hale, F., 'The Scandinavian Corps in the Second Anglo–Boer War', *Historia* 40 (2000), pp.220–236
Hall, J., *The Coldstream Guards 1885–1914* (Oxford: The Clarendon Press, 1929)
Hattingh, J., 'The British blockhouse system', in F Pretorius, (ed), *Scorched Earth* (Cape Town: Tafelberg, 2017), pp.216-229.
Hofmeyr, N., *Zes Maanden bij de Commando's* (Gravenhage, W.P. van Stockum & Zoon, 1903)
Jeans, T.T., *Naval Brigades in the S. A. War* (London: RN Sampson Low, Marston & Co. Ltd, 1901)
Kruger, R., *Goodbye Dolly Grey The Story of the Boer War.* 5th Edition (London: Pan Books, 1964)
Laband, J., *Rope of Sand: The Rise and Fall of the Zulu Kingdom In The Nineteenth Century* (Johannesburg: Jonathan Ball Publishers Pty Ltd, 1995)
Lane, J., *The War Diary of Burgher Jack Lane 1899–1902* (Cape Town: Van Riebeeck Society, 2001)
Maurice, F., *History of the War in South Africa 1899–1902* (London: Hurst and Blackett Limited, 1906), vol. 1.
Maurice, F., *The History Of The Scots Guards* (London: Chatto and Windus, 1934), vol. 2
Maydon, J.G., *French's Cavalry Campaign* (London: C. Arthur Pearson Ltd, 1902)
Meintjes, J. *De La Rey: Lions of the West* (Johannesburg: Hugh Keartland Publishers, 1966)
Menpes, M., *War Impressions Being A Record in Colour* (London: Adam & Charles Black, 1901)
Meriwether, J.L., 'The uncertain path: War Office administration and the journey into war, South Africa, 1896–1899', *Military History Journal*, 11:3/4, (1999)
Methuen, P.S., *Despatch of Belmont Action,* 26 November 1899, as reproduced in *The True History of the War Part II* (London: Harrison & Sons)
Methuen, P.S., *Minutes of Evidence, Royal Commission on the War in South Africa* (London: Wyman and Sons Ltd, 1903), vol. 2
Meyer, J.H., *Kommando-Jare 'n Oud-stryder se persoonlike relaas van die Tweede Vryheidsoorlog* (Cape Town and Pretoria: Human & Rousseau, 197I)
Miller, S.M., *Lord Methuen and the British Army: Failure and Redemption in South Africa* (London Portland, Frank Cass, 1999)

Mohlamme, P.S., 'African refugee camps in the Boer Republics', in F. Pretorius, (ed), Scorched Earth, 110-133 (Cape Town: Tafelberg, 2017)

Nasson, B. & Grundlingh. A.M'., (eds), *The war at home* (Cape Town: Tafelberg, 2013)

O'Meara., (1926), *Lt-Colonel Kekewich in Kimberley,* as quoted in T. Pakenham, *The Boer War* (Johannesburg: Jonathan Ball Publishers, 1978)

Pakenham, T., *The Boer War* (Johannesburg: Jonathan Ball Publishers, 1979)

Peddle, D.E., 'LONG CECIL The Gun made in Kimberley during the Siege', *Military History Journal* 4:1 (June 1977), pp.1-16.

Pemberton, B., *Battles of the Boer War* (London: Leo Cooper, 1964)

Phillips, M., *With Rimington* (The Project Gutenberg EBook, 2005)

Pretorius, F., Scorched Earth (Cape Town: Tafelberg, 2017)

Prothero, R.C., Despatch of Belmont and Graspan Actions, 4 December 1899 as reproduced in *The True History of the War Part II* (London: Harrison & Son, London, 1902)

Ralph, J., *An American With Lord Roberts* (New York: Frederick A Stokes Company, 1900)

Ralph, J., *Towards Pretoria: A Record of the War between Briton and Boer to the Hoisting of the British Flag at Bloemfontein* (London: C. Arthur Pearson Ltd, 1900)

Reay, W.T., *Australians in War: With the Australian Regiment from Melbourne to Bloemfontein* (Melbourne: A.H. Massina & Co., 1900)

Russell, A.V.F.V., *Letters From South Africa During the Boer War of 1899–1902* (London: JJ Keliher & Co. Ltd, 1909)

Spiers, E.M. *Letters from Kimberley Eyewitness Accounts from the South African War* (London: Frontline Books, 2014)

van den Heever, C.M., *General J.B.M. Hertzog* (Johannesburg: APB Bookstore, 1946)

van Onselen, C., *The Seed is Mine: The Life of Kas Maine, a South African Sharecropper 1894–1985* (Johannesburg: Johnathan Ball Publishers SA, 1996),

Von Heister, C., 'The Orange Free State Artillery', *Royal United Services Institution Journal* 45:276 (1901)

Wallace, R.L., *The Australians at the Boer War* (Canberra: The Australian War Memorial and Australian Government Publishing Service, 1976)

Warwick, P., *Black People and the South African War 1899–1902* (Johannesburg: Ravan Press Pty Ltd, 1983)

Weale, J., *Paper III Siege of Kimberley Report of the Royal Engineers* (London: Royal Engineers, 1903)

Wilson, H.W., *After Pretoria: The Guerrilla War* (London: The Amalgamated Press Ltd, 1902) vol. 2

Wood, W., *The Northumberland Fusiliers* (London: Grant Richards, 1901)

South African Heritage Resources Agency

WG/39, Volume 4: Circular from British Forces Committee to members of Ad Hoc Committee, 29 November, 1962

WG/39: Letter from the Highland Colonels, 1967

WG/39: Volume 4, Letter from A.C. Long to Secretary British Forces Committee, 5 May 1974

WG/39: RE Stevenson, included in: Notes by G.E. Brink, 12 February 1967

Unpublished thesis

Benneyworth, G., MA Research Report, *Reinterpreting Military Landscape* (Johannesburg: University of Witwatersrand, 2002)

Benneyworth, G., Traces of forced labour – a history of black civilians in British concentration camps during the South African War, 1899–1902 (Cape Town: University of Western Cape, 2007)

War Museum of the Boer Republics, Bloemfontein, South Africa

05784/00014: Recollections by P.J. Bekker
02005/00001: War Memories by P.J. Horak, Bloemfontein
04220/00034: Letter by A. Joubert to F. Joubert, 6 December 1899
03213/00001: Recollections by J.S. Kruger
04426/00001: Recollections by Burgher (later General) J.J. van Niekerk

Western Cape Archives and Records Service

GH 35/197: Vol. 3, Reference 172
GH 35? Vol 2, Reference 197
PAS, Volume 2/1078: Reference GX/MISC/7

Websites

Anglo Boer War Museum, "Introduction to the war: Second British offensive", <https://www.wmbr.org.za/view.asp?pg=research&pgsub=intro1&pgsub1=5&head1=Introduction%20to%20the%20War>, accessed 22 Apr. 2021

Anglo Boer War Museum, "Introduction to the war: The mobile war begins" <https://www.wmbr.org.za/view.asp?pg=research&pgsub=intro1&pgsub1=6&head1=Introduction%20to%20the%20War>, accessed 22 Apr. 2021

Benneyworth, G., 'Land, labour, war and displacement: A history of four black concentration camps in the South African War (1899–1902)', Historia [online], 64/2 (2019), 14–15 DOI 10.17159/2309-8392/2019/v64n2a1

Benneyworth, G., Traces of forced labour – a history of black civilians in British concentration camps during the South African War, 1899–1902, <http://etd.uwc.ac.za/xmlui/handle/11394/5466>, accessed 22 Apr. 2020)

Index

Abon's Dam, 97, 145
Afghanistan, 124
African babies, 26
African refugee camps, 232, 240
African workers, 20, 21, 22, 24
Afrikaner nationalist ideology, 234
Agterryers (African Auxiliaries), 44, 82, 89, 118 119, 132, 143, 167, 184, 187, 196, 209
airburst shells, 63, 150, 173, 187
Albrecht, Major F.W.R., 13, 42–43, 54, 62-63, 87, 96, 112, 115, 224, 226
ambulances, 113, 117, 160, 191–92
ambulance wagons, 35, 193
ammunition, 13, 47, 56, 77, 86, 105-06, 149, 153-54, 162, 170, 174, 190–91, 221
Anderson, Private H., 189
Anglo-Afghan War, 99
Anglo-Egyptian War, 75
Anglo-Zulu War, 11, 29
Argyll and Sutherland Highlanders, 97, 99, 103, 109, 112, 122–23, 125, 136, 148, 157, 163–66, 194, 207, 211
Army Circular, 231
artillery, 23, 24, 54, 63–64, 88, 90, 94, 96, 114–17, 136–37, 145–46, 152, 154, 170–71, 176–77, 188, 189, 204
Australians, 51, 62–63, 81–82, 107

Babington, General J.M., 141, 172, 174, 190
Baerentzen, Burgher William, 164-66
Bakenlaagte, 155
balloon, 144-46, 176–77, 180, 182, 185, 187, 201
bandoliers, 165, 173
Bannatine-Allason, Major R., 172
Barkly West, 31,38
battalion commanders, 50, 66
Battery Royal Field Artillery, vii, 69, 75–76, 97, 101, 110, 112–13, 122, 150, 174–76, 187, 189, 190
Battery Royal Horse Artillery, 142, 144, 146, 150, 172, 174, 187, 194
Beaconsfield, 20, 26–28, 230
Bearer company, 146, 147
Bechuanaland, 15, 16, 18, 120
Beit, Werner, 12
Bekker, P.J., 86, 89
Bell, Private H., 123
Belmont, 30–33, 35–36, 38, 40–42, 44–45, 47–83, 85, 88, 93, 120, 139–40, 144–45, 202, 204, 236–37
Belmont Farm, 41, 50, 56, 59, 61, 79, 221, 237
Belmont Station, 30, 38, 43, 48, 50, 55, 59, 78
Benson, Major G.E., 139, 141, 155–56, 180–81
Berkley, T. M., 162, 167, 170–71
Bermuda, 185
Bethlehem, 129, 133
Bethulie, 15, 18, 39
Bettington, Corporal A., 207
Bissett, 129-30, 214–15
black civilians, 232, 234
black concentration camps, 234
Black Watch, 97, 148, 150, 152–53, 155, 157–60, 162–64, 166–67, 170, 197, 199, 203, 205–7, 211–14, 235–36
  memorial, 206, 212, 215
blockhouses, 228, 231, 234
Bloemfontein, 14–16, 31–32, 39–40, 43–44, 86, 91, 112, 143, 223–24, 227, 233, 235, 238, 240–41
Bloemfontein Commandos, 67, 131
Bloemfontein Conference, 14
Bloemhof, 112, 129, 132–33
Blundell, Lieutenant W.A., 70
Boer artillery, 25, 33, 42, 57, 62, 112, 116, 193-94
Boer casualties, 34, 81, 90–91
Boer commandos, 15, 89, 131, 171, 208, 231, 233
Boer forces, 15, 17, 21–22, 31–32, 38–42, 44, 46–47, 75–76, 92, 94, 98, 100–101, 126, 171, 228–30
Boer Generals, 12, 42, 128, 133, 204, 224
Boer guns, 96, 101, 104, 110, 112, 170
Boer laager, 33, 54, 58, 76–77, 127, 139, 143, 195
  main, 49, 196, 223
Boer Republics, v, 9–10, 13–15, 37, 43, 72–73, 77, 83, 228, 230–32, 234, 240–41
  annexed, 230
Boer trenches, 95, 101, 110, 125, 134, 152, 160–61, 163, 176, 183, 188
Boshof, 31, 82

Boshof Commandos, 44, 132
Botha, Louis, 210
Botha, Paul, 92, 186
bridges, 31, 61, 120, 127, 228, 237
broken railway, 102
damaged Modder River, 126
damaged railway, 94
destroyed railway, 102
deviation, 126–27
pont, 40
strategic, 15
Brine, Lieutenant R.W.M., 64–65, 74, 80
Brink, 222, 240
British army, 11, 15, 18, 37, 48, 53, 80–81, 117, 228, 232–34, 239
British artillery, 63–64, 110, 117, 132, 144, 167, 178, 204
British casualties, 79, 90, 149, 235
British Cavalry, 41–42, 69, 76, 89, 183, 238
British Government, 10–12, 14–15, 17–18
British graves, 91, 216, 219
Brodie, Captain 217
Brown, Lance Corporal E. T., 162, 235
Brown, Private J., 123
Brown's Drift, 97, 126, 130, 137,141, 145, 152, 172
Buist, Major J., 217
Buller, General Sir Redvers, 10, 17, 20, 22–24, 29–30, 32, 35, 39–41, 45, 52–53, 59, 88, 90, 98, 200, 223–24
Burger, Willem, 92
Burgergrafte Komitee, 219
Burgher Monument, 208, 212
burghers, 14–15, 44, 46–47, 67–71, 73–77, 81–82, 85–86, 88–89, 91–94, 96–97, 100–101, 110, 127, 129, 131–32, 153–54, 157, 170–71, 184–88, 191–94, 212, 229
burials, 82, 122–25, 205–8, 211, 213, 217
burial sites, 79, 90, 120–21, 123, 205–8, 211–16, 219, 221-22
Burtchaell, Lieutenant-Colonel C.H., 57, 66, 71, 79, 81, 89–90, 101, 184, 193–94, 196–97

Cameron, Major A.R., 211–15
Canada, 23
soldiers, 82-83
Cape Colony, 10, 13, 15, 17–18, 22, 28–29, 37, 53, 211
central, 15, 29, 39, 53
eastern, 200
Cape Town, 16, 20, 22, 79, 81, 96, 98, 100, 117, 215, 217–18, 231–33, 236–41
Carter, Captain J.E., 193–95
Carter's Ridge, 26
carts, 41, 64, 74, 100, 106–7, 141, 143
mule, 79, 106, 117
ration, 66, 100
casualties, 21, 26, 59–61, 80, 89–90, 93, 98, 119–21, 124, 186–88, 191, 196–97, 208
figures, 90, 196–97
identified, 182
Casualty List, 167, 213
Cemetery, 79, 122–24, 158, 167, 188, 205, 208, 211, 217, 219
Chandos Pole Gell, H.G., 44, 66, 79, 119, 158, 179, 192
civilian population, 21, 27, 30, 39, 228, 231
Codrington, Lieutenant Colonel Alfred. E., 74-76, 105, 178–81, 197
Coetzee, Hansie, 117, 182
Coetzee, Veldkornet K.J.C., 182, 197
Coldstream Guards, 44, 56-57, 60, 66, 74–76, 99, 102–3, 105–6, 114, 119, 178–81, 188–89, 192, 208
Coldstream Hill, 43, 50, 56–58, 60, 68–70, 72, 74
Colenso, 200
Colesberg, 15, 20, 30, 39–40, 128
Colley, Major General G., 12
Colvile, Major General H.E., 49, 51–52, 57, 66–67, 74–76, 81, 102, 104, 114, 139, 141–44, 147, 178–81, 195–96, 201–2
commandos, 9, 12, 15, 26, 28–29, 44, 53, 59, 61, 86, 115–17, 126, 129, 132–33, 170, 184, 196–97, 228–29, 233–34
concentration camps, 230–31, 234
black, 232–34, 241
Coode, Lieutenant Colonel J., 148, 159-61, 197, 207, 208, 211
ordered, 159
Cooksey, Lance Corporal W., 196, 221
Cox, Lieutenant, E.S., 167, 217
Crabbe, Lieutenant-Colonel E.M.S., 58, 66–70, 79, 178–79, 209, 220
Creusot guns, 13
Long Tom, 21
Cronjé, General P.A., 40, 86, 92, 94, 96, 100–101, 114–17, 120, 127–29, 131–34, 136, 142, 141, 152–53, 156–59, 181, 184, 204, 209, 223-24, 226, 230
Cumming-Bruce, Captain, 155

Danie Theron's Reconnaissance Corps, 133
Dauth, Dick, 182
DCM. *See* Distinguished Conduct Medal
De Aar, 18, 20, 28–29, 32, 38, 40, 53
De Beers Consolidated Mines, 10, 13, 20–25
Denmark (Danish), 130, 173, 213
Danish Consul, 213–14
Despatch of Belmont Action, 63, 66–67, 75–77, 81, 239
Despatch of Belmont and Graspan Actions, 66, 76, 240
Diamonds (mining), 9–10, 12, 18, 20-2, 232
Dickie (Fox Terrier), 88, 91
Diederichs Commandant A.P.J., 170–71, 184, 204, 208
Distinguished Conduct Medal (DCM), 73, 114, 188, 207
Distinguished Service Order (DSO), 140, 184
Division, 30, 39, 41, 45, 47, 52–54, 62, 64, 81, 85–87, 98–99, 117, 120, 180–81, 237
doctor, 70, 115, 117, 160, 205, 207
Doornkop, 13

Douglas, Colonel C.W., 141, 144, 178, 180-81
Douglas, Lieutenant H.E.M., 183-84
Downman, Lieutenant Colonel G.T.F., 183, 188-89, 197, 217
Driefontein, 19, 135, 224, 227
drinking water, 20, 38, 63
driver, 107, 122, 174
Dry Harts, 234
Dum Dum, 186, 221
Dundee, 15–16, 18
Durban, 16, 29, 96, 100, 107, 113, 115, 144, 161, 164–65, 177

earthwork, 131, 154, 167
Eastern Cape, 9, 29–30
East London, 16, 214
Edenburg, 126
Edwards, Lieutenant N.G., 207–8, 211
Egypt, 23, 39, 137, 139, 189
Elandslaagte, 54
Enslin, 31, 85, 90-92, 128-29, 136, 140–41, 170, 201
Enslin Station, 91–92, 140
entrench, 126–47
entrenching, 98, 128, 132
entrenchments, 42, 134, 204
Ericson, Mr T., 216
Ewart, Lieutenant Colonel J.S., 57, 137–43, 145, 148–49, 152, 155–59, 161–63, 179, 182–83, 189–90, 192, 195, 199–203, 205–8

Fagerskjold, Baron, 164
Falconer, Keith, 35
farmhouse, 46, 52, 64, 97, 109, 112–13, 116, 170, 191
farms, 38, 41, 55–56, 64, 79, 94, 106, 109, 129, 228, 231
Fauresmith, 31, 44, 86, 129
Fauresmith Commando, 30, 96, 100, 104, 106, 133, 187, 192, 212
fences (fencing), 133, 212, 216, 231
  wire, 112, 157, 163-64, 167, 171-72, 179, 206, 211
Ferreira, General I (Naus)., 42–43, 141, 170, 184-85, 187, 204
Fetherstonhaugh, Major General R.S.R., 59, 67
Fichardt, Captain, 136
Ficksburg, 18, 129, 133, 184
Ficksburg Commando, 18, 170–71, 184, 186
Ficksburgers, 171, 186
Field Company Royal Engineers, 110, 238
field glasses, 49, 63
field guns, 13, 21, 28, 33, 42, 44
field hospital, 78, 90, 98, 130, 147, 195, 208
Fincham, Mr, 46, 50
Fincham's Farm, 33, 41, 46, 48, 58
First World War, 39, 163, 184, 189, 197, 221
Fischer, Abraham, 129
Flygare, Captain/Veld Kornet, J., 130, 165
Forrest, Captain J.V., 89–90
Fourie, Kommandant P., 131, 186
fox holes, 94–95, 125
France, 13, 60, 189
franchise, 12, 14
Franco Prussian War, 43
Fraser's Farm, 112, 121
Frederick's Kop, 30
French, Major General J.D.P, 29, 30, 39, 53, 126, 224
French's Cavalry Campaign, 115, 137, 141, 143, 201, 239
Friction firing tubes, vii, 63, 175
fuses, 62, 150
Fynn, W.D., 24–26

Gangers, 51, 143
Ganger's Hut, 49, 51, 59, 66, 68, 142–43
Garden of Remembrance, 79, 81, 124, 205, 207, 219, 222
garrison, 18, 21, 27, 30, 39–40, 85, 121, 140
Geneva Convention, 117, 194
Glegg, J.A., 99
Goff, Lieutenant Colonel G., 148, 158, 160–61, 197, 217
gold, 12, 228, 232
gold mines, 130
Gordon Highlanders, 147, 158, 176, 182-83, 188, 200, 202
Gough, Lieutenant Colonel George Hugh, 30, 35, 38, 43, 60, 76, 97
Gough, Lieutenant Colonel Bloomfield (9th Lancers), 32-35, 38, 90
Graspan, 19, 31, 35, 85, 87–89, 91, 93, 97–98, 127, 131–32, 138–39
Graspan action, 35, 66, 76, 86, 92, 140, 144-45, 204, 230, 236, 240
Graspan Station, 85, 87, 90
graves, 80–82, 90–91, 119, 121, 123–24, 158, 167, 205–8, 211–16, 219, 221–22
  fenced, 211
  isolated, 90, 216
  original, 211, 214, 219
  single, 213
  solitary, 221
  unfenced, 212
greatcoats, 47, 54, 66, 149
Grenadier Guards, 52, 58–60, 68–69, 72–73, 102, 114, 178, 180, 195–96, 202, 209, 221
Grenadier Hill, 58, 69–70, 82
Greyling, Kommandant B., 96, 187
Griequaland West, 15
Guards Brigade, 54–56, 60–61, 66, 68, 70, 79, 81, 102, 104, 106, 114, 144–45, 178–79, 202, 237
guerrilla war, 228, 231-32, 240
  escalating, 229
  protracted, 17
guides, 33, 68, 138, 155–56
Gun Hill, 49–50, 57–58, 60, 62–63, 66–75, 82
  climbed, 75

descending, 72
indicated, 68
Gun Kopje, 55, 58
gunners, 62–63, 122, 172, 174
naval, 194
gun pits, 141
gun positions, 26
prepared, 62
guns, 35, 44–46, 54–55, 62–63, 75–76, 96, 100–101, 110, 112–16, 144–46, 150–51, 162, 172, 174–75, 189–90
gun team horses, 64, 116

Hall, Lieutenant Colonel F.H., 63, 150, 174, 176

Hamman, Burgher Eddie, 185
Headquarters Hill, 145, 154, 176, 178, 180, 187, 189–90, 192
heat, 32,43, 49, 54, 61, 162, 185, 207
Heilbron, 129
Heilbron Commandos, 133
Heliograph, 48, 63
helmet, 70, 159, 174
Henderson, Private Robert, 213
Henniker, Major A., 119, 178-79
Hertzog, Judge/General J.B.M.(Barry)., 85, 96–97, 100, 120, 128, 191, 240
Highland Brigade, 120, 136–38, 141, 145–46, 148–49, 152–55, 162–63, 171–72, 174, 177–83, 187–90, 193–95, 197, 199–200, 202, 205–7
retreating, 193
strong, 144
Highland Brigade Memorial, 168
Highlanders, 109–10, 154, 164–65, 167, 170–71, 178–80, 184–85, 188–89, 195, 202, 211, 213
Highland Light Infantry, 113–14, 137, 148–49, 157–58, 163, 205
Highland Regiments Memorial, 220
High Ridges, 58, 69–70, 76
Hill, Padre Eustace St Claire Hill, 64-65, 70, 73-74, 80, 115, 119, 121, 123, 125
Hodgsen, Lance Corporal W.C.H., 188
Hofmeyr, N., 133, 159
Hoopstad, 44, 86, 129, 131, 133
Hoopstad Commandos, 69, 131, 158, 212
Hore-Ruthven, Lieutenant C.M., 152, 156, 161, 164–65, 188, 190, 197, 199–203
Horse Artillery Hill, vii, 153, 172, 174–75, 180, 187–89, 192, 208
horses, 33, 35, 41, 48, 61–63, 76-77, 86, 89–92, 114–17, 127, 167–68, 170–72, 174, 190, 192
howitzers, 144, 146, 150–51, 172, 176
shells, 170
Hughes-Hallet, Lieutenant Colonel, J.W., 148, 157–58, 187-89, 199–200
hunger, 99–100, 105, 112, 154, 185

Hutchinson, Sir W.H., 211, 213

India, 39, 41, 60, 184, 189
Indian Cavalry Corps, 60
infantry, 33–34, 46, 48, 54, 56, 59–61, 63–64, 70, 72, 87, 91, 93, 101, 105–6, 111–12
Isandlwana, 11

Jackson, Gunner E., 172
Jacobsdal, 31, 44–45, 91–92, 94, 97, 99, 114, 126, 129–30, 137–38, 141, 143–44, 194–95
captured, 224
Jacobsdal Commando, 92, 94, 133, 229
Jacobsdal hospital, 117
Jacobsdal memorial, 82
Jameson Raid, 13
Jeppe, Julius, 42, 44–45, 52–53, 61, 64
Johannesburg, v, 11–13, 17–18, 23, 47, 85, 92–93, 185, 187, 232, 238–40
seized, 228
Jooste, Lieutenant K., 133
Joubert, Burgher A., 88
Joubert, General P.J., 12–13, 196
Joubert's commandos, 18

Kaffir Kop Farm, 30, 43, 49, 54, 58, 76
Kekewich, Lieutenant Colonel R.G., 20, 23–24, 26–28, 83, 201
Kelham, Lieutenant Colonel H.R., 140, 148–50, 158–59, 183, 189, 197
Kidd, Private J., 73
Kimberley, 20–28, 30–31, 35–41, 45–47, 51, 53, 83, 120–21, 126, 137–38, 143–44, 150-51, 158–59, 172, 189, 205, 211, 234
Kimberley diamond mines, 12, 232
Kimberley Relief Column, 39, 126
King, Lieutenant W.B., 164, 207-08, 211, 216
King's Own Yorkshire Light Infantry, 67, 82, 90, 103, 107, 109-110, 123-24, 145, 184
Kitchener, Lord, 126, 223, 230–32
Kitchener's Fighting Scouts, 208
Klokfontein, 92, 97–98, 103, 110, 113, 121–22
Knight, E.F., 30, 32
kopjes, 74, 82, 84, 87-88, 103, 140, 172
great southern, 68
koppies, 74, 92, 140, 145, 157, 224
steep boulder strewn, 82
kraal, 94, 96, 106, 109–10, 231
small, 116
Krag-Jorgensen rifle, 173
Kroonstad, 16, 44, 82, 129, 131, 133, 158
Kroonstad Commandos, 184-85
Kroonstad railway line, 229
Kruger, S.J.P., 12–13, 17, 35–36, 42–43, 127, 129, 136, 185, 187, 239, 241

Kruger government, 13–14
Krupp, 13, 45, 86, 96, 116, 131, 133, 170, 172, 189–90
  guns, 13, 26, 42, 62, 86, 96, 132, 140
Krygsraad (council of war), 94, 114, 129

laager, 33, 42–43, 46, 55–56, 59–60, 76–77, 127,129-30, 143, 152, 156, 194-95
labour, 10, 232–33, 241
  coercing, 232
  forced, 232, 234, 241
  manual, 115
  redirecting, 232
labourers, 132
  agricultural, 232
  black, 207
  forced, 233
Labram, George, 22
Ladybrand Commando, 129, 133, 170, 184-87
Ladysmith, 16, 18, 26, 28–29, 223–24, 230
  isolating, 15
  rescuing, 29
Lambton, Captain A.F., 205-06, 211
lancers, 33, 54–56, 76, 89–92, 98, 101, 136, 140, 143–45, 147, 172, 180, 239
  squadron, 55
Lane, Burgher Jack, 98, 100-101, 105, 117, 143, 153, 156, 182, 188, 192, 194–96, 203
Lang, Lieutenant B., 100, 107, 113, 115, 144, 161, 164–65, 216, 238
Langberg, 130-31, 142–45, 184, 202
Langberg hills, 126
Last Post, 80, 91, 188, 208, 239
Leeuw Gamka, 81
Lennox, Gordon, 209
Lichtenberg Commando, 94, 154, 182, 185
Lichtenburg, 86, 112, 129, 133, 185, 196
Lindstrom, 166
Logan, Mr J.D., 217–18
Long Cecil, 20–22, 240
Loyal North Lancashire Regiment, 24, 61, 90, 103, 110, 112, 121, 123, 145
Lt-Colonel Kekewich, 23, 240
Lt Douglas, 184
Lubbe, Commandant (Kommandant), D., 91–92, 229–30
Luiperds Kop, 33, 58
Lynne, Private J., 81

Macfarlane, Captain W., 167, 208, 211
Mafeking, 15–16, 18, 26, 28, 37, 92, 126, 223, 230, 233
Magersfontein, v–vii, 10–240
  abandoned, 134
  entrench, 129
  farm, 213
  occupied, 128, 141, 143
  outflanked, 224
  penciled sketch of, 162, 167, 170, 235
Magersfontein Action, 57, 66, 90, 126, 150, 172, 174, 176,191, 204, 208, 215 236–37
Magersfontein Battlefield Museum, v, 177, 182, 185–86, 192, 196–97, 212, 238
Magersfontein Burgher Monument, 81, 219
Magersfontein Despatch, 178, 236
Magersfontein Farm, 130, 182, 190, 208
  farmhouse, 170, 191
Magersfontein Hill, 131, 133, 145, 149–52, 156–58, 162, 166–67, 171, 174, 189, 193, 203, 208
  main, 144–45, 148, 210
  northern slopes of, 133, 167
  scaling, 167
Mainwaring, Colonel A.E., 139, 141, 152
Majuba, 18
Majuba Day, 224
March Phillips, Lieutenant L., 84, 103, 106, 119
Martini Henry, 34, 89, 132, 154, 183
Matjiesfontein, 217–18, 238
Mauser rifles, 13, 77, 101, 104, 117, 143, 154, 173
maxim machine gun, 35, 74, 86, 96, 106
McDonald, Lance Corporal John, 213
McFarlane, Captain W., 207–8
McKay, Corporal Piper Jimmy, 161
McNeil, Private A., 123
Medical Corps, 46, 57, 66, 81, 89–90, 116, 119–20, 145, 184, 193–94, 197
memorials, 28, 79–82, 91, 124–25, 182, 205–11, 214–15, 218–22
Merwe van der, Kommandant P.T, 30, 35, 38, 187
Methuen, Lord, 17, 24, 27, 30, 34–41, 45–46, 49, 51–55, 57, 59–61, 63–64, 66–67, 74–77, 81–83, 87–88, 90, 93, 96–99, 101–4, 106-07, 109, 114, 120, 126, 128, 136–44, 149–52, 155, 176, 178–83, 187, 192, 193, 195, 199–205, 217, 224, 229
Methuen Despatch, 98-99
Methuen Unpublished Despatch, 150
Meyer, Burgher Izak., 94, 101–2, 104, 116, 128, 131-32, 151, 153–55, 158
Milner, Sir Alfred (later Lord), 14, 22–24, 220
Minaar, Kobus, 101
mines, 12–13, 20–21, 27, 232–33
  diamond, 18, 20
Minutes of Evidence, 37–41, 51, 61, 63, 69, 76, 236, 239
Modder River, 17, 19, 31, 37, 40–42, 45, 51-52, 57, 67, 83, 85, 92–94, 97–103, 107, 110, 116–17, 119–21, 123–24, 126–33, 136–42, 144–46, 149, 150, 153, 158, 167, 175, 177–78, 180, 182, 183, 187–88, 192–95, 198, 200-201, 203–5, 208–9, 211, 217–19
Modder River Camp, 103, 128, 136, 142, 145, 177, 194, 198, 217
Modder River Station, 57, 93–94, 97, 99, 126, 128, 138, 141, 183, 195, 211

Modder village, 94
monuments, 81, 205–7, 213–14, 216, 219, 221
morphia, 71, 184
Moss Drift, 131, 133, 172, 174, 183–84
Mount (Mont) Blanc, 43–44, 49, 50, 55, 57–60, 64, 67, 69–70, 74–75
mounted infantry, 55, 60, 83, 86, 89, 143–44, 146, 165, 172, 180, 183
mounted troops, 48, 54–55, 58, 60–61, 64, 76, 87, 90, 117, 172
mules, 41, 64, 73, 76, 192

Natal, 11–12, 14–18, 23, 26, 29–30, 32, 54, 151, 224, 234
Natal Campaign, 26, 228
Native (African) Drivers, 64, 105–7, 114, 193, 198
Native Refugees Department, 232–34
Naval Battalion, 45, 66, 87–88, 145
Naval Brigades, 27, 45, 55, 88, 90, 146, 239
naval guns, 29, 39, 40, 45, 60, 66, 76, 110, 117, 143, 145, 150, 174, 194–95
  4.7-inch, 142, 144, 172, 174, 194
New South Wales Lancers, 62
Northamptonshire Regiment, 67, 71, 73, 79, 90, 103, 140, 145
Northcott, Lieutenant Colonel H.P., 114, 123
Northumberland Fusiliers, 46–47, 64, 67, 71, 73, 80, 83, 90, 103, 110, 122–24, 207, 211
Norvalspont, 15, 18, 39
Norway, 173, 130, 213
Noupoort, 29, 40, 53
Noupoort junction, 39

Oafontein, 31
officers, 35, 39, 46, 51–53, 67, 69–70, 74–75, 80–81, 88, 91–92, 109–10, 152–55, 163–67, 190–91, 194-95, 197, 199–200, 204, 216–17
Ogg, Private John, 213
Ogilvy, Lieutenant Colonel D.S.W.(10th Earl of Airlie), 143
Olivier, General J.H., 20
Omdurman, 137, 167
Orange Free State, 9–15, 16, 20, 34, 39–40, 45, 77, 85, 126, 131, 224, 229, 232, 234
Orange Free State Artillery, 42, 44-45, 131, 240
Orange Free State forces, 15, 86, 94, 96, 127
Orange River, 15, 22–23, 31, 39–40, 47, 51, 53, 99, 128
Orange River Colony, 129, 233
Orange River Station, 20, 22, 24, 30–31, 33–34, 37–39, 41, 81, 91, 97, 138–39, 233–34, 238
Outpost Ridge, 146

Paardeberg, 43, 94, 165, 224, 226
Pietermaritzburg, 16, 29
Pietersburg, 16
du Plessis, Sergeant W., 96, 112, 115
du Plooy, Kommandant F.J., 170, 204, 208
Pole-Carew, Major General R., 57, 66, 99, 102-06, 109-112, 114, 137, 139, 141-43, 146, 201
Pom-Poms (gun), 42, 44, 62, 86–87, 96, 105, 116, 131, 133, 172-74, 190, 192
Poplar Grove, 224
Potchefstroom Commando, 86, 94, 129, 131–33, 158, 184
Potgieter, Kommandant F.J., 133
Pramberg, 92
Pretoria, 14–15, 21, 32, 34, 40, 42, 47–48, 64, 67–68, 74, 228, 231–33, 236–40
  occupied, 228
Prinsloo, General Marthinus, 36, 42–43, 85–86, 94, 96–97, 116, 128, 136, 140-1
Prinsloo's commandos, 30, 45, 52-53, 85, 96, 116
prisoners, 65, 81, 85, 90, 117, 165, 171, 185, 191, 194–95, 197
Prussian Army, 43
Pulteney, Lieutenant Colonel W., 69, 73, 75

Queenstown, 29

Radford, Sergeant J., 123–24
railway, 27, 30, 38, 50, 52, 55–56, 59, 63, 94, 102–3, 131, 139-40, 143, 146, 228, 234
  embankment, 73–74
  employees, 51, 143
  infrastructure, 140, 228–31
RAMC. *See* Royal Army Medical Corps
Ramdam, 31, 85, 91
Ramdam area, 229
rationing, 25, 231
  inadequate, 232
rations, 25, 39, 76, 232–33
  half, 146, 154
reconnaissance, 30, 32–35, 38, 42, 49–51, 57, 59, 87, 98, 128, 137, 141–43, 146, 153, 193, 201–2
Red Cross, 119
regiments, 38, 56, 80, 90, 99, 112, 149, 153, 157, 161, 163
reinforcements, 14, 16, 30, 40–41, 98, 115, 126–27, 136, 138, 144, 151, 178, 180–81, 184
Remembrance, 79, 81, 124, 205, 207, 219, 222
Rennie, Captain George 155-56, 195
Rey, de la, Adriaan, 113, 114, 116–17
Rey de la, Jacobus Herculaas (Koos) 30, 40, 47, 85–86, 91–94, 96, 100-101, 112–14, 116–17, 126–29, 131–32, 196, 204, 224, 228
Rhenoster River, 229
Rhodes, Cecil John, 10, 12–13, 20–25, 27–28, 39
  disgraced, 13
  ignored, 28
Rhodesia, 12, 15, 16, 18
ridge, 32, 35, 42–44, 55–60, 64, 67, 69, 75–76, 82, 146–47, 164, 172, 178–79, 202
  bushy, 181
  low, 63, 153, 202–3

low rocky, 96
parallel, 58
series of, 43, 58
southern, 71
Riet River, 31, 92–94, 96–97, 101, 105–6, 109–11, 113–14, 117–18, 120-122, 127, 130, 145
rifles, 22, 30, 69–70, 90, 104, 106–7, 110, 112, 151, 153-54, 158–59, 166–67, 170, 172, 179, 181, 183–85, 189, 191
Rimington, Major M.F., 56, 60-61, 76, 98, 141, 155
Rimington's Guides, 54–55, 60, 98, 103, 146, 155
Roberts, Lord v, 52, 66, 99, 165, 223-24, 226, 228–29, 231
isolated, 229
Robertson, Chaplain J., 194, 207
Rolfontein Farm, 126
Roll of Honour, 182, 185–87, 192, 196–97, 238
Roos, Burgher J.H., 192, 212
Rosmead, 93–94, 96-97, 102, 110–13, 115–16
Rostel's Farm, 94, 95, 123
Royal Army Medical Corps (RAMC), 71, 79, 89–90, 119–20, 183–84, 196–97, 235
Royal Canadian Regiment, 83
Royal Commission on the War in South Africa, 24, 37, 49, 69, 97
Royal Engineers, 20, 54, 112, 126, 144–45, 176–77, 205, 240
Royal Field Artillery (RFA), 60, 76, 87, 117, 140, 146-47 150, 180
Royal Horse Artillery (RHA), 142, 146
Royal Hotel, 94, 126, 139, 144, 175
Royal Marines, 90–91
Royal Munster Fusiliers, 66–67, 145
Royal Navy, 137
Royal United Services Institution, 42
Ruggles-Brise, Major H.G., 66, 75, 179, 208-09
runners, 23, 83, 113
Russell, Lieutenant A.V.F.V, 66, 68, 70, 79, 209, 220
Russell Cowie, Lieutenant W., 205, 211
Rutherford Clarke, Captain J., 163, 205-06, 211

Scandinavian burial site, 209, 214
Scandinavian Corps, 133, 129, 208, 214
Scandinavian Memorial, 210, 213, 215, 225
Scandinavians, 166, 211–12, 213–16, 239
Scandinavian volunteers, 130, 156, 208, 238
Schoeman, H.J., 18, 20, 112, 128
Scholtznek, 126–29, 140
Schulenburg, Burgher A.C., 154, 181, 185, 191
Schweizer-Reineke Commando, 173, 187
scorched earth policy, 229-30, 232
Scots Guards, 55, 59–60, 63, 67–69, 72–73, 102, 104–5, 114, 121, 178, 180, 190, 193
scouts, 30, 140
colonial, 193
forward, 47
Scrub Ridge, 131, 144, 152–54, 159, 165, 170–74, 176, 178–80, 182, 184, 187–88, 190–94, 202–3, 208
attacking, 200
comprised, 133
scurvy, 25
Seaforth Highlanders, 140, 148, 157, 159, 162, 164, 166-67, 170, 188, 194, 197, 205
Second Anglo-Afghan War, 99
Sekhukhune's War, 86
Senussi campaign, 65
le Seur, Trooper E.M., 98, 121-22
Shaul, Corporal J., 163
sheep, 38, 77, 116
shellfire, 27, 63, 64 75, 81, 87, 94, 110, 131, 143, 150-54, 170, 172, 185, 187, 190, 208
shells, 21–22, 62–63, 76–77, 90, 93, 104, 107, 110, 117, 119, 142, 150–51, 172, 174, 176
lyddite, 150, 174, 176
percussion, 150
seventy, 140
single, 116
shelters, 27, 61, 119, 146, 232
bomb, 27
makeshift, 225
shrapnel, 55, 63, 75, 88, 117, 150, 170
rapid, 189
siege, 12–13, 18, 20–28, 30, 85, 224, 238, 240
Skandinaviskåkåren, 129–30, 153, 156, 163–66, 172, 208–11, 214, 216
Skandinaviskå-kåren burial site, 216
Skandinaviskå-kåren graves, 210, 213
Smit, Ignatius, 91
Smuts, General J.C., 210, 216
South Africa, 9–10, 13, 17–18, 23–24, 27, 37, 39–40, 51–52, 67–70, 79–80, 96–98, 112, 114, 158–60, 162–63, 200–201, 216–17, 220–21, 235–36, 238–39
South African Field Force Casualty List, 62, 86, 91, 124, 167, 174, 184, 196, 237
Soutpansburg Commando, 129, 131
Spytfontein, 31, 40–41, 52, 97–99, 101, 114, 126, 128, 141, 144
Stellenbosch, 35
Stellenbosched, 35
Stewart, Major C.E., 97, 143, 149–50, 157, 160, 162, 190–91, 235
Steyn, President Marthinus Theunis,13-14, 36, 85, 127–131
Stopford, Colonel H.R., 74, 119, 123
Stormberg, 200
Streatfield, Colonel, 53
stretcher bearers, 74, 79, 163, 196
stretchers, 195–96
Sudan, 23, 39, 52, 137
Sudan Campaign, 47, 64, 167
Sudan Frontier Field Force, 139
Sugar Loaf Hills, 38, 43, 55–59, 75–76
burghers defending, 60

Superintendent Refugee Camps (SRC), 233
supplies, 16, 20, 22, 27, 31, 38, 46, 126, 129, 136, 234
Sweden, 213
Swinkpan, 31, 87

Table Mountain, 43, 50, 55, 57–60, 67, 69, 71, 73–76, 82
Tafelberg, 228, 231–33
Tait, Lieutenant F., 160, 190
telegrams, 22–23, 35, 39, 128–29, 143, 238
  official, 85–86
Tel-el-Kebir, 47, 149
telescopes, 32, 133, 149
tents, 46, 146, 148, 198, 224
  surgical, 64
  ward, 46
thirst, 48, 71, 73, 105, 107–8, 112, 162, 166, 185
Thomas, Native Driver Matthew, 106, 114
Thomas, Mr, 49, 51–52, 56, 58, 64
Thomas's Farm, 41, 48, 51–52, 54, 61, 79, 80, 83
tins, 119, 191, 216
  condensed milk, 216
  cooking mess, 47
  emergency ration, 154
  rusted British army ration, 61
towns, 20–24, 28, 38, 131, 228, 231, 239
  key, 18
  shanty, 10
  small, 228
Towse, E.B., 188-89
trains, 27, 38–39, 86, 136, 217, 228
  armoured, 86
  hospital, 80
  laden, 32
transport, 41, 139, 151
  given, 139
  mule, 38
  wheeled, 38
transport carts, 64
transport column, 41
transport drivers, 48
Transvaal, 9, 11–12, 14, 16, 37, 85–86, 151, 228, 234
Transvaal forces, 11–13, 15, 94, 127
Transvaal War, 11, 18, 23, 55, 69, 239
trenches, 117, 131–32, 134, 136, 140, 151-55, 157–61, 166, 171, 174, 176, 178, 183, 190, 193–94, 203, 205–6, 208

uitlanders, 12, 14, 86

Vaal River, 15, 20, 31, 228
Van Eck, Mr, 49
van Graan, Veld Kornet, 132
van Niekerk, Burgher (later general) J.J., 112, 170-71, 186-87
van Rensburg, Burgher J., 96, 112, 141, 170, 185–87, 191–92, 194, 196, 212
van Rooyen, Jacobus, 35
van Tonder, Burgher J., 143
veld, 32, 48, 54, 70, 71, 73, 79, 81, 93, 99, 100-01, 105-06, 123, 126, 136, 154, 157, 164, 170, 190
Venter, Veld Kornet., 92
  Verner, Lieutenant Colonel W., 33-35, 38, 48-52, 66-67, 92
Verner's Hill, 49, 52, 54, 54-58, 61–64, 66, 68, 76, 79
Victoria Cross (VC), 23, 29, 163, 184, 189
Victoria, Queen, 199-200
Vissers Drift, 31
Viviers, Kommandant, 96
Voetpads Drift, 145, 180, 184, 194
  known, 146
Volksrust, 16, 233
Von Heister, Carl, 42
Voortrekkers, 9
Vryburg, 16
Vryheidsoorlog, 86, 90, 92–94, 96, 113, 117, 119, 126–29, 131–33, 136, 238–39

wagons, 30, 76–77, 100, 139, 143, 177, 193, 224
  mule, 41
  ox, 41
  supply, 137
  tube, 177
Waldemaar Crosses, 212
  twin, 164, 210–11, 216
Walker, Private G., 166
War Graves, 91, 124, 211
War Memories, 39, 67, 112
War Office Plan, 15, 18, 29, 40, 223
Warre, Dr, 51
Warren Expedition, 37, 60
Warrenton, 16
water, 41, 48, 61, 90, 92, 105, 107, 109–10, 128–29, 162, 164, 171, 191–92, 194–95
  boiling, 191
  event, 129
  insufficient, 87
  rain, 134, 155
  shallow, 201
  wounded, 190
water bottles, 61, 66, 70–71, 73, 107, 190
water carts, 107–8, 189
water mania, 48
water resources, 41, 48, 144
Waterval, 31
Wauchope, Major-General Andrew Gilbert, 53, 57, 97, 125, 136–45, 148–49, 152, 155–57, 159–60, 167, 187, 193-95, 197, 200–201, 203, 206, 217-18, 224
Wauchope, Lieutenant Arthur Grenville, 155, 193
Wauchope, Lady 217
Wepener, 36
Wessels, Kommandant C., 85

Wesselton, 20, 24
Westerman, Mr, 213
Wet de, General C.R., 228-29
Wet de, Veldkornet H.J., 170-71, 204, 208, 228
Whiteman's Farm, 56
Wigston, Lance Sergeant H.,123
Wilson, Sergeant F., 123
Wilson, Lieutenant R.S., 167
Winburg Commando, 19, 44, 86, 97, 135
Witkop Farm, 97, 128
Witteputs, 31, 33–35, 41, 47–48, 54–55, 57–59, 61, 63, 66
Witte-Putts Farm, 55
Witwatersrand gold mines, 12
Wolmaransstad, 133
Wolmaransstad Commandos, 112, 129, 133
Wolseley, Lord, 15, 17
Wood, Major General E., 32-33
wounds, 79–81, 90, 114, 117, 119–20, 124, 126, 129, 139, 162–63, 166, 186, 194, 196–97, 199, 202

Zulu, 11, 29, 60